INVESTING SECRETS OF THE MASTERS

INVESTING SECRETS OF THE MASTERS

Applying Classical Investment Ideas to Today's Turbulent Markets

Charles E. Babin

William J. Donovan

McGraw-Hill

New York   San Francisco   Washington, D.C.   Auckland   Bogotá
Caracas   Lisbon   London   Madrid   Mexico City   Milan
Montreal   New Delhi   San Juan   Singapore   Sydney
Tokyo   Toronto

Library of Congress Cataloging-in-Publication Data

Babin, Charles E.
   Investing secrets of the masters : applying classical investment
ideas to today's turbulent markets / by Charles E. Babin, William J.
Donovan.
      p.   cm.
   Includes bibliographical references.
   ISBN 0-07-134100-5
   1. Investments.   I. Donovan, William J.   II. Title.
HG4521.B17 1999
332.6—dc21   99-15633
                                                 CIP

McGraw-Hill

A Division of The McGraw·Hill Companies

1 2 3 4 5 6 7 8 9 0   DOC/DOC   9 0 9 8 7 6 5 4 3 2 1 0 9

ISBN 0-07-134100-5

*The sponsoring editor for this book was Jeffrey Krames, the editing supervisor was
John M. Morriss, and the production supervisor was Elizabeth J. Strange. It was
set in Times New Roman by North Market Street Graphics, Lancaster, PA.*

Printed and bound by R. R. Donnelley & Sons Company.

McGraw-Hill books are available at special quantity discounts to use as premiums
and sales promotions, or for use in corporate training programs. For more information, please write to the Director of Special Sales, McGraw-Hill, 11 West 19th Street,
New York, NY 10011. Or contact your local bookstore.

This publication is designed to provide accurate and authoritative information in
regard to the subject matter covered. It is sold with the understanding that neither the
author nor the publisher is engaged in rendering legal, accounting, or other professional service. If legal advice or other expert assistance is required, the services of a
competent professional person should be sought.
—*From a Declaration of Principles jointly adopted by a Committee
of the American Bar Association and a Committee of Publishers.*

To Anna, my wife and best friend, and my daughters, Debora and Michelle, who enrich my life beyond measure. Finally, to my mother, Marcia, without whom all is impossible.

Charles E. Babin

To my parents, Bill and Mary Donovan, for their support through the years. And to my wife, Laura, and my children, Brenna and Will.

William J. Donovan

Foreword

SOMETHING AMAZING AND EXCITING is happening all over this country. Main Street is taking over Wall Street.

A new generation of investors is on the rise. More Americans than ever before—about 125 million—now own securities. And it's not the same old crowd. Women, minorities, and middle class workers from all walks of life are investing their hard-earned money in stocks, bonds, and mutual funds in unprecedented numbers. They are drawn by a strong economy and a growing confidence that they can get a real return on their money—and create lasting wealth for themselves and their families—if they put their trust in the magic of the markets.

Americans today are increasingly excited about the opportunity to invest and build up what I call "family capital." Just look at the explosion in popularity of Individual Retirement Accounts, 401(k) plans, stock options, and the like. Witness the enormous interest in the Internet, which is opening new doors to business news, research, and on-line investing. Behold the proliferation of new business-oriented cable television networks, radio programs, books, newsletters, and magazines.

A cultural sea change is underway. Seemingly ordinary people are creating extraordinary wealth. Americans no longer trust Big Government to provide for their economic security as much as they once did. They increasingly trust themselves and the free market. All this is very good news. And if we remove the tax and regulatory obstacles that continue to stand in people's way, even more Americans will be able to join in. After all, no one should be left behind. Everyone should be free to participate in this new era of prosperity.

That said, we must always keep in mind that a well-informed public is essential to a healthy marketplace. As more Americans invest in the markets, it is absolutely critical that everyone has access to accurate information, solid education, and wise advice.

That's where this book comes in.

Charlie Babin—a first-rate investment strategist at State Street Global Advisors in Boston, not to mention a FORBES columnist—and William Donovan—a business writer for the *Providence Journal* in Rhode Island—have written a wonderfully informative primer on the classic, time-tested principles of successful investing. There are pearls of wisdom and nuggets of gold in these pages. Read them carefully and ignore them at your peril.

New investors will be well served by the discussion of the human side of investing, the dynamics of the stock market, and the authors' emphasis on *discipline* and *prudence*. Discipline is key because markets do fluctuate. They can—and do—go through *sustained* downturns, as well as upturns. With discipline, you should come out well ahead rather than be whipsawed. More seasoned investors will find thought-provoking investment strategies and tactics, as well as interesting technical data. Everyone will benefit by learning from—and about—the masters of Wall Street and the principles they employed to reach new heights.

Which brings me to the title of this book. There's a slight misnomer to *"Investing Secrets from the Masters"* because they're not really secrets at all. They have been in the public domain for generations, waiting to be studied by those ready to succeed. What Babin and Donovan have done is to bring them together under one roof.

One final thought: My grandfather, B. C. Forbes, a Scottish immigrant came to this country with little money and barely a grade-school education. He founded FORBES in 1917. The magazine prospered spectacularly in the 1920s, but was nearly destroyed in the 1930s by the Great Depression. During those hard times, my grandfather never gave up because of his deep faith in his adopted country. "You never get rich for long by selling America short," he would say. My grandfather never made that mistake and we shouldn't either when hit by detours, disappointments, and setbacks.

That said, enjoy!

—STEVE FORBES
New York City
July 7, 1999

Contents

Appendixes

Preface

That which has been is that which will be, and that which has been done
is that which will be done. So, there is nothing new under the sun.

Ecclesiastes 1:9

THIS BOOK IS FOR INVESTORS, not speculators. Readers looking
for tips on "day trading" or how to earn a "fast buck" in the
stock market will be disappointed. Our mission is to put a new
face on timeless investment practices—classical ideas with a
tradition in literature—and to test them for relevance in today's
volatile environment. Simply put, we seek to develop quantifiable, disciplined ways to create and preserve wealth through tried-and-true investment principles.

Given what's at stake, it's not surprising that investment advice
abounds. It is also easy to understand why truths unearthed long ago now
play second fiddle to Wall Street pundits. After all, thinkers such as Fisher,
Sloan, Graham and Dodd, and Babson are unavailable to defend their views
or apply them to current-day investment problems. So investors have little
choice but to trust prevailing opinions. Unfortunately, high technology and
multimedia communication networks notwithstanding, the course of world
events often defeats modern-day observers and belies their ability to anticipate the events destined to shape stock market returns.

These days established ideas are seldom voiced; they are unwelcome
when introduced and rarely followed. But smart money realizes the importance of heeding bygone practitioners. And it has good reason for doing so:
These ideas have weathered the test of time.

Our study draws on the history of investment thought to develop long-term equity strategies, a subject of some import to a growing number of today's investors. But it wasn't always so. Prior to the turn of the century, substantive analysis was reserved for fixed income investments. As a class of securities, common stocks were considered "speculative." Since then, attitudes have shifted—quite considerably.

Given the scope of our inquiry, the "masters" upon whose ideas we rely so heavily are chiefly 20th century thinkers. And, as we'll see, their ideas have an enduring quality. As Benjamin Graham and David L. Dodd, patron saints of modern-day security analysis, put it 50 years ago:

> **It is our own underlying thesis that the principles of sound investment have not changed materially over the past half century, in spite of the tremendous and tragic events of the period and in spite of the major transformations in the economic, social and political scene.[1]**

Today, Graham and Dodd's words still ring true.

When it comes to the stock market, technical material is hard to avoid. To assist the reader, we've organized *Investing Secrets of the Masters* into two parts. In Part I: The Master Plans, we detail the salient features of viable investment programs. Here we discuss the pitfalls of human emotions, identify the prime determinants of stock market behavior, and provide an analytical framework for evaluating investment opportunities. In a nutshell, our early chapters are intended to establish, briefly, the underlying logic of our classical investment approach.

In Part II: The Master Plans in Action, we set out a number of strategies designed to exploit equity market returns while controlling risk. The centerpiece is our Total Return Portfolio—a cost-efficient, disciplined way to beat the Dow Jones Industrial Average. At root the strategy is based on the turn-of-the-century *Secret* that dividend growth is the key to long-term performance.[2] What's more, in Appendix E, we present the step-by-step annual procedures necessary to "rebalance" the Total Return Portfolio. Actually, this is one of the more refreshing aspects of the strategy. Once constructed, the portfolio requires minimum maintenance, resulting in lower costs and tax liabilities. And make no mistake, in the investment business especially, a penny saved is a penny earned.

Armed with our model portfolio, we address other issues of importance to investors. How to invest fresh capital into a "topsy-turvy," top-heavy stock market; diversification strategies; coping with concentrated equity positions; and identifying extreme market valuations are just some of the topics explored.

The pages that follow weren't written to be read from a recliner or while sitting at the beach with an eye on the surf. We plan to put you to work, so sharpen your pencil. Some of the material is challenging, but stick with it. If you're serious enough about investing to open this book, you're likely to find the *Secrets* ahead worth learning. And while the practical applications presented in *Secrets* are straightforward, some readers eager to embrace them may prefer to have someone else "crunch the numbers." So updated information—including instructions for implementing and maintaining the Total Return Portfolio without ambiguity—will be available via our Web site (www.topthedow.com).

Of course, we aren't the first to explore this territory in pursuit of opportunity. The seminal work, at least to our knowledge, was contributed by Laurence Sloan, whose survey of the field and thoughtful insights frame the guidelines treasured by today's investor. Not surprisingly, from time to time our charted course intersects with Sloan's well-marked trail. While our product differs, we possess a commonality of purpose:

> [T]he objective of all this ado will be to emerge, enfin, with a body of definite conclusions which it is hoped may be of aid to those who are seeking to formulate and carry out a conservative long term common stock investment program.[3]

Charles E. Babin
William J. Donovan

Boston, Massachusetts
September, 1999

Acknowledgements

WRITING IS DEMANDING SPORT, especially when it involves statistics and arcane principles long since buried in the archives of investment thought. Many hands lightened our burden and contributed to the value we hope readers find in this book. Three individuals deserve particular recognition.

Those who have traveled this path realize that book projects are, in a word, tedious. So first, we express our sincere thanks to Nicholas A. Lopardo, Chairman and Chief Executive Officer of State Street Global Advisors, without whose enthusiastic support, encouragement, and thoughtful insights this book would not have been possible.

Then, of course, there's Steve Forbes whose kind words grace our foreword. Only those who know him would have guessed that he could find the time, and muster the stamina, necessary to critique this work while on the stump for the Presidency of the United States. But that's Steve. We are humbled by his generosity and complimented by his findings.

To our colleague and friend, Venkat S. Chalasani, goes our deep appreciation, indeed admiration, for his unbounded energy and extraordinary contribution. Venkat's research and analysis, especially with respect to the practical applications found in *Secrets of the Masters,* was critical. If we have satisfied our objective, it is largely due to Venkat's efforts.

We are grateful to a number of other individuals as well. And while none approached the project with the same perspective, each enriched its style and content. Dolores G. Beck provided an invaluable perspective on the average investor, and the challenges he or she faces in financial dealings. Our biographical sketches benefited from Mark S. Brochu's genius in scouring the Internet. Professor Samuel B. Graves of Boston College's Wallace E. Carroll Graduate School of Management and Larry L. Martin, CFA of State Street Global Advisors, provided invaluable technical assistance. Special thanks to Suzanne M. Sergi for the countless hours she sacrificed unearthing obscure manuscripts, editing, and proofreading. Thanks also to L. Clarke Hill, H. Alan Tubman, and Paul O. Schofield whose ideas and counsel rehabilitated us when fatigue set in. Finally, we're indebted to Steven Levingston, former director of the Business and Economics Journalism Program at Boston University and now an editor with the *International Herald-Tribune* in Paris, for his advice about the publishing industry and suggestions on how to make a collaborative effort a success.

We would be remiss if we failed to recognize two individuals at McGraw-Hill. It was, after all, Jeffrey Krames who conceived *Secrets* and choreographed our production. Thank heavens for Kelli Christiansen whose writing skills shaped our discussion and enhanced the final outcome.

PART ONE

THE MASTER PLANS

CHAPTER ONE

The Human Side of Investing

We must recognize the psychology of the speculator militates strongly against the speculator. For, by relation of cause and effect, he is most optimistic when prices are highest and most despondent when they are at bottom. Hence, in the nature of things, only the exceptional speculator can prove successful, and no one has a logical right to believe that he will succeed where most of his companions must fail.[1]

Benjamin Graham and David L. Dodd
1934

NVESTING SECRETS OF THE MASTERS focuses on principles espoused by some of the 20th century's great investment minds. As such, our aim isn't to advance fresh ideas. Rather, we revisit classical investment theories, test them for relevance in today's environment, and develop disciplined structures capable of exploiting equity market returns while controlling risk, taxes, and costs.

All such undertakings have biases, of course. We're impressed that the investment principles embedded in modern-day practice are the ideas of bygone generations, ideas that have survived world wars, economic crises of varied intensity, oil embargoes, and countless currency debacles. In short, time—not the pundit—is the arbiter of wisdom.

Before we delve into investment strategy and portfolio construction, though, let's start by recognizing an overriding problem: investors are often their own worst enemy. Emotions, ill-focused motivations, and peer pressure often compromise otherwise sound investment plans. Empty wallets and squandered opportunities are the price of ignoring psychological influences.

All too often, carefully orchestrated investment strategies are discarded in the face of steep stock market declines. Good news can have the opposite effect. Euphoria of intense "bull" market rallies sweeps unwary investors into a buying frenzy. To borrow from Federal Reserve Chairman Alan Greenspan, "irrational exuberance" is the stuff that fosters appetites for easy money. Failure to temper return expectations by the risk of achieving them is prescription for disaster.[2]

This, in a nutshell, is the human side of investing. And it's important. So *Secrets* begins with a simple assertion. Effective strategies—whatever their stripe—take into consideration the psyche's impact on investment decisions. They also include disciplined ways to protect against rash decisions.

The groundwork for successful investing, then, begins with a few critical, personal questions. How well do you know yourself? Do you have the intestinal fortitude to stick by your plan as you watch the stock market nose-dive? Will you remain even-keeled in a raging bull market when your friends are urging you to sink every last cent into stocks?

For many, the prospect of "going it alone" is frightening. As a result, vast numbers of potential investors are inclined to believe that Wall Street issues are above them. Not necessarily. There is a very human side to investing (see Figure 1-1). Novice investors shouldn't get "psyched out" by technical jargon and impressive-sounding analysis. The computer age notwithstanding, investing remains an art form—not rocket science. In this arena, truth cannot be demonstrated via physical experiments. Outcomes cannot be guaranteed.

Effective portfolio strategies need not be complicated. Common sense, a handful of concepts, and an understanding of classical investment theory as supported by the historical record go a long way. For those individuals thinking about exposing hard-earned capital to equity risk or looking to

FIGURE 1-1
The Human Side of Investing

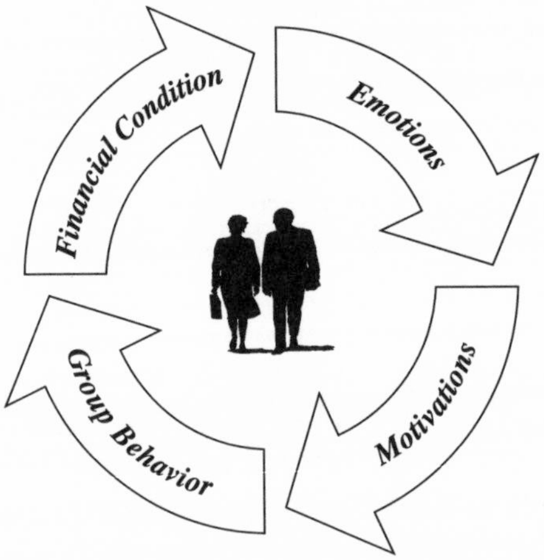

enhance their long-term investment prospects, the time-tested "secrets" in the chapters to follow will, we trust, prove helpful.

ARE YOUR EMOTIONS IN CHECK?

It's the human factor that often distinguishes investors from pretenders. Solid investors recognize the pitfall of emotions and they devise ways to insulate their decision-making process from it. Self-awareness is a prerequisite for successful outcomes.

Emotions are best saved for romantic dinners, junior's graduation, or cheering ol' alma mater. When it comes to equity investing, though, they're a hazard. It's easy to understand why. Our vision of what lies ahead is colored by recent events. We're programmed for extrapolation. The human mind just works that way. But betting on the "stock du jour" or pursuing investment fads can prove costly, especially at inflection points in the stock market cycle.

The bull market of the mid-1980s is a case in point. On the heels of a 50 percent cumulative return (1985–1986), the Dow Jones Industrial Average opened with a bang in 1987, skyrocketing an additional 30 percent through September. The allure proved irresistible. Individuals with little or no capacity for losses rushed into the stock market. It was a mistake. Equity markets surrendered a fifth of their value in the ensuing month.

As those of us who experienced "Black Monday" (October 19, 1987) will attest, only disciplined investors were able to hold their ground as pandemonium reigned on Wall Street. Pity the jittery stockholder, torn between selling or holding, who turned to the television for intelligence. All around the dial the assessments were bleak. With the type of coverage usually reserved for assassination attempts and plane crashes, news anchors and experts wrung their hands as they watched the market tumble, solemnly speculating about the implications of a Wall Street meltdown. Who knew when (or even if) investors would recover their losses? As the *New York Times* put it: "Is It 1929 Again?"

So it wasn't surprising that carefully assembled portfolios became unglued as skittish investors scuttled well thought-out investment plans. As sell tickets piled up on the floor of the stock exchanges, even the pundits were absorbed by panic. A lot of people—unable to weather the financial and psychological strain—bailed out.

In time they regretted that decision. The tailspin created one of the great buying opportunities in generations—an opportunity that many investors squandered as emotions overwhelmed their ability to remain calm and objective. Within a year or so stock prices had fully recovered, and the bull market got under way once again.

1987 is hardly an isolated case. While not always as severe, "corrections" occur with great regularity. Indeed, as we discuss more fully in Chapter 6, since 1961 the Dow Jones Industrial Average has suffered monthly declines roughly 43 percent of the time—many of them in excess of 10 percent.

Remember when Iraq invaded Kuwait (August 1990) and the world found out about Saddam Hussein? Again we were glued to our televisions as seasoned news anchors sketched out a scenario that, for investors, was downright scary. If the military experts were correct, war was inevitable. Conflagration of the Kuwaiti oil fields was probable. The implications for the world economy were, at best, bleak. And with the United States already slipping into recession, seriously increased energy prices were sure to ignite inflationary pressures and exacerbate the economic downturn.

Memories of the OPEC oil embargo, long lines at the gas pumps, and two crushing years of economic decline (1974 and 1975) flooded our consciousness. The bottom line seemed clear: sell stocks—all of them. The market responded with a vengeance, quickly shedding 13 percent. Even if you didn't abandon your portfolio, you certainly wouldn't have been in a buying mood. After all, who was to say that the market wouldn't drop yet another 13 percent?

Some of the predictions materialized, of course. There was a war and the oil fields were set ablaze. But we didn't see quadrupled oil prices. Inflation didn't run rampant, and the recession was relatively mild and brief. Once again, amid hard times, 1991 was a spectacular year for stocks, with the Dow Jones Industrial Average appreciating some 20 percent. Had you allowed emotions to cloud your thinking, you would have missed another stellar buying opportunity.

At root, this is what happens when emotions rule and discipline is abandoned. It's the plausible explanation for why so many people dump stocks just as prices scrape bottom, and why they expose themselves to equity risk at market peaks. Fortunately, there are ways for investors to minimize their exposure to the problem. We'll discuss them in the chapters that follow.

WHAT'S MOTIVATING YOU?

So how well do you know yourself? Ask yourself why you're in the stock market or think you ought to be. What's motivating you? Simple questions, true enough. Making money might seem to be the obvious response, but that's not always the case. The answers, however, can be pivotal to the effectiveness of your investment plan.

Actually, the very factors that drive human behavior are applicable to understanding our investment needs and, in turn, identifying the means to satisfy them. Here we rely on a body of work developed by Abraham A. Maslow (1908–1970), the eminent psychologist who established a hierarchy of motivational factors.[3] Importantly, Maslow observed that individuals provide economic activity in hope of satisfying present and future needs (see Table 1-1). Remember, investing is a forward-looking process. Past performance is of no consequence.

It's easy to understand why self-preservation is paramount in Maslow's model. Absent the necessities of life, all other needs evaporate. Boiled down, there are but a few ways to maintain those necessities: work effort, income from savings and investment, and charity.

Let's take a closer look as to how Maslow's hierarchy might apply to investors. Imagine a couple looking to fund their retirement years. They realize that, at a point in life when they'll no longer be working, they'll still need to eat. They'll have medical bills. Even if the homestead is paid for, they'll still need heat, electricity, and water. Added up, it's a powerful incentive to maximize savings and investments, while they enjoy earnings capacity.

Other motivational factors come into play as well. Consider safety. There's a lot of uncertainty with retirement planning. Beyond the essentials, will our hypothetical couple be able to maintain their lifestyle? Will they need to remain working into their 60s or, even, their 70s? What happens if they outlive their money? Certainly corporate pension plans aren't the safety blankets they once looked to be. Then there's our Social Security system. Yes, it continues to hum along. But with each passing year, we hear more about its inevitable demise.

A lot of "baby boomers" are probably counting on inheriting wealth from their parents—a group whose own investments and real estate holdings have blossomed in the post–World War II era. But even here, expectations could fall short of reality. As the boomers' fortunes grow, so do their respon-

TABLE 1-1
Maslow's Need Hierarchy

Motivational Factor	Description
Self-preservation	Necessities of life
Safety	Freedom from fear and anxiety
Affection and belonging	Desire for family and friends
Esteem	Self-respect and admiration of others
Self-actualization	Creative satisfaction

sibilities. An impressive number of them are now finding themselves as caregivers to their parents or loved ones. Regrettably, runaway medical costs could easily swamp a lifetime of hard work, savings, and investment. So the challenge is not simply to create wealth, but to preserve it.

Beyond self-preservation and safety, people often buy stocks to satisfy nonmaterial needs. For some, investing provides a common interest among friends and family. Investment clubs have gained widespread popularity. Others derive self-esteem from their investment activities. They speak confidently at cocktail parties about the 500 shares they bought in a biotech company with the sure cure for cancer. Or the subject comes up after the stock they bought turned out to be a winner ("I got in at $27 and sold at $44. Now it's back down in the low $30s."). Think they'd be so chatty if the stock had bombed? Would they boast as loudly if the biotech company went bust?

Then there are those who dabble in the stock market because it strikes an inner chord. As Maslow observed, poets write and musicians create music to be "at peace with themselves." So too, these investors relish the educational aspects and the challenge of picking stocks and charting their own course. They prefer to go it alone, rather than hire a professional money manager. They're serious about the process and enjoy its different facets.

BEWARE OF GROUP BEHAVIOR

As you continue your self-analysis, ask yourself another question: Can you make your own decisions and stick by them even when the going gets tough? Will you keep your head when the market turns wildly bullish and at every turn you hear: BUY! BUY!

The influence of group behavior on financial decisions is another threat to happy outcomes. Solid investors are ever mindful of this problem. They realize they're not deaf to what others say or immune to the power of persuasion. But they understand that the reliability of investment advice isn't a function of the number of commentators spouting it. Success is not, necessarily, a by-product of consensus thinking. There's no comfort in losing money along with everyone else. The wily veterans on Wall Street shy away from the stock tips no matter how many chums at the club are touting them or investment firms are recommending them. If it doesn't fit the plan, they resist.

Is it not possible that individual investors are unduly influenced by the well deserved reputations of such financial institutions for conservative investment, and overlook the fact that they, as individuals, are investing with the purpose of providing real wealth, not the changing symbol of value for their later years, or for the next generation?[4]

Themes can be dangerous. An idea becomes popular and gains momentum on radio and television investment programs. Suddenly it's hot. One example is the argument that the market has nowhere to go but "up" given the massive, nationwide inflows to equity funds. The alternatives for pension money, bonuses, 401ks, and the like simply couldn't compare with double-digit gains on equities. Surely all this "buying" power spells higher share prices. It only makes sense. Right?

Maybe, but if stock values did ratchet higher, we'd be hard pressed to attribute the move to an imbalance of demand. True, these days there is a lot of money flowing toward stocks, especially as the government urges people to invest as a safeguard to a potential collapse of Social Security. But wait a minute. For every buyer, there's a seller. So who's the fool who would sell stocks if everyone realizes that market prices will grow to the sky? And how can there be an imbalance? Wouldn't sellers, since they are in equal numbers to all those buyers, provide a countervailing force and push prices down?

Obviously, something doesn't compute. There must be some other explanation for stock market fluctuations. One plausible explanation, for example, is that stock prices reflect the general expectations of market participants. When new information becomes available, expectations change. And, in a dynamic stock market, prices quickly change to take account of it. The point is, you'd better not commit funds to the stock market on the basis of ideas that don't add up. The beauty of well thought-out investment plans is that they don't rely on story lines and "greater fool" theories.

DOES YOUR PLAN REFLECT YOUR FINANCIAL CONDITION?

So how's the introspection going so far? Have you figured out why you want to risk your finite capital in the equity market? Have you concluded that you can be a detached investor guided by your head and not your heart?

Well, you're still not ready. Ask yourself if you're financially equipped to start buying stocks. Every investor has different income needs and tolerance for risk. If losing principal would be catastrophic, then your risk tolerance is low. And in rational markets, lower-risk instruments yield lower returns. On the other hand, if the core of your financial plan can withstand the pressure of a market setback, your tolerance for risk is undoubtedly higher and your potential returns over the long haul ought to be greater.

Managing the human side of investing means assessing where you are along life's path, the resources you have available, the financial commitments you face, and the goals you'd like to reach. Your ability to participate in the stock market might be limited by your need to put food on the table, clothe your kids, put a roof over their heads, and provide for their education. Maybe you're not at a point where you're financially capable of being an investor. Rather, you're more of a consumer. Or maybe you're a saver on the way to becoming an investor. Maybe you're a speculator willing to "bet the farm" in pursuit of quick gains.

When it comes to financial dealings, there are a lot of ways to categorize people. Let's start by defining four. Figure 1-2 presents a convenient way to "compartmentalize" people from a 4-D perspective: time horizon, price appreciation, dividends, and risk tolerance. To understand the device, let's first examine the rubrics.

Consumers

By choice, or necessity, consumers spend their money. They may live from hand to mouth. The items they purchase tend to be the essentials of life. Or they may have sufficient income and savings, but simply have a compulsion to buy things. Consumers operate on a fairly short time horizon. They have the cash. Its worth is its purchasing power—today's purchasing power. Inflation is of little concern. They don't worry what something will cost tomorrow, because they're going for it now.

They have no interest in investing for the future because, often, their needs boil down to putting food on the table and a roof over their heads.

FIGURE 1-2
What Are Investors All About?

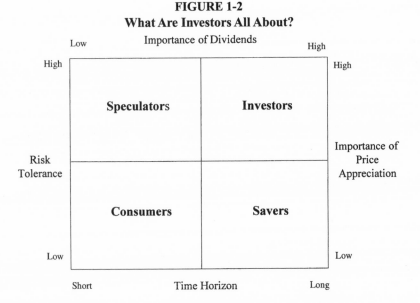

Their ability to risk the hard-earned money they have is nil. What they earn is what they spend. Savings and investment portfolios are a dream.

Consumers are described by the lower left-hand quadrant of Figure 1-2. They have a short time horizon and are unable to accept risk in pursuit of appreciation and dividends.

Savers

The key differences between savers and consumers are time horizons and income flows. Savers have the necessities of life covered to the point where they can set money aside for a rainy day. Savers tend to have a low tolerance for risk. It could be college education, a house, perhaps retirement. Despite their long-term objectives, savers loathe stepping out on the risk curve to accomplish them. For them, lower rates of return are the price of a comfortable night's sleep. Conservation of principal is paramount.

Savers could be people with an extra $100—or even $1,000—a month to put aside for a rainy day. Naturally their choices as to how best to manage their savings varies, depending on the size of their available funds. People with $100 per month to save may turn to money market accounts, certificates of deposit, or interest-bearing checking accounts. They may open a brokerage account, but place their money in something conservative such as short-term Treasuries.

Savers with $1,000 a month have more options. They could create a fixed income portfolio, mixing in "cash equivalents" such as riskless Treasury bills or high-quality, short-duration municipal bonds.

The lower right sector of the graph describes savers, given their long-term orientation. And while they value dividend income, they're unwilling to accept the risk associated with equity investments.

> **Simple saving is the process of denying oneself the utilization of a portion of one's income or assets, and of employing the sums so derived with the minimum of risk.[5]**

Speculators

Unlike savers, speculators have a short-term outlook. If their stock achieves a price target in 5 minutes, they'll sell and move on to something else. This is also the group that may praise a company's management, applaud its product, and champion its industry. But if the stock wavers for a moment, they dump it without a second thought.

> **The trouble with many people is that they proceed on a blind plan of buying and selling, hoping that they may be able to make a profit.**

These people are, in effect, merely gambling, therefore most of them fail.[6]

Speculators fall in the upper left quadrant. They're driven by price appreciation. It's just a matter of how high, how fast? They're willing to assume more risk to get what they perceive to be "supernormal," quick returns. Speculators often fancy themselves as superb stock pickers with an uncanny ability to anticipate the next Microsoft.[7] And the stocks they pick are probably different from the shares of the electric company or railroad line that their grandparents held. Reliable, predictable, dividend-paying stocks make speculators yawn.

Start-ups, little-known companies, firms with unproven but promising products all catch their eye. When they hear about a company that's going to cure baldness, their attention is held—and not because their hairline is receding. In short, tips, hunches, and rumors fuel their trading day.

> Bull or bear a man may be, and he still be an investor rather than a speculator, so long as he looks to dividends rather than to price changes to justify the cost of his stock. There exists another large class of traders, however, made up of speculators, whose business it is to buy and sell for changes in price alone. To these speculators dividends are inconsequential because they hold for too short a time to receive many dividends.[8]

Investors

Beyond consumers, anyone who has a long-term view, a family, and a degree of affluence should be an investor. Investors prize carefully designed plans that strike a happy balance between the need for creating and growing wealth while controlling risks.

Investors have their lifestyle needs covered and savings accounts in place. They take the long view, look for price appreciation, and realize that with no risk, there's no glory.

Investors are constantly trying to optimize the trade-off between risk assumption and return. They devise highly disciplined ways of identifying how much risk is being taken and how much return can be expected. Investors are often concerned with intergenerational wealth preservation and creation. Once constructed, portfolios are often passed down to the next generation and may never be sold.

Investors are depicted by the upper right quadrant of Figure 1-2, where a high desire for price appreciation meets a strong belief that dividends count. Investors also have a long time horizon and are willing to take appropriate risk for commensurate rewards.

> Throughout, the viewpoint will be that of the long term investor. The "long term," for our present purposes, will be a period of a year or more—perhaps five years, ten, twenty, a lifetime, several consecutive lifetimes. . . . An "investor" will be one who purchases securities of any type with the intention, all other things being equal, of retaining what he has bought for a year or more, i.e., for the long term. In other words, the time limit of the security purchaser's intent defines his status as between a speculator and an investor.[9]

Investors tend to be rational. Just like our readers, investors are operating in their own best interest to optimize their after-tax, cost-adjusted returns. Nobody risks capital expecting to lose it.

Don't be surprised if you see yourself in one or more categories. If you do, think hard about the characterization that best fits your motives for investing. If you're a saver who's emboldened to take on equity risk convinced that a tip you've heard will give you an edge, you are, in truth, a speculator.

To borrow from Graham and Dodd's postmortem of the 1927–1933 "boom-bust" stock market:

> That enormous profits should have turned into still more colossal losses . . . that unlimited optimism should have been succeeded by the deepest despair are all in strict accord with age-old tradition. That out of the intensity of the debacle there will arise new opportunities for large speculative gains appears almost axiomatic; and we seem to be on firm ground in repeating the old aphorisms that in speculation when to buy—and sell—is more important than what to buy, and also that almost by mathematical law more speculators must lose than can profit.[10]

You may see yourself in one of our quads now, but may recall that you would have fit in another quad 10 years ago. That's not unusual. In fact, most of us transition through the categories as we travel through life. Here's the typical route of a freshly minted young professional. Let's call him Johnny Grad.

At the end of his college years, Johnny Grad is "chomping at the bit" to make his mark. Shedding the cap and gown for pinstripes and bow ties, he's ready for the "real world." The value of Johnny's parchment notwithstanding, it's probably a safe bet that today's graduate is also a pocket of poverty. Even when there's a legitimate job, often there are college loans to pay off. Affordable housing, in many instances, means sharing an apartment with one or two other people and, if reliable transportation's critical to employment, throw a car loan into the mix.

The first job isn't likely to be at the top. It'll be entry level, with entry-level pay strapped by taxes, Social Security contributions, and a health care plan that Johnny's undoubtedly required to join. Survival, not saving and investing, is the big priority. In a word, while Johnny has prospects, at the start our young grad is a consumer.

The early years pass. Initial raises and bonuses get chewed up paying off the educational loans. Not infrequently, competitive forces persuade many young professionals back to the classroom in pursuit of an advanced degree as they seek to position themselves for success. As weekly income builds, they start migrating (albeit slowly) into the "savers" quadrant. Every inch of the way, expenses seem to meet income, especially as big-ticket items come into play. Perhaps by now Johnny's married and wants a house for his family. Kids are fun, but doctors' bills and dance lessons add up. The difference is that now his consumption devours a smaller portion of his income. Savings, finally, emerge as a priority.

The initial priority continues, onward and upward. Promotions, merit raises, and then the big leap: *partner.* The bills are under control and savings plans are in place and funded. It's time for investing.

The first goal might be a comfortable retirement. If Johnny's 35 when he's financially able to get serious about it, he'll have a full 30 years to invest—plenty of time to adequately supplement his Social Security benefits (assuming they're available when he retires). Goal number two could be investing for the kids' college education. Whether it's Harvard or State U., the cost of higher education is no small matter. Fortunately, time is an ally. Unless Johnny's eldest child is a genius, it will be about 18 years before she goes off to college. That means her parents have that much time to raise the money.

Assuming our hypothetical young professional opts for a long-term, carefully orchestrated investment plan, he will fit neatly in the investor quadrant of Figure 1-2. Time horizons are distant, share price appreciation is highly desired, and dividends are valued. Given the time advantage, a higher level of equity risk can be tolerated, particularly in the early years. At this point, the possibility of Johnny Grad moving into the speculators' quad depends as much on personality as it does finances. So far, he's moved gradually and predictably from one group to the next. The behavior has been rational, based on current and future needs.

OK. Once all the costs and investment programs are covered, maybe there's something extra. Perhaps it's time to loosen up a bit. Our hero may treat himself to a larger house or a flashy car. If he's doing especially well, maybe it's a boat or Harley that gets him excited. Or maybe he'll take that money and indulge the speculative urges he suppressed while getting his foundation in place. Why not? Johnny's earned it—fair and square.

SECRETS OF THE MASTERS

You know you like your pasta *al dente.* You know you love the color of money. And you know you'll keep your cool when deadline pressures arise at the office. But do you know if you're prepared to be an investor? Do you know if you'll stay faithful to an investment plan when your money's on the line and the market is on a long, intimidating decline?

Successful investing doesn't begin with a call to your broker. It starts with a "psychological checkup" to understand why you're investing and if you're prepared for it. There's really no point in launching a financial plan if you don't first know yourself as an investor.[11]

Remember this: as surely as there's a seller for every buyer, the market will have its highs and lows. Some drops will be drastic, some gains will be sublime. Most will be in between. If that's disconcerting, already you've learned something about your investing profile. But even that uneasiness can be overcome and buying equities can be profitable, if a sound plan is developed and followed. What constitutes a sound plan? It's one that "promises safety of principal and a satisfactory return," to quote Graham and Dodd yet again.

In the end, then, it's not enough simply to identify a viable strategy, even if it's wholly appropriate to your need for returns and tolerance for risk. Equally important is your capacity to stick by that plan when those inevitable market swings occur. And failure to understand your position in the consumer-investor spectrum increases the odds of snatching defeat from the jaws of victory. So before you put money on the line, ask yourself the tough question: Why? And make sure the answers are compatible with your inner nature as well as financial circumstances. In sum:

1. Insulate investment decisions from emotions.

2. Think, and think about the long-term objectives, before you leap.

3. Maintain sufficient cash reserves in case of turbulence.

CHAPTER TWO

What Drives the Stock Market, Anyway?

The matters that concern the investor most immediately are (1) the general price level, (2) interest rates, (3) business profits, (4) dividends, and (5) security-price movements.[1]

Benjamin Graham and David L. Dodd
1951

PERHAPS YOUR KNOWLEDGE OF AUTOMOBILES is limited to which way the key turns. Or maybe all you really want to know about your computer is which side of the mouse to click. No problem. You can still function without being a "techy." But when it comes to variables that determine if you'll have enough money for retirement or your children's college education, it's a different story. Equity investing will require a working knowledge of the forces destined to shape your financial returns.

There's no mystery why investors attach so much importance to understanding what makes Wall Street tick. Absent this knowledge, how can they hope to construct a viable strategy? Unfortunately, when it comes to the stock market, theories abound. For every three "experts," there seem to be four opinions about what lies ahead and how to capitalize on it.

The litany is impressive and ranges from "fundamental and technical analysis" to such tried-and-true indicators as "hem lines," "Super Bowl champs," and the "January effect." But, to steal a line from Bill Clinton, in our view "it's the economy." Understanding the linkage, however loose, between economic activity and share prices is as fundamental to investing as knowing how to run the diamond is to baseball.

PROSPERITY SPELLS PROFITS

Make no mistake, economic prosperity is the stuff that fuels bull markets. And while any number of extraneous factors influence prosperity, given the crucial role of the economy in portfolio performance, it's worth establishing a plausible explanation of the linkages, using a handful of established ideas. Before we explore that relationship, let's take a moment to define the economy.

When we talk about "the economy," we're referring to an official government statistical measure of the nation's output called real Gross Domestic Product (GDP)—that is, the market value (adjusted for inflation) of all goods and services produced within our borders.[2] As you can imagine, it's a big number. The 1997 GDP, for instance, amounted to a whopping $7.3 trillion.

Expressed in dollars, as we've done here, the size of the economy is referred to as the "level" of GDP. Curiously, when investment professionals discuss GDP, few do so in terms of its level. Indeed, fewer still could probably even cite the dollar value. They're interested in whether the economy is expanding or contracting (and to what extent). So Wall Street conversations usually focus on the "growth" or percentage change in the level of GDP.

Although the midpoint in mathematics is zero, meaning there's an infinite amount of numbers (positive and negative) to either side of the numeral zero, when we're describing the growth of Gross Domestic Product the average rate has hovered around 3 percent. Measured on a calendar-year basis over the 1959–1997 interval, Gross Domestic Product averaged some 3.2 percent growth. Generally speaking, economic outcomes that fall short of this "potential" rate are considered anemic, while outcomes above it are viewed as robust. Historically GDP growth has ranged from a high of 7.4 percent in 1959 to a low of −2.1 percent in 1982. Fortunately negative growth years, though painful, are the exception. Indeed, there have been only 5 subzero GDP years since 1959.

Beyond the gross figure, investors are also interested in understanding how the various components of GDP are contributing to the growth of the economy. Actually, GDP can be viewed from a number of different angles—all of which add up to the same $7.3 trillion figure. The first, which we've already mentioned, breaks down GDP according to the so-called supply-side accounts. This methodology dissects GDP according to the dollar value of goods and services produced within the United States. The market value of cars produced by General Motors, Microsoft's computer software, the electricity generated by your local utility company—all contribute to the GDP figure.

The demand-side accounts divvy up GDP according to expenditures by U.S. residents and businesses. Things like personal consumption on motor vehicles, furniture, food, and clothing as well as medical care, transportation, residential and nonresidential structures, and business and industrial equipment are but some of the line items.

Finally, GDP can be viewed from the perspective of incomes. And it is this measure of the economy that is of critical importance to establishing the linkage between economic vitality and the stock market. Think about it this way. By official definition, Gross Domestic Product equals the total amount of income generated by the economy. From an income perspective, the chief components include wages and salaries paid to employees, proprietors' income, rents, interest, and *importantly* corporate profits. Profits, of course, are the driving force behind dividends and, as we'll see in Chapter 5, share prices.

At first glance, this point may seem innocuous. After all, measured as a level, profits are only a small sliver of the GDP pie (see Figure 2-1). But when you consider that annual fluctuations in corporate profits explain roughly 60 percent of the year-over-year growth in Gross Domestic Product, you start to appreciate why Wall Streeters worry so much about the path of the economy.[3]

Even a "back of the envelope" graph of the data hints at the strong association between corporate profits and the economy (see Figure 2-2). Notice the volatility of corporate profits relative to GDP. It's the tail wagging the dog.

The historical record indicates that, on average, corporate profits (adjusted for inflation) advanced some 6.2 percent during periods when GDP exceeded trend-line growth. Conversely, during those years when GDP failed to achieve potential (there were 17 such years between 1959 and 1997), profits tended to be "in the red." Indeed, measured across all 17 years, profit growth averaged −2.6 percent even though GDP growth remained in positive territory during 12 of them.

FIGURE 2-1
1997 GDP Contributions

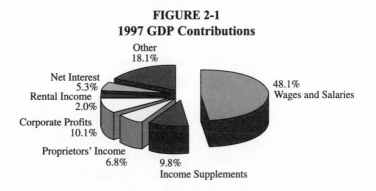

FIGURE 2-2
Corporate Profits and GDP

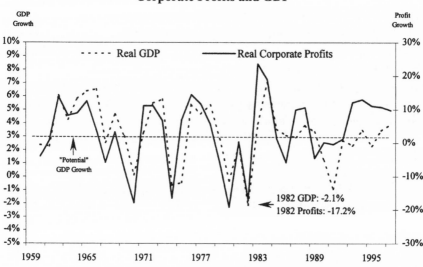

Recessions are especially damning. Look at the 1982 experience. As shown in the graph, GDP declined roughly 2 percent. How did profits hold up? They didn't. They were crushed (−17.2%). The bottom line is that economic vitality spawns corporate profit and dividend growth. The bigger the economy, the bigger the celebration on Wall Street.

FISCAL POLICY: WHAT STIMULATES OUTPUT, SAVINGS, AND INVESTMENT?

So what makes the economy tick? The current-day science of political economics, especially fiscal policy, is traceable to 1776, when Adam Smith (1723–1790) published *The Wealth of Nations*. Ironically, Smith's message was elegantly simple: government can only interfere with the efficient operation of the economy. Nothing could cause markets to operate with more precision than individual self-interest. According to Smith, the individual never

> **intends to promote the public interest . . . he intends only his own gain, and he is in this, as in many other cases, led by an invisible hand. . . .**[4]

Smith's philosophy formed the bedrock of U.S. fiscal policy during the first 140 years of the Republic, and through the 1920s there remained conservative beliefs about the economy that were rooted in Smith's doctrines. The budget should be balanced every year at a modest level; debtors—particularly those in charge of public funds—should be scorned; a government is no different from a family—its spending should be limited to its monthly income. Does this philosophy sound familiar? It should. After a 50-year intermission, it resurfaced as "Reaganomics," which marked an inflection point in the way America governs. Now, as we bridge into the 21st century, these classical ideas have reclaimed their hold on the political landscape.

In between Smith and Reaganomics came the Great Depression and John Maynard Keynes. In the face of 25 percent unemployment, Keynes veered from Smith's economic model with his breakthrough work *The General Theory of Employment, Interest, and Money*. In it Keynes argued that economies don't always resolve inefficiencies naturally. Instead, the nation could slump into a permanent state of stagnation and underemployment. If the market was unable to right itself and keep capitalism growing, government spending should replace private spending to stimulate growth and employment and keep the economy on track. In a nutshell, Keynesian economics sought to manage the economy by propping up consumer spending (the so-called demand side of the economy) via an elaborate system of "automatic stabilizers" or "transfer payments" to those disadvantaged by economic downturns.

In a political economy, it didn't take long for Keynes' prescriptions to catch on in Washington. After all, pocketbook issues translate into votes. But there was a problem. Keynes looked to cease government intervention once the economy rebounded. But once the transfer payments started to flow, cutting them off was political suicide. The path of least resistance was to invent labels like "entitlements" and "social responsibility" to camouflage a burgeoning welfare system and wealth redistribution.

Not surprisingly, the U.S. economy sputtered. A half-century of the Keynesian tax-cum-transfer prescriptions coincided with an increasing number of recessions, rampant inflation, mind-boggling budget deficits, and rising crime and unemployment. Gerald Ford's WIN buttons (Whip Inflation Now) and Jimmy Carter's hand wringing about the country's "malaise" just didn't cut the mustard. Consumer price inflation (the "insidious tax") was clocked at 17.3 percent, and in 1981 the so-called prime rate—the interest rate that banks offer their choice customers—climbed above 20 percent. Imagine what the rest of us were paying. What Americans saw was an economy in crisis. As early as 1980 voters had begun looking for solutions, not for economists and politicians.

Fortunately, there was a silver lining in all the bad news. In a political economy, change is born of extreme adversity. Only then are politicians willing to abandon course. And the sea of change arrived in the form of Ronald Reagan's incentivist policies.

After years of stagnation and inflation in the U.S. economy, Reagan was intent on putting the country back on a steady, noninflationary growth path. His then controversial prescription was to stimulate economic growth through massive budget cuts and tax rate reductions. From the "get-go," he mounted a frontal attack on the Keynesians, arguing that the basic problem with the U.S. economy was too much government interference and ill-focused incentives. Prohibitively high federal tax rates were sapping America's productive resources and encouraging nonwork, leisure, and crime. In Reagan's world, it was axiomatic that the economy would reap more of what it subsidized and less of what it taxed. The secret to unleashing American enterprise was to allow productive factors to keep more of what they earned. The answer, in Reagan's view, was to slash marginal tax rates and reduce onerous government regulations (i.e., de facto taxes). Adam Smith was back.

It took a while for the benefits to show up. But then, supertankers aren't turned around on a dime. The 1982 economy—the transition year—suffered the biggest recession in postwar history. But the pain was short-lived. Over the ensuing 16 years, the U.S. economy went on a tear, expanding every year but 1990, when Saddam Hussein swallowed Kuwait and the Gulf War crisis erupted. While cynics still dispute a cause-and-effect relationship between America's new-found prosperity and a return to classical economics, the fact remains that Reaganomics marked an inflection point in fiscal policy that coincided with waning inflation, lower interest rates, and the greatest bull market in generations. We were rolling again.

THE FISHER FORMULA: ARE INTEREST RATES LINKED TO THE ECONOMY?

Unfortunately, few economic theories have withstood the test of time. One survivor, though, is the preeminent Yale economist Irving Fisher's turn-of-the-century observation that the market rate of interest is forward-looking, influences economic activity, and enters into the pricing of securities.

> **The truth is that the rate of interest is not a narrow phenomenon applying to only a few business contracts, but permeates all economic relations. It is the link which binds man to the future and by which he makes all his far-reaching decisions. It enters into the price of securities, land and capital goods generally, as well as into rent, wages, and the value of all "interactions." It affects profoundly the distribution of wealth. In short, upon its accurate adjustment depend the equitable terms of all exchange and distribution.[5]**

It's a profound statement, with a number of implications relevant to our discussion. Before we travel too far down this path, though, let's establish the framework. Here, again, we rely on Fisher's scientific writings to provide insight. In his view, the chief components of the market rate of interest (the "nominal" interest rate) boil down to creditworthiness (the factor that compensates lenders for assuming loan risk) plus a markup for expected inflation. Certainly taxes are a reality too. So the nominal interest rate would also contemplate the government's levy on interest income.

In a world of technical arguments, few observers would quibble that borrowers worry about the impact of inflation and taxes on the gross interest rate, as Fisher rightly argued. Lenders, on the other hand, are concerned only about how much ends up in their pocket net of inflation and taxes.

Importantly, as the gap between inflation and taxes fluctuates, so does credit extension. It's hard to imagine a vibrant credit market if lenders can anticipate losing principal, having their interest payments expropriated by taxes, or suffering lost purchasing power. More likely the market would dry up altogether if Fisher's formula produced a negative after-tax "real" rate of interest.[6] Ceteris paribus, the level and volatility of interest rates, together with the terms and conditions of the loan, are critical to corporate expansion and consumer spending. There's also the linkage between interest rates and the economy. Lumped together, these two components account for the lion's share of GDP.

To see Fisher's formula in operation, look at Figure 2-3. In a world free of inflation and taxes there would be no distinction between the gross interest rate paid and that received. Loan rates would be priced to reflect the credit rating of the borrower plus a factor for the time value of money. For the sake of illustration, we've assumed the after-tax real rate of interest to

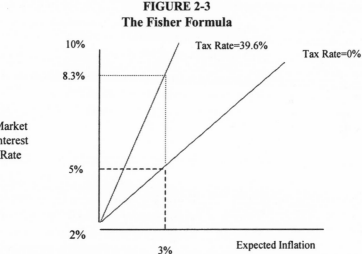

FIGURE 2-3
The Fisher Formula

be 2 percent. Set this value to be at the "point of origin" in the graph (that is, the point where the horizontal and vertical axes intersect).

Now let's introduce inflation at, say, a modest 3 percent and pose a simple question: What gross interest would yield the same after-tax real rate of interest? The answer is easily derived from Figure 2-3 by drawing a straight line up from the horizontal axis (over the tick mark labeled "3%") and allowing it to intersect with the diagonal line (labeled "Tax Rate = 0%"). Now connect the diagonal with the vertical axis using a horizontal line. There's your answer. Under the Fisher formula, the market rate of interest would have to balloon to 5 percent, of which 3 percent would be eroded by inflation, leaving lenders and borrowers in the same relative position. Therein lies the problem. Even before we allow for taxes, interest rates would have more than doubled just because of the inflation factor.

Any number of tax curves could be superimposed on the graph, of course. But we've elected not to clutter it up. For demonstration purposes, we've assumed that a 39.6 percent marginal tax rate applies. So here's the next question: Holding expected inflation constant at 3 percent, what's the implication for nominal rates? Up, and up a lot. To get the answer, operate the graph as before using the newly added tax line. Without concern for the precision of the outcome, loan rates would have to at least quadruple if the status quo ante is to be preserved—a significantly different outcome with all sorts of ramifications for the economy. In short, tax rates are a gearing mechanism that exacerbates inflation's impact on nominal interest rates.

While you wouldn't guess it from the last two decades, tax rate reform isn't a regular event in Washington. Between John F. Kennedy's term and Ronald Reagan's there were no permanent changes in our progressive marginal tax system. Given the reductions now in place, further cuts seem unlikely. So, if there are to be any surprises, they would probably be fueled by a sudden increase in prices. A simple exercise provides an important, albeit worrisome perspective.

Suppose an investor is thinking about putting $100,000 to work in a 5-year Treasury note. As indicated in Table 2-1, in a zero inflation environment, it would take a 2.8 percent nominal interest rate to offset the tax bite and still produce a 2 percent after-tax real rate. Hardly an earth-shattering figure. But don't forget, we're talking about zero inflation.

Now, holding our tax rate assumption constant, look at what would happen if inflation reignited to even a modest 5 percent. T-note yields would have to rise to 9.8 percent, practically double-digit territory, in order to generate that same 2 percent return. Don't forget, interest rates are forward-looking. So even the specter of higher inflation could trigger

TABLE 2-1

Taxes, Inflation, and the Nominal Interest Rate

	Inflation Environment	
	0%	5%
Principal investment	$100,000	$100,000
Plus: Real interest (2% Rate)	$2,000	$2,000
Plus: Inflation offset*	$0	$5,050
Plus: Tax offset (39.6)	$792	$2,792
Equals: Gross return	$2,792	$9,842
Divided by: Principal	$100,000	$100,000
Equals: Nominal interest rate	2.8%	9.8%

* Inflation adjustment applied to principal and 50% of income

an interest rate spiral, putting pressure on the economy and the financial markets.

In sum, taxes and inflation are a nasty brew. Fiscal policies that embrace higher tax rates are a recipe for disaster, especially if market forces expect inflation to heat up. Given the leverage involved, nominal interest rates would skyrocket, sapping economic growth potential. Moreover, since expectations change swiftly (and radically), the credit market would likely experience severe turbulence.[7] Gross Domestic Product would falter.

The reverse logic would also hold. Policies that lower tax rates ought to calm credit market volatility and foster an improved interest rate environment. Go back to the early 1980s again. When Ronald Reagan took command of the Oval Office (1981), the calendar-year average 3-month Treasury yield was a whopping 14 percent (don't forget, that's a "riskless" return). Investors armed with Fisher's formula wouldn't have been shocked. After all, they would have realized the implication of a 70 percent maximum tax bracket coupled with double-digit inflation.

Over the ensuing years, a number of "phased-in" tax cuts were introduced that condensed some 13 tax brackets to a handful and reduced the top marginal rate to 33 percent. Even today, despite some recent jiggering, the highest tax rate (39.6%) is seriously lower than what it was 17 years ago. There was good news on the inflation front too. Over this same interval, growth in the Consumer Price Index subsided to a paltry 2.3 percent. Did Fisher's formula hold up? Judge for yourself. Treasury bill yields declined to less than 5 percent. The economy prospered.[8]

WHO, OR WHAT, CONTROLS INTEREST RATES?

Paul Samuelson of the Massachusetts Institute of Technology, dean of the collegiate economic curriculum, wrote about the role of the Federal Reserve on interest rates decades ago:

> [T]he vital function of the Federal Reserve Banks [is] as creator and controller of the community's supply of money, and as a vital factor determining the level of interest yields on government and private securities.[9]

We don't dispute the Samuelson gospel. But we suspect the process of controlling rates is far more subtle, even indirect, than most observers believe.

In its efforts to defeat inflation and curb the business cycle, the Federal Reserve has a number of weapons at its disposal. Chief among them is the ability to manipulate interest rates directly.[10] But the Federal Reserve's Board of Governors aren't the only people focused on interest rates. If interest rates are forward-looking, as Fisher states, then market participants would be alert for any changes in factors that can shape the price of credit—including likely Fed actions. That probably has as much or more to do with fluctuating market prices than direct Federal Reserve initiatives.

There's some suggestive evidence that supports this view. Between January 1994 and December 1997, the Federal Reserve adjusted the discount rate on five occasions. Figure 2-4 traces the path of 3-month Treasury bill yields during the period between Federal Reserve policy initiatives to see if market participants make any attempt to anticipate directional shifts in Fed interest rate policy. If they do, then we ought to discern movement, up or down, in market rates during intervals when the administered rate was stable. Then it's only a matter of observing if the Fed's next move followed suit.

Let's walk through the exercise illustrated above using the January 1994 example. As shown in the graph, as the year unfolded, the discount rate was set at 3 percent. Notice that the T-bill yields were ratcheting higher even though the Fed maintained a constant policy through May 16. One day later, though, the Fed bumped the discount rate to 3.5 percent—a 17 percent increase in the price of credit. Market prices had already discounted the news.

IS THE STOCK MARKET FORWARD-LOOKING?

Fisher also contributed to the idea that the values people place on financial assets are based on rational expectations. When a rational market is disrupted by information that differs from the norm, such as the Asian finan-

FIGURE 2-4
Do Market Participants Anticipate Fed Policy Initiatives?

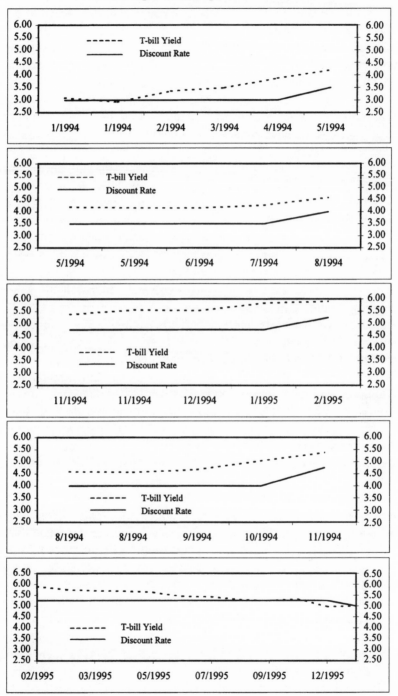

27

cial crisis in the late 1990s, expectations change and prices reequilibrate to take account of the shift.

To see his point, consider the impact on share prices of market participants anticipated that interest rates would double. Few observers would expect the equity market to remain calm and unaffected. After all, only the uninitiated would wait around to see if such dire expectations pan out before redressing their investment strategy. But by then, it's a safe bet that market prices would have already discounted a severely deteriorated credit market environment.

Sure, there's the ever-present danger that events will fail to mirror anticipations. Here's the important point to remember. When it comes to the pricing of financial assets, perceptions count. Reality is of lesser consequence. So even if an anticipated event never occurs, it matters little. The market has already moved on what it thought would happen.

This nuance is of critical importance to the cause-and-effect relationship between economic outcomes and stock market performance. If the theory holds water, then it's the *expectation* of economic growth and expanding corporate profits that causes stock prices to move today. From this perspective, it's irrelevant whether expectations actually prove out— whether tomorrow's economy "zigs" or "zags." All that's needed is a *belief* that GDP will expand or contract. The challenge, then, is to find a reliable, unbiased method for discerning constantly changing market opinions.

Imagine an omniscient investor. She would certainly enjoy a serious advantage over her Wall Street competitors. For starters, she'd know if the economy was headed for prosperity and could anticipate when corporate profits—the stuff that fuels dividends and share prices—would boom. The advantage would also hold in reverse. At the first sniff of recession, our investor would reposition her portfolio to weather the coming storm.

Clairvoyance isn't part of the human makeup, of course. To be sure, all investors suffer their share of incorrect judgments, a natural consequence of which is to produce "winners" and "losers." But the important distinction is that they try, desperately, to "get it right." After all, they have a big incentive to do so. In this arena, participants have their wallets on the line— unlike the pundits in the financial press or on the television. So even though investors' ability to foresee events is necessarily limited, there ought to be some evidence that market participants, in their collective wisdom, tend to anticipate changing economic conditions, especially at inflection points in the economic cycle. If the exceptional test proves the rule, then a simple exercise ought to tell us something.

Over the 35-year period ended December 31, 1997, the Dow Jones

Industrial Average posted an impressive calendar-year average return of some 8.6 percent. During this interval, the United States suffered five recessions, one of which (1982) proved to be the worst U.S. economy in postwar history. If our framework for analysis has merit, then "bear" markets ought to presage economic downturns and recession periods should spawn "bull" markets. After all, amid the red ink, market participants would look for recovery.

Figure 2-5 contrasts the Dow's performance for the 6-month period leading up to, during, and following economic slowdowns. The results are highly suggestive that the stock market is forward-looking. Notice how the DJIA tended to slump prior to the onslaught of recession. Equally impressive are the extraordinary gains that preceded the recovery periods. And remember, these big market moves occurred even though the nation was still mired in recession.

There's another lesson to be gleaned from this exercise. As we discussed in Chapter 1, investors who allowed their emotions to shape their investment decisions probably couldn't understand why the champagne was flowing on Wall Street in the face of economic collapse. Too bad. As we see in Figure 2-5, with the exception of the 1969–1970 episode, by the time the recession clouds had lifted, the big surge in share prices was over. Buying opportunities were squandered.

Analysis of the empirical record also confirms that the stock market leads the economy. More specifically, regression analysis reveals a statistically significant relationship between year-over-year changes in Gross Domestic Product (the value of all goods and services produced within the borders of the United States) and previous-year fluctuations in the Dow Jones Industrial Average.[11] But we were unable to find a contemporaneous relationship between the two variables.

Finally, consider this. The evidence discussed here suggests that economists should be listening to what the ticker tape is signaling rather than telling us what it ought to be saying. Careful examination of the historical record yields more than a confirmation of Fisher's hypothesis that market prices are forward-looking and intelligent. It points to an efficient, highly objective way for investors to handicap economic forecasts and anticipate shocks to consensus thinking—a potentially valuable input.[12]

SECRETS OF THE MASTERS

Investors can't buy the Gross National Product. But they can own the factors that produce it. In a very real sense, the stock market's capitalization (share price multiplied by the total number of shares outstanding) repre-

FIGURE 2-5
Is the Stock Market Forward-Looking?

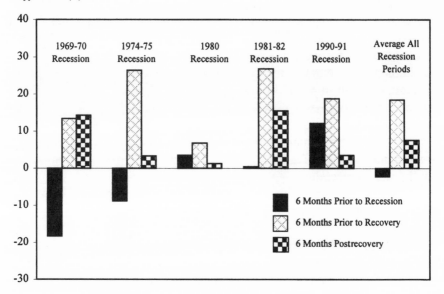

	6-Month Investment Period		
Recession	Prerecession	Prerecovery	Postrecovery
1970	-18.3	13.4	14.3
1974-75	-8.8	26.4	3.3
1980	3.5	6.8	1.3
1981-82	0.5	26.8	15.5
1990-91	12.1	18.8	3.5
Average:	-2.2	18.44	7.58

sents the value of the corporations that generate the nation's output of goods and services. As such, the stock market is the price of the economy. It's what market participants judge the economy to be worth.

The bottom line, to be drawn from the foregoing analysis, is that the stock market's fortunes are inextricably linked to the economy. Just as the knee bone is connected to the shin bone, fiscal and monetary policy influence credit prices that ripple through the economy. And as the economy goes, so go profits and dividends—the stuff investors crave. After all, in a rational expectation model, stock prices are the distillation of prospective capital gains and income flows (see Figure 2-6).

Disciplined investors don't rely on gut reactions and pundits. They ferret out empirical evidence to confirm the wisdom of opinions. Unlike stargazers, they have to live by their decisions. Small wonder, then, that market participants have little choice but to stay alert for anything that might change the economic climate. Certainly the advent of computer technology and the information highway has enabled vast numbers of investors to stay ahead of the curve. And judging from their demonstrated ability to foresee events, the collective wisdom of the marketplace is tough to beat.

Graham and Dodd had it right! Cause and effect run from the economy to the stock market. But remember, the financial markets are forward-looking. So what counts with equity investors is *expected* economic growth and, in turn, business profits and dividends.

Hence we are accustomed to say that the markets are "barometrical," or that they "discount the future." The careful security holder's eyes turn eternally toward the future. No system of evaluation can be of much account, no line of analysis can lead to any point of consequence, no long term investment program can promise any degree of satisfactory achievement, without full consciousness and acknowledgement of this underlying principle.[13]

FIGURE 2-6
Economic Prosperity and Stock Market Performance: The Linkages

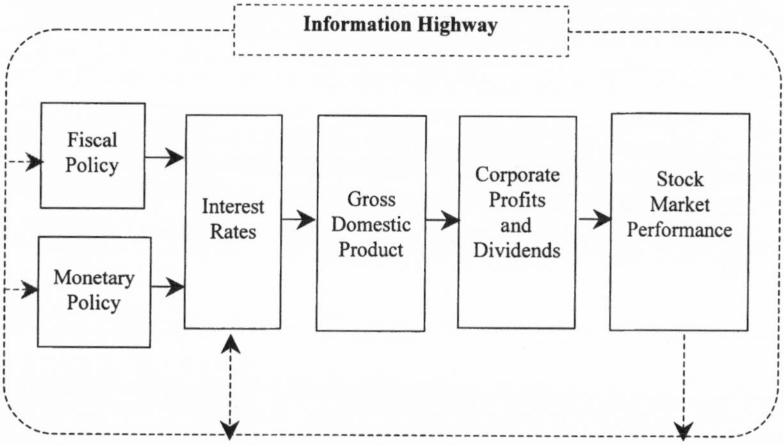

To sum up:

1.   Economic growth spurs corporate profits, dividends, and share
     price values.
2.   Fiscal and monetary policy initiatives, especially those that influ-
     ence taxes and inflation, are prime determinants of economic pros-
     perity.
3.   Changing perceptions drive market prices.

CHAPTER THREE

Be Disciplined,
Exercise Prudence

Do what you will, the capital is a hazard. . . . All that can be required of a trustee to invest, is that he shall conduct himself faithfully and exercise a sound discretion. He is to observe how men of prudence, discretion, and intelligence manage their own affairs, not in regard to speculation, but in regard to the permanent disposition of their funds, considering the probable income, as well as the safety of the capital to be invested.

Supreme Judicial Court of Massachusetts
Harvard College and Massachusetts General Hospital v. Francis Amory, 1834

MORE DURABLE WORDS WERE NEVER WRITTEN. For more than a century Justice Putnam's opinion has formed the overarching principle by which fiduciaries are judged.[1] Today the "Prudent Man Rule" enunciated by Putnam is often invoked, but few practitioners appreciate its history. The case revolved around the estate (c. 1823) of John McLean, who placed $50,000 in trust. The trustees, Jonathan and Francis Amory, were instructed to "loan the same (funds) upon ample and sufficient security, or to invest the same in safe and productive stock either in the public funds, bank shares or other stock, according to their best judgement and discretion."[2] Profits and income were to be paid over to McLean's wife, and upon her death, the residue was to be distributed to Harvard College and Massachusetts General Hospital. Unfortunately, at the time of distribution, the trust was a shadow of its former self, owing to depreciation in common stock valuations. Harvard and Mass General sued to recover the difference.

Upon review, the Court determined that the trustees had conducted themselves "honestly and discreetly and carefully, according to the existing circumstances in the discharge of their trusts" and could not be held liable for capital losses. "If this were held otherwise, no prudent man would run the hazard of losses which might happen without neglect or breach of good faith."[3]

The critical point is that the Prudent Man Rule establishes the standard for conduct—not investment performance. Prudence is a function, not of return on capital, but rather of the care, skill, and effort exercised in achieving it. Personal assets should be treated with no less regard, and a few rules of thumb ought to help guide the process.

RULE 1: DO UNTO YOURSELF WHAT FIDUCIARIES ARE REQUIRED TO DO FOR YOU.

Investors don't always act in a fiduciary-like manner. Just as some mild-mannered people suffer "road rage" when they get behind a steering wheel, otherwise conservative individuals frequently toss discretion aside when it comes to managing their financial affairs. Often they don't scratch for the information destined to shape their returns or are unduly trusting of the "expert" opinions they hear on talk shows or read in the financial press.

Examples abound. We recently bumped into a senior executive who had entrusted her financial affairs to her stockbroker, figuring that the safe-guards of a regulated industry would protect the integrity of her financial objectives. It was a mistake, not because the broker was a "bad guy" but because the executive failed to exercise diligence and disregarded the incentives operating on her account.

In the brokerage industry, it's a fairly simple business model: no trades; no commissions; no income. In this instance commissions, "minimum ticket charges," and an active trading program summed up to nearly 3 cents of every transaction dollar.[4] True, 3 cents is a modest amount. But think about it from a different perspective. Calculated on a "round trip" basis, it's equivalent to a 6 percent return on every equity investment.[5]

Unfortunately, there's more to the story. The broker advised the senior executive to move a quarter of her account into mutual funds, two of which had a scanty 12-month track record. And one year does not a record make. Plus they were expensive. On top of a 1.8 percent expense ratio, all the funds paid an additional 1 percent to the brokerage house each year ("12b-1 fees") and carried a 4 to 5 percent "deferred load" phased out over a 5-year period ("contingent deferred sales charges"). So, in effect, the executive was "locked in" if she wanted to avoid these contingency fees. Wow!

None of this should be construed as an indictment of the brokerage community. There are always a few bad apples in every harvest. Forget about the broker. Our allegory is intended to illustrate what can go awry when investors become complacent or relax their defenses. Fiduciaries don't put themselves in harm's way. They're ever mindful that the wisdom of their investment decisions must withstand scrutiny. They do their homework even if it means wading through the fine print in a prospectus and consulting mutual fund rating services like Morningstar.

Above all, fiduciaries never lose sight of a basic tenet put forth long ago by Laurence Sloan:

> **The waste of capital is an abhorrent thing. And we are not thinking of waste in the sense of destruction, but rather dissipation. We consider capital to have been dissipated, or wasted, when it is needlessly lost. It is needlessly lost, in most cases, through ignorance or carelessness.[6]**

RULE 2: WORRY ABOUT THE RETURN OF YOUR MONEY AS WELL AS THE RETURN ON IT.

Credit Will Rogers for this insight. While he may have played the rube on occasion, he knew how to hang on to his money. He recognized the importance of striking a happy balance between capital preservation and capital creation. Too often unsuspecting investors are dazzled by the allure of above-average dividend yields or extraordinary interest rates. They don't question why some securities yield more than others. Usually, those reasons boil down to risk.

Think back to the 1980s, when high-yield ("junk") bonds were fashionable—even a symbol of cachet—with high rollers. Though the bonds were considered less than investment grade by the rating services, a lot of fixed income investors bragged about the 17 percent yield they were pocketing, which was roughly 11 percentage points higher than what they'd earn on "no-brainer" Treasuries.

But those high-yield bonds often went to fund high-priced hostile takeovers or overextended leveraged buyouts. When the economy crashed in the 1990–1991 recession, the high-yield bonds earned their nickname. Many of the debtors were wiped out and default rates soared! All of a sudden, that 17 percent interest rate didn't mean very much.

Surprisingly, in the late 1990s junk bonds made a comeback as investors stepped out on the risk curve to "pick up" some extra return. By mid-1997 the average junk yield was down to around 9 percent and junk bond fund managers were encouraging investors to get the highest yield they could.[7] We'd certainly agree with that attitude, to a point. In the strong economy of the late 1990s, the potential risks of high-yield investments seem, well, a remote possibility, much as they did at the height of the boom of the 1980s. But just as the 1990–1991 recession converted potential risk into reality, another economic downturn would probably exact a similar toll—in a hurry.

Junk bonds aren't the only example. A lot of investors probably couldn't believe their bad luck when the Three Mile Island nuclear accident (March 27, 1979) blew a hole in General Public Utilities' share price. If you were living on dividend income, GPU undoubtedly showed up on your radar screen and, possibly, in your portfolio. After all, the company was likely to maintain its franchise as the electricity provider for New Jersey and Pennsylvania, and its dividend yield topped 18 percent—three times that of the general market.

The situation was a trap. And even though the company survived, the crisis was financially devastating. As shown in Figure 3-1, over the balance of 1979 the company halved its dividend and eliminated it altogether in early 1980.

It shouldn't have been a surprise. Forward-looking market prices were flashing the danger signal well in advance of the cut. Look at the change in GPU's share price during the period leading up to the dividend cut. More evidence of the market's intelligence is visible in the graph. Notice the price action of the stock prior to the reinstatement of the dividend.

The lesson here is that it's tough to outsmart the market. When investors think they spot an anomaly in the pricing of financial markets, they should think again before risking a divergent strategy. In effect, they're betting against the collective wisdom of market participants. While they may be justified in their opinion, savvy investors ask themselves what they know that the marketplace either is unaware of or is unwilling to pay for. They consider the answer carefully.

As the saying goes, if something seems too good to be true, it probably is.

RULE 3: BE DISCIPLINED. WAIT FOR THE FASTBALL.

In baseball, good hitters study the opposing pitcher early in the game to see if he has his best "stuff." Is he wild or does he have his control? Is he throwing hard or lacking velocity? Are his pitches lively or flat?

Let's say he's a great curveball pitcher. The hitters know that if he's sharp, they're going to be seeing that bender all day long, and not many of them will be hitting it. But if he can't find the strike zone with the curves, eventually he's going to have to start throwing fastballs—perhaps fat, flat,

FIGURE 3-1
Beware of Extraordinary Deals
General Public Utilities

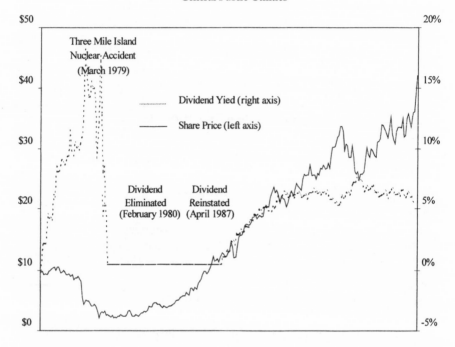

hittable fastballs. So they stay away from the curves and wait for their opportunities.

The hitters are poised for the advantage, just as investors should capitalize on opportunities when they appear. If it's possible to recognize, even in some small way, that one moment is more favorable than others to invest, market players could reduce the risk that comes with buying stocks. And if they could determine those moments through some sort of quantifiable measure, rather than the educated guesses of others, they could invest more aggressively.

As you'll read in Chapter 6, patient investors looking to put money to work in the stock market could follow an approach we call "dynamic hedging." The methodology is highly disciplined and manages two critical variables: time and volatility. In a nutshell, half the equity portfolio is funded straightaway. Then the strategy turns opportunistic. Whenever the market suffers a "correction," the technique allows investors to shift incremental funds into the portfolio according to the magnitude of the downturn. Absent volatility, though, the balance of the cash position is "averaged into" the market at regular intervals.

RULE 4: AVOID ALL-OR-NOTHING BETS. MAINTAIN ADEQUATE DIVERSIFICATION.

Diversification is the means by which investors exploit turbulent markets while mollifying risk. At root, it's a simple idea that recognizes that asset classes and investment styles don't move in lockstep fashion. So why put all your eggs in one basket? As Roger Babson summed up the point:

> **By a division of funds into separate parts, the investor is always in position to take advantage of every contingency and benefit from every change. Such a plan eliminates the worry and trouble of wondering what is going to happen next and the danger of placing all one's eggs in one basket.**[8]

Go back to our General Public Utilities example. Obviously, there had never been a nuclear accident on the scale of Three Mile Island. (And there hasn't been one since.) But for GPU shareholders, once was quite enough. Obviously, it would have been a huge blunder to chase a double-digit dividend yield at the exclusion of other investment vehicles.

Beyond single-stock portfolios, there are a host of ways to paint yourself into a corner. Imagine a portfolio consisting entirely of utility stocks. Sure, investment risk would be spread across a number of issues, but the problem is far from over. Think about the effect on portfolio values of legislation creating the Environmental Protection Agency.

The moral here is to spread your money around. Depending on your investment objectives and the size of your nest egg, consider diversifying across asset classes, investment styles, geographical borders, and investment philosophies. Listen, again, to Roger Babson:

> **Prudence demands diversification, not only among companies, but also as to geographical distribution of industries, types of securities and time of purchase and sale. Planning to do this sometime in the future is not enough. Action in establishing immediately a proper investment program is most important; it is the foundation for the other steps.**[9]

And be aware that all-or-nothing bets can occur in the time domain as well. As we discuss more fully in the chapters ahead, typically the problem surfaces when investors worry about missing a bull market. Many people just pile right in, figuring that stock prices have nowhere to go but up. In effect, the investor is betting that a specific moment will prove to be the optimal time to expose capital to equity risk. Maybe so, but the odds seem slim.

Finally, keep in mind that market fluctuations can throw asset allocations out of kilter. Consider an investor who determined at the end of 1994 that an appropriate asset mix was 70 percent equities, 25 percent bonds, and 5 percent cash. Over the ensuing 36-month period, assuming that there was no rebalancing activity and that the various components of the portfolio kept pace with their respective benchmarks, the asset mix would become meaningfully different (equities, 80%; bonds, 17.5%; and cash, 3%)—leaving the investor overly exposed to equity risk.[10] So it's a good idea to subject your asset allocation plan to an annual checkup and rebalance as needed.

RULE 5: EXPLOIT REPEATING PHENOMENA.

In an earlier chapter we talked about the linkage between interest rates, gross domestic product, and corporate profit outcomes—the stuff that drives equity prices. So the interest rate outlook is important. Just imagine the impact on equity prices should riskless Treasury bill yields rise to double-digit proportions, as they did in the early 1980s. Few observers would expect the equity market to remain unaffected. Small wonder, then, that investors worry so much about the path of interest rates.

But here's a question: Why ask an economist which way interest rates are headed when you can easily find out what market participants are saying with their checkbooks? Futures contracts for Treasury bills have traded on the International Monetary Market (a division of the Chicago Mercantile Exchange) since January 1976 and provide an example of a repeating phenomenon that you can consult daily.[11] Participants in the futures market can express their view (today) as to where T-bill yields are headed, up to 2 years in advance.

History shows that futures market quotations can provide an unbiased, reliable estimate of the upcoming year's average T-bill rate. Assuming you buy the financial dailies anyway, the marginal cost of acquiring this implicit market forecast is "zip." But even if these implicit forecasts mirrored expert opinion, why pay for something when you can get reliable information for nothing?

Dividend policy, as we'll see in Chapter 5, is another example of a repeating phenomenon. Some companies pay no dividends, of course. But that's still a policy. Others are stingy or have spotty records, occasionally cutting (or even forgoing) their dividend. However they set dividend policy, you can bet management will adhere to it doggedly.

Consider General Electric, the only company in today's Dow Jones Industrial Average that was a constituent of the index when it was invented 100 years ago. GE not only boasts an uninterrupted record of dividend payments dating from 1899 but, impressively, has religiously increased its dividend every year since 1975. That's a repeating phenomenon.

These days a lot of investors don't attach much importance to dividends. Too bad, because dividends contribute significantly to share price. Think about a $100 stock that pays $1 in dividends. Its current yield is a paltry 1 percent ($1 ÷ $100 = 1%). No big deal.

Now imagine that the dividend increased by 10 percent a year for the next quarter century. What's the "yield on cost"? Some 10.8 percent.[12] But there's an even bigger point. In the 25th year, the current yield isn't likely to be 11 percent. Other factors being constant, if the stock was priced to maintain the same current yield over time, the share price would have to appreciate from $100 to $1,080. That's significant. What's more, when the stock market turns choppy, it's always nice to have dividends to lean on.

RULE 6: TAKE ACCOUNT OF COSTS AND TAXES.

Sounds like a simple enough proposition, doesn't it? But you'd be amazed how often investors forget what counts: the jingle that ends up in *their* pocket. Thinking about buying a mutual fund? You'll be hard pressed to find any that fully adjust their historical performance for costs and taxes, even if the adjustment is based on a hypothetical example.

Figure 3-2 illustrates a real, albeit extreme case. Consider this: a hedge fund reported a whopping 72 percent gross return for calendar year 1997—eclipsing the S&P 500 stock index by a wide margin. As with many hedge funds, the excess return was subject to a performance fee "kicker" (20%). Assuming the portfolio was fully taxable with short-term gains subject to a 50 percent combined state and federal tax rate, the gap between the fund's performance and that of the general market nearly evaporated.[13] And that's before any allowance is made for risk differentials.

Unfortunately, there's reason to believe that taxes and costs take a heavy toll on investment returns generally. A recent study examined the differences between gross and net returns accruing to a large number of actively managed equity mutual funds over a 25-year period. The conclusion was astonishing and worth reading if investors are to avoid getting the short end of the stick.[14]

RULE 7: DON'T THINK OF VARIABLES AS CONSTANTS.

Beanbags have memory. They tend to retain the shape of the last person who sat on them. But whatever their configuration, nobody would think it's permanent. When it comes to variability, few things rival the financial markets. Yet even though we know instinctively that equity markets are turbulent, our perception of the future is shaped by recent history. We're inclined to extrapolate current market trends—a phenomenon that can be

FIGURE 3-2

Tax-Aware Investing

1997 Investment Performance

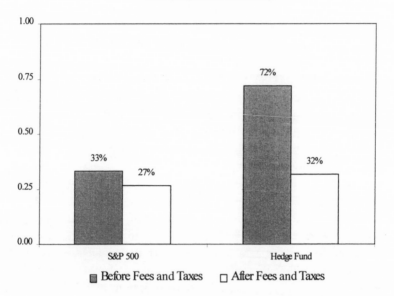

☐ Before Fees and Taxes   ☐ After Fees and Taxes

hazardous to investment results, especially at inflection points in the market cycle.

The 1995–1997 bull market is a case in point. On the heels of a 120 percent cumulative gain in the Dow Jones Industrial Average (including dividends), investors were positively giddy over their newly minted wealth. The stock market was hailed as the only game in town. Why go for 5 or 6 percent fixed income securities when equities were providing double-digit returns? Measured over the last quarter century, the DJIA's average annual return was an impressive 14.5 percent, roughly twice that of cash equivalents.

So what's to worry about? Even a bad year for stocks would probably beat safe money. Maybe. A simple exercise illustrates the point. In Figure 3-3 we've plotted the cumulative value of a dollar invested in the DJIA from the end of 1972 through 1997 against the value of 3-month Treasury bills mindlessly rolled over during the same period. As shown, over the first half of the period, equity investors were kicked to death by a rabbit. Over the initial 12-year period, T-bills outperformed the Dow in half the years. Through 1985 at least, investors would have done just as well with riskless Treasuries. You can bet that investors in 1985 weren't quite so enamored of the stock market as they are currently.

But just as investors ought to resist the temptation to extrapolate bull markets, it is equally important for them not to allow the bear market environment to jaundice their thinking about equity investments. As Figure 3-3 shows, over the ensuing period (1986–1997) the Dow's average annual return zipped up to nearly 20 percent versus a paltry 5.7 percent for Treasury bills.

RULE 8: DISTRUST STORY LINES.

Investors always seek comfort in their decisions, especially when the going gets tough. Unfortunately, there's no safety in numbers. Just because a lot of people profess the same viewpoint doesn't make it right. Omniscience isn't part of the human psyche. Simply put, there's no substitute for homework and a carefully orchestrated game plan.

Just imagine the beleaguered investor who, having just regained consciousness from the 1987 crash, reentered the stock market at the end of 1989. Uh, oh. Months later, in the aftermath of the Iraq invasion, equity returns were decidedly negative. Worse, according to the financial press at the time, recovery prospects were bleak. If the experts were right, the impending war would precipitate conflagration of Kuwait's oil fields and trigger a surge in energy prices, rampant inflation, and a deeper, longer-lived recession.

FIGURE 3-3
The Stock Market in Perspective

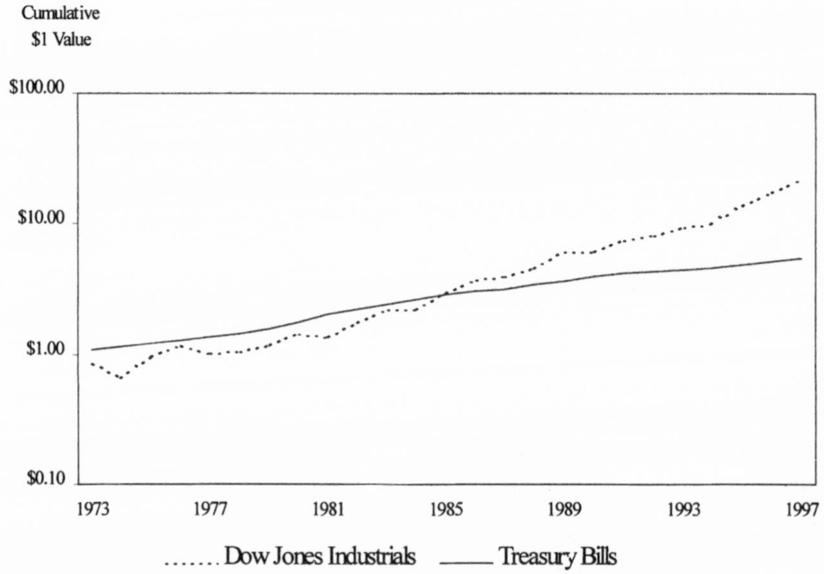

Cumulative
$1 Value

.... Dow Jones Industrials _____ Treasury Bills

Discouraged, many equity investors bailed out after the market plunged roughly 15 percent during the August–October 1990 period. Too bad. As shown in Figure 3-4, undisciplined investors suffered a double whammy. The Saddam factor notwithstanding, stock prices rebounded. In the face of armed conflict, burning oil platforms, and recession, the stock market appreciated better than 20 percent in 1991. So what's the message? Turn off the TV and stick by your plan. Don't let the evening news guide your investment decisions. Stay disciplined.

RULE 9: THINK ABOUT LIQUIDITY.
Liquidity is yet another problem faced by investors. Don't let untimely cash requirements compromise sound investment decisions. You could trigger a tax event and may not be able to reestablish the position at favorable price levels. Don't overextend yourself. Keep some cash in reserve so you can take advantage of corrections to round out positions or meet unexpected household needs.

Also, be aware that some stocks are thinly traded, especially in the Nasdaq market. "Bid" and "ask" quotations are for the first round lot (100 shares). There's no telling what the price of the "nth" lot will be. Depending on the size of your position, you could influence the price, especially if your trade coincides with a big market move. A lot of investors learned this lesson the hard way in 1987 as sellers rushed for the exit en masse.

FIGURE 3-4
Distrust Story Lines: The Desert Storm Experience

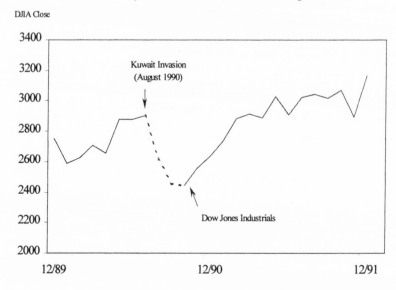

Even the most carefully selected stocks purchased with any funds are subject to severe price declines in sympathy with other stocks in a readjustment of the market. Hence it is essential that the investor should be in a secure financial position so that he will not be forced to liquidate his good holdings.[16]

RULE 10: PROPER PRIOR PREPARATION PREVENTS POOR PERFORMANCE.

Now for the cardinal rule: expect the unexpected, and plan accordingly. As much as we like to think we're in control of our destiny, reality says otherwise. In our fully integrated global economy, it matters what central bankers, politicians, and multinational corporate leaders are doing worldwide. The key to successful investing revolves around a few critical elements:

- Know yourself.
- Understand your objectives.
- Devise a responsive plan.
- Remain disciplined.
- Think defense.

Portfolio management is—and always should be—a defensive process. The goal of the portfolio manager is to control or manage risk in pursuit of wisely determined and explicitly stated objectives of the investor or beneficiaries.[15]

SECRETS OF THE MASTERS

Navigating the financial markets can be hazardous. It pays to understand the rules of the road. Boiled down, investors are advised to:

1. Exercise prudence and cautious risk taking.
2. Be skeptical.
3. Be methodical; devise a long-term plan and stick with it.

CHAPTER FOUR

Risk/Return Trade-offs

The most important questions of life are, for the most part, really only problems of probability.

Pierre Simon De Laplace
1749–1827

"CONGRATULATIONS," YOUR INVESTMENT ADVISER tells you one day, "you lost only 10 percent in last year's market. If you had been across the street, you would have lost 20 percent." Imagine being handed that line. It's a strange point of view when investors are expected to be grateful to their money managers for steering them on a course that leaves them with less in their pocket. Believe it or not, though, such statements are heard with surprising regularity when "relative" return (performance relative to a benchmark or peer group) is the game and "absolute" return (whether the portfolio finishes in the "red" or "black") is ignored.

Investment return is important, that's for certain. But it's not enough to base our money management decisions on. Defending ourselves against risk is also integral to every investment program. Wall Street is littered with "hot tips" that ended up on the ash heap. Effective plans reconcile investors' return expectations with their tolerance for risk, tax bracket, and investment horizon. That's a lot to consider. Beyond absolute and relative risk, the list of portfolio killers includes volatility, inflation, taxes, and transaction costs.

In this chapter we'll explore some basic concepts, sort of an investor's tool kit, effective in portfolio analysis and construction. Yes, a degree of instruction is required. And just as it takes a moment to learn the correct way to use a circular saw or router, so the numerical measurement devices described in the pages ahead require a bit of concentration. But a tool worth having is worth using. Once this knowledge is mastered, the utility gained will, we trust, outweigh the cost of acquiring it. Laurence Sloan put it this way:

> There is intended no intimidation here that a high degree of expertness is absolutely necessary in the use of these tools by the average investor. A working knowledge of them will ordinarily suffice.... Increasing knowledge of the tools of security market analysis over a period of time can assuredly do no harm; this writer holds that it can do nothing in the world but enhance the probability of attaining more satisfactory results.[1]

WHAT RETURN?

When investors swap equity ideas, conversations tend to center on returns. In a nutshell, people crave performance and want to know the likelihood that it will continue. That's to be expected. After all, if capital is to be put at risk, investors need to feel reasonably sure that their expectations will pan out. One way to anticipate future outcomes is to understand the past. The process starts by identifying a stock's historical average return—a term used to describe a number of statistical measures.[2] Here's what Sloan believed:

> Statistics provide the tool with which one digs . . . with which one discovers relationships . . . gives mathematical values to these relationships . . . computes and detects the true significance of mathematical facts . . . reveals comparisons and contrasts . . . produces derived data that are highly helpful. Statistics function as a searchlight. By their use one reveals and illuminates.[3]

The Mean

The arithmetic mean of a series of returns is the most popular definition of "average." It's determined by dividing the sum of the returns by the number of values in the sample. Table 4-1 illustrates. Company A's annual returns over the past 5 years add up to 50 percent. So its mean return is: 10 percent

TABLE 4-1
Company A Calendar-Year Returns

	Return
Year 1	8.0%
Year 2	9.0%
Year 3	10.0%
Year 4	11.0%
Year 5	12.0%
Sum:	50.0%
Mean:	10.0%

(50 ÷ 5 = 10). But, as we're about to learn, the mean isn't the only definition of average. And different measures give different impressions—some dramatically so.

The Median

The median value of a series of numbers is another definition of "average." Although few investment professionals pay much attention to it, often it provides a more robust indication of what's termed the "central tendency" of a stock's performance. By definition, the median is the central point of a distribution such that an equal number of returns fall to either side.

Look again at Table 4-1. Here we can quickly see that the median of Company A's data is 10 percent (year 3), since two of the calendar-year returns are below and two are above this result. But what if there's no "middle number" that conveniently bisects the data? In this instance, the median is calculated as the arithmetic mean between the two middle values. Using the example at hand, erase the final row (year 5) from the table. The middle values are now 9 and 10, giving a median of 9.5 percent ((9 + 10) ÷ 2 = 9.5).

At first glance, the significance of the median (and hence its usefulness) as a separate statistic from the mean may not be apparent. So imagine an investor who is contemplating a purchase of Company A's common stock. While speaking with a broker, the investor learns about Company B, a competing firm that has an identical 5-year mean return and that looks to be "cheaper" in price. Shouldn't the investor go with Company B if both companies generated the same return?

Maybe, but looks can be deceiving. The pattern of returns could hold a secret. And the median statistic can unlock it. To see how, observe Table 4-2. True enough, both companies achieved the same mean return (10%). But that's where the similarity ends. Company B's performance was far less impressive—a fact that is obscured by the 50 percent return in year 4. The median is far less susceptible to distortions caused by a few extreme outcomes. In Table 4-2, the median shows a "central tendency" or "average" outcome of zero. All of a sudden, there are issues worth investigating.

The Mode

Though rarely used, the mode provides another interesting barometer of a stock's potential. Briefly, the mode is the most frequently observed or commonplace value. Again, Table 4-2 provides a good illustration. Just "eyeballing" Company B's data reveals another disturbing characteristic: the mode of its returns is 0 percent. When the mode is viewed in combination with the median, few observers would expect the stream of well-behaved double-digit returns suggested by the arithmetic mean.

TABLE 4-2
Mean vs. Median Stock Market Returns

	Company A	Company B
Year 1	8.0%	25.0%
Year 2	9.0%	-25.0%
Year 3	10.0%	0.0%
Year 4	11.0%	50.0%
Year 5	12.0%	0.0%
Sum:	50.0%	50.0%
Mean:	10.0%	10.0%
Median:	10.0%	0.0%

What about Company A? All its calendar-year results occurred with the same frequency ("1"). Hence the mode of its returns is nonmeaningful. This brings us to another point. When it comes to the mode, don't worry about precision. Perspective is the objective. If you get caught up on accuracy to the "*n*th" decimal place when describing year-to-year investment results, you may never find a mode. Indeed, all the values are likely to be different, even if only by a smidgen. So forget decimals. Round off the returns to the nearest integer (8, 9, 10, etc.) and then check.

Better yet, sort the values according to descriptive intervals (e.g., 0–4%; 5–9%; 10–14%) and calculate the frequency of returns falling in each range. With respect to the data in Table 4-2, we could still separate the wheat from the chaff. Company A would fall into the 10–14 percent bucket while Company B would be viewed as a 0–4 percent performer.

The Geometric Mean

Returns are the stuff investors prize. Statistics merely provide a convenient way to envision probable outcomes. As is already evident, reliance on one or two calculations can be hazardous. Caution should also be exercised when using the arithmetic mean to compound investment returns over time. For this exercise, the geometric mean is the handy statistic.[4]

Examine Table 4-3. After the initial 2-year period, some Company B shareholders may have concluded that their portfolio was at breakeven. After all, they were up 25 percent after the first year and down 25 percent in the second. Unfortunately, that's not the way breakeven works. In reality, the investment would be underwater.

To see why, think about portfolio values in terms of dollars, not percentage changes. A year into the cycle, every $1 would have grown to $1.25. Now think about a 25 percent decline in the second year. The loss

TABLE 4-3
What Return? Is It the Mean, Median, Mode, or Geometric Mean?

	Company A		Company B	
	Return	Cumulative Value per $1 Invested	Return	Cumulative Value per $1 Invested
Year 1	8.0%	1.08	25.0%	1.25
Year 2	9.0%	1.18	-25.0%	0.94
Year 3	10.0%	1.29	0.0%	0.94
Year 4	11.0%	1.44	50.0%	1.41
Year 5	12.0%	1.61	0.0%	1.41
Sum:	50.0%		50.0%	
Mean:	10.0%		10.0%	
Median:	10.0%		0.0%	
Mode:	N.M.		0.0%	
Geomean:	9.99%		7.06%	

would have been $.31, not $.25 (1.25 · 0.25 = 0.31). So instead of being at breakeven, the portfolio of Company B shareholders would show only 96 cents for every dollar invested.

As shown in the table, over the entire period, a $1 investment in Company B would have compounded to $1.41. By comparison, the identical investment in Company A shares would have achieved a cumulative value of $1.61, even though both companies had the same "average" return as measured by the arithmetic mean.

The geometric mean circumvents this mathematical quirk. It enables investors to identify the average annual (or "annualized") rate of return required to generate these ending values.[5] Check it out. Multiply a dollar by a constant 7.06 percent rate (the geometric mean of Company B's returns) each year for 5 years. You'll end up with $1.41. If we judge from the geometric means, there's no mystery why Company B looks "cheap" compared with Company A. Close to a 30 percent differential in the compound rate of return separates the investment alternatives.

Statistical analysis demonstrates that market participants are discerning and recognize the indicators of inferior performance. The importance of returns notwithstanding, savvy investors never pursue "cheap" stocks without understanding the risk factors associated with them. Here's a final distinguishing point. The geometric mean describes the "typical" multiple-year performance, while the arithmetic mean measures the "typical" single-year outcome.

How are you doing with these numbers so far? If something's not clear, we recommend that you reread the relevant section before moving forward.

WHAT RISK?

Just as there are a host of definitions and measures of investment returns, so there are a variety of ways to think about risk. Fortunately a fairly simple tool, "distribution analysis," can yield valued inputs sufficient for most investor needs.

Distribution analysis rounds out a stock's performance profile by examining the variability or dispersion of its returns. Here's a quick example. The "range of returns" measures the difference or spread between the worst and best result in the series. In the case of Company A, the distribution is bordered by 8 percent to the south and 12 percent to the north. Hence the range is 4 percent. What about Company B? Even though it had the same mean, the range of its returns is 75 percent. Is a picture emerging? We're talking volatility. And make no mistake. Investors aren't cavalier about it. In the investment world, volatility *is* risk.

The Standard Deviation

Good investors never chase returns without knowing the risks involved. In addition to the range of historical returns, we could develop an idea of a stock's volatility by calculating the "deviation" of each year's performance relative to its average outcome. For instance, Company A's first-year return was 8 percent versus its mean of 10 percent. So the year 1 deviation was minus 2 percent. Obviously, the "sign" of the deviation (negative or positive) is simply a matter of whether the particular year's result was lower or higher than average. Over the entire 5-year interval, Company A's annual deviations fluctuated between −2 and +2 percent while Company B's deviations bounced between −35 and +40 percent. From this angle, Company B is obviously far more volatile (i.e., riskier) than Company A.

While the spread in deviations tells us something, why not reduce this perspective to a single number that captures a stock's average deviation—its volatility—in one fell swoop? In other words, let's define its typical or "standard deviation."[6]

As we'll discuss in the pages and chapters that follow, the standard deviation is enormously useful. It allows us to shape our thinking about the likelihood of an event. For some high-stake players, Company B's volatility might not be all that alarming. After all, if it earned a 50 percent return once, it could always do it again. Perhaps, but the odds seem awfully slim. Maybe these players would be less enthusiastic if they realized that two-thirds of the possible outcomes were likely to fall between −18.5 and 38.5 percent and that the chance of suffering a loss (a 36% chance) was a lot higher than witnessing another grand slam (an 8% chance). The standard deviation statistic enables us to develop this perspective.

Given the importance of the standard deviation, let's take a moment to talk about its construction (see Table 4-4). Our first step is to "square" all the annual deviations. The year 1 calculation for Company A is −2 · −2 = 4. Then we sum all the squared values and divide by the number of returns in the series. In statistical parlance, the result at this point is the "variance." Hence, as shown in Table 4-4, Company A's variance is 2.

While understanding the variance is helpful, the initial step in the process (i.e., squaring the deviations) produces large numbers relative to their original magnitude. And large numbers can be unwieldy. Certainly Company B's variance (650) seems remarkably out of context when its largest single-year deviation is 40. The remedy is to create a new statistic, the "standard deviation," by taking the square root of the variance.[7] As shown in Table 4-4, it would be an understatement to say that Company A's risk factor, as captured by the standard deviation of its returns, is lower than that of Company B (1.58 vs. 28.5). It is by far.

Just as returns shouldn't drive investment decisions, so volatility (or the lack of it) shouldn't be the sole determinant of a security's investment merit. The bigger issue is whether investors will be compensated for exposing themselves to the marginal risk. In some instances, the extra headache

TABLE 4-4
Measuring Volatility

	Company A			Company B		
	Return	Deviation	Deviation (Sq)	Return	Deviation	Deviation (Sq)
Year 1	8.00	-2.00	4.00	25.00	15.00	225.00
Year 2	9.00	-1.00	1.00	-25.00	-35.00	1,225.00
Year 3	10.00	0.00	0.00	0.00	-10.00	100.00
Year 4	11.00	1.00	1.00	50.00	40.00	1,600.00
Year 5	12.00	2.00	4.00	0.00	-10.00	100.00
Sum of deviations (Sq)		10.00				3,250.00
Variance:		2.00				650.00
Standard deviation:		1.58				28.50
Mean return:		10.00				10.00
Return per unit of risk:		6.32				0.35

may be worth it. Fortunately, there's an easy way to determine how much return a stock is likely to deliver per unit of risk. We just divide its mean return by its standard deviation.[8] Once again, if history's a guide, Company A wins hands down (6.32 vs. 0.35 in Table 4-4).

OK. Now that we understand that volatility equals risk and how to measure it, let's discuss some practical applications of the standard deviation. We realize that formulas can be heavy. But stick with it. Even a cursory understanding of this subject matter can be helpful.

Estimating Absolute Risk

As we mentioned earlier, the standard deviation enables us to measure the odds of a general outcome using a statistical rule of thumb. The genealogy of statistical inference, using the standard deviation to estimate the frequency of probable outcomes, has a rich history in mathematics. The most recent (classical) contributor was P. L. Tchebyshev, a 19th century Russian mathematician who posited that, given a series of random values, at least $1 - 1/k^2$ of them will lie within k standard deviations of their mean value, where k is a number *greater than or equal to 1*.[9]

To envision Tchebyshev's Theorem, look at Figure 4-1. From our previous discussion, we know that Company A's mean return is 10 percent with a standard deviation of 1.58 percent. For the purpose of this exercise, the mean locates the midpoint of the graph. Now, from Tchebyshev's formula, how many returns will be contained in an interval defined as the mean, plus and minus 2 standard deviations? The answer, as we're about to see, is at least 75 percent of the outcomes.[10]

While the answer is easily derived from the formula, rather than going through the math every time, Table 4-5 schedules the frequency of outcomes falling within various intervals using Tchebyshev's Theorem. For the example at hand, then, 2 standard deviations for Company A would

FIGURE 4-1
Tchebyshev's Theorem: Measuring the Frequency of Returns
Company A Returns

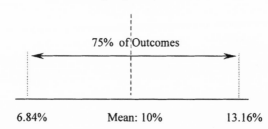

75% of Outcomes

6.84%   Mean: 10%   13.16%

TABLE 4-5
Tchebyshev's Distribution Values

Interval about the Mean (Standard Deviations)	Percentage of Outcomes Contained in Interval
1.0	00.0
1.5	55.6
2.0	75.0
2.5	84.0
3.0	88.9
3.5	91.8
4.0	93.8
4.5	95.1
5.0	96.0
5.5	96.7
6.0	97.2
6.5	97.6
7.0	98.0
7.5	98.2
8.0	98.4
8.5	98.6
9.0	98.8
9.5	98.9
10.0	99.0

equal 3.16 percent. Hence, as we see from Table 4-5, at least 75 percent of Company A's returns are likely to fall between 6.84 and 13.16 percent, as depicted in Figure 4-1.

By the same fashion, we could easily figure out how many outcomes would fall within any number of standard deviations (k) about the mean, as long as the k is *greater than or equal to 1.* Say an investor is comfortable with the perspective that at least 75 percent of Company A's returns are likely to fall between 6.8 and 13.2 percent, but wants to know how frequently the outcomes are likely to fall within a narrower range—say, between 7.5 and 12.5 percent. As before, the initial step is to express the interval in terms of standard deviations. In this case, we're talking about bracketing Company A's average return by 2.5 percentage points, which is 1.58 standard deviations on either side of its mean.[11]

By interpolating from Table 4-5, we can quickly determine that better than 55.6 percent of the potential outcomes ought to be contained in an interval from 7.5 to 12.5 percent.[12] Not bad.

Here's another exercise. What's the chance of losing money with Company A? Stated a bit differently, the question boils down to estimating the frequency of returns below zero. Since zero lies 6.33 standard deviations below Company A's average return ($10 - 0 = 10 \div 1.58 = 6.33$), according to Tchebyshev at least 97 percent of the outcomes would be expected to fall between 0 and 20 percent. So *fewer than* 3 percent of the outcomes are likely to be negative, since some of the remaining possibilities would exceed 20 percent.

While the frequency of a negative outcome is a rough-and-ready calculation, an important point is resolved. The odds that investors will suffer a principal loss (absolute risk) with Company A shares are low. And since investing is an art form, that's probably all we need to know.

In sum, Tchebyshev's Theorem offers investors a highly useful, straightforward way to estimate probable stock market outcomes, with two advantages:

• It yields gross (or conservative) approximations.
• It's applicable to any distribution of returns, not just those that are neatly described by the symmetrical "normal" or "bell-shaped" curve.

But here is the serious limitation of Tchebyshev's formula:

• It requires that the interval (or range of returns) subject to measurement be at least 1 standard deviation on either side of the mean.

Think about Company B. Given a mean value of 10 and a standard deviation of 28.5, what fraction of Company B's returns would be expected to fall below zero? As before, the interval between 0 and 10 percent is the same as in the Company A exercise. But when we express it in terms of standard deviations, the resulting value is only 0.35 ($10 - 0 = 10 \div 28.5 = 0.35$). So there's a problem.

As we emphasized in our opening comments, Tchebyshev's Theorem yields nonmeaningful answers when the range of possible outcomes is less than 1 standard deviation removed from the mean. Hence the absence of values in Table 4-5 for measurements less than 1 standard deviation. So what now?

One solution is to rely on other statistics listed in Table 4-3. Since Company B's median return is zero, for instance, the chance of losing money in a given calendar year is fairly high, probably around 50 percent. For our purposes, that may be as good a "signal" as any. But there's an alternative.

We could assume that our returns are "normally distributed" and use an empirical rule introduced in the early 1700s by Abraham DeMoivre to estimate the odds of a subzero performance.[13] More specifically, DeMoivre's empirical rule defines the following intervals:

• The mean ± 1 standard deviation will contain 68 percent of the probable outcomes.

- The mean $\pm$ 2 standard deviations will contain 95 percent of the probable outcomes.
- The mean $\pm$ 3 standard deviations will contain 99.7 percent of the probable outcomes.[14]

To simplify matters, Table 4-6 presents the "normal distribution values" associated with various outcomes as measured in terms of standard deviations about their mean value—including those that are less than 1 standard deviation from the mean. Again, rather than fretting over formulas, we can get to the answer by referring to the table.

Here's an illustration using the Company B exercise. Rounded off, a negative return would describe all outcomes more than 0.4 standard deviations below the mean. Now look at Table 4-6 to the right of 0.4. As shown, roughly 34 percent of the probable outcomes are likely to be less than zero—not exactly an inconsequential number.

Estimating Relative Risk

The procedure for calculating the chance of underperforming a benchmark (relative risk) follows along the same lines, except that we'll need to convert our return data much as we did for Table 4-3. For the sake of discussion, assume that the Dow Jones Industrial Average is the appropriate benchmark for comparison. To keep the numbers simple, imagine that the Dow generated a 7.5 percent return every year.

TABLE 4-6
The Normal Distribution Values

Standard Deviation	Normal Distribution Value	Standard Deviation	Normal Distribution Value	Standard Deviation	Normal Distribution Value
0.0	0.5000	1.0	0.1587	2.0	0.0228
0.1	0.4602	1.1	0.1357	2.1	0.0179
0.2	0.4207	1.2	0.1151	2.2	0.0139
0.3	0.3821	1.3	0.0968	2.3	0.0107
0.4	0.3446	1.4	0.0808	2.4	0.0082
0.5	0.3085	1.5	0.0668	2.5	0.0062
0.6	0.2743	1.6	0.0548	2.6	0.0047
0.7	0.2420	1.7	0.0446	2.7	0.0035
0.8	0.2119	1.8	0.0359	2.8	0.0026
0.9	0.1841	1.9	0.0287	2.9	0.0019
				3.0	0.0013

Begin by converting the return data to dollars. If Company A posted an 8 percent return in year 1, then every dollar invested in Company A would have grown to $1.08 by the end of the first year. Hence its relative return, rounded off, would be 1.005.[15] Table 4-7 lists the fully converted data series.

As with our earlier discussion, relative returns equal to 1 indicate that the security's return was identical to the Dow's. Values greater than 1 reflect positive relative returns and vice versa. Estimating the relative risk associated with Company A shares, then, is a matter of figuring out how often Company A's relative returns are likely to be less than 1. As with absolute returns, the starting point is to subtract 1 from the mean relative return and express the distance in terms of standard deviations; in this instance, the distance is equal to 1.53 standard deviations.[16]

According to Tchebyshev's formula, *at least* 57 percent of the outcomes ought to fall at the mean plus and minus 1.53 standard deviations. If so, *fewer than* 43 percent of the outcomes should be above and below this range. As a gross approximation, we could deduce that *less than* 21.5 percent of Company A's relative returns would be less than 1, since roughly half the remaining possibilities would be in the lower end of the distribution.

Did you notice the italicized language in our previous statement? It's important to reemphasize that Tchebyshev's formula yields rough estimates. If we wanted to fine-tune our number, we'd derive the answer from the normal distribution values in Table 4-5. Here we see that only about 6 percent of Company A's relative returns ought to underperform the DJIA. So Tchebyshev's estimate is confirmed.

Company B's relative risk profile isn't so "bullish." Given its standard deviation (0.24), the interval measures roughly 0.01 standard deviations—which rounds to zero. As shown in Table 4-6, Company B would be expected

TABLE 4-7
Measuring Relative Returns

	DJIA	Company A				Company B			
	Return	Return	Relative Return	Deviation	Deviation (Sq)	Return	Relative Return	Deviation	Deviation (Sq)
Year 1	1.075	1.08	1.005	-0.019	0.00035	1.250	1.16	0.14	0.02
Year 2	1.075	1.09	1.014	-0.009	0.00009	0.750	0.70	-0.33	0.11
Year 3	1.075	1.10	1.023	0.000	0.00000	1.000	0.93	-0.09	0.01
Year 4	1.075	1.11	1.033	0.009	0.00009	1.500	1.40	0.37	0.14
Year 5	1.075	1.12	1.042	0.019	0.00035	1.000	0.93	-0.09	0.01
			Sum of deviations (Sq):		0.001				0.28
			Variance:		0.000				0.06
			Standard deviation:		0.015				0.24
			Mean relative return:		1.023				1.023

to underperform the DJIA roughly half the time. The bottom line is clear. No matter how you slice it, Company B is a lot riskier than Company A.

A FEW ADDITIONAL THOUGHTS

Over the years, the investment community has wrangled with the problem of fairly and uniformly presenting performance. Considerable progress has been made. Today the Association for Investment Management and Research (AIMR) promulgates important standards and practices that enable investors to compare money manager results.[17]

AIMR performance standards are extensive. Our purpose in mentioning them here is to ensure investor awareness. Readers considering a money manager are encouraged to request AIMR-compliant historical returns for analysis. Still, as helpful as the AIMR standards are, no small effort should be expended to verify that investment returns are fully adjusted for management fees, transaction costs, sales charges, and taxes. So dig deep. Inquire about portfolio turnover (the percentage of the assets bought and sold annually). As a rule, higher turnover spells increased taxes and costs. Don't forget. What counts is the amount that ends up in the investor's pocket.

Once all the facts are in hand, adjust for inflation. After all, the value of investment returns is purchasing power. And beyond direct charges, inflation saps purchasing power. Revisit the cumulative investment data presented in Table 4-3. Remember, we assumed that company shares were bought and held for 5 years. Let's imagine there were no dividends involved and that the performance numbers were net of management fees and brokerage costs. At some point, of course, investors will need to liquidate their positions if they are to reap the fruits of their labors.

Figure 4-2 charts the cumulative performance of Company A and Company B shares adjusted for inflation and taxes. In converting the pretax returns, we assumed that prices (as measured by the Consumer Price Index) increased by 3 percent each year. Then we deducted a small commission (0.025 percent of principal) and 20 percent capital gains tax at the conclusion of the 5th year, when the portfolios were closed out.

The results are striking. To lend perspective, we added the solid line in the graph (across the chart at $1) to reflect the cumulative value of a portfolio that merely kept pace with the CPI. Whenever stock market performance sinks below this benchmark, investors suffer a loss of purchasing power.

Look at Company B. Here we see the point we raised earlier. After the initial 2-year period, the value of the portfolio is less than what we started with. Worse, over the initial 3-year period, the investment wasn't able to

FIGURE 4-2
Inflation, Taxes, and Investment Performance

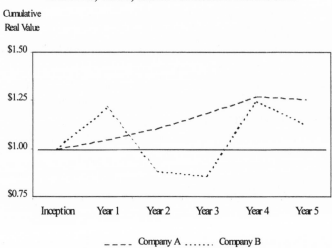

Cumulative
Real Value

- - - - Company A .... Company B

keep abreast of inflation. It took a 50 percent return in year 4 to rescue the stock's "real" performance.

SECRETS OF THE MASTERS

When it comes to investments, you start with some money, you end with some money, and the difference determines your rate of return. What could be simpler? Try brain surgery.[18]

Most investors realize instinctively that there's no such thing as a "free lunch." They know that every investment opportunity carries risk. Often, though, they lack a quantifiable structure for measuring risk exposures in light of their potential for return. Here's where some basic mathematical descriptions come into play.

Mathematics can properly claim no place in economic discussions except as they add something not expressible, or at any rate only imperfectly expressible, in ordinary language.[19]

We've concentrated on a few essential analytical measures based on three criteria:

- Ease of calculation
- Universal application

• Ability to measure the risk-return characteristics attendant to competing investment choices

Statistical analysis, of course, is a tool—not the solution to investment management. But because numerical descriptions are objective, they protect against speculative urges.

Analysis connotes the careful study of available facts with the attempt to draw conclusions therefrom based on established principles and sound logic. It is part of the scientific method. But in applying analysis to the field of securities we encounter the serious obstacle that investment is by nature not an exact science. The same is true, however, of law and medicine, for here also both individual skill (art) and chance are important factors in determining success or failure. Nevertheless, in these professions analysis is not only useful but indispensable, so that the same should probably be true in the field of investment and possibly in that of speculation.[20]

In brief, then:

1. Balance the need for investment returns with the risks of achieving them.

2. Analyze investment returns from different angles. Evaluate returns by calculating their mean, median, and mode.

3. Understand that volatility is risk and measure it by calculating the standard deviation of historical returns.

PART TWO

MASTER PLANS IN ACTION

CHAPTER FIVE

Creating the Total Return Portfolio: The Importance of Dividend Growth

> If earnings not paid out in dividends are all successfully reinvested at compound interest for the benefit of the stockholders, as critics imply, then these earnings should produce dividends later; if not, then they are money lost. . . . Therefore we must say that a stock derives its value from its dividends, not its earnings.[1]
>
> *John Burr Williams*
> *Harvard College, 1938*

I N TRUTH, ANY NUMBER OF extraneous events shape equity prices. But trying to identify them all is like counting stars in the sky. They seem to go on and on. Even if counting events were possible, investors would still face the challenge of anticipating their occurrence and quantifying their impact. This is a serious handicap. So, rather than suffer "analysis-paralysis," we've elected to concentrate on what might be characterized as the prime determinants of stock market behavior.

Armed with these basic concepts, we now shift our focus to developing practical, disciplined ways to exploit stock market returns while managing risk, taxes, and transaction costs. Our launching point is a way of creating a common stock portfolio. We call it the Total Return Portfolio.

In the turbulent world of equity investing, few techniques have withstood the test of time. One that persists is the generations-old hypothesis that share prices are linked to dividend flows.[2] This is an important point.

As we discussed earlier, investors don't risk capital just for the fun of it. Rather, they operate to optimize their returns net of taxes, inflation, and transaction costs. Boiled down, there are only two ways to profit from common stock investments: dividends and price appreciation. Combined, these two factors add up to "total return."

> **In the selection of securities for investment, we must consider more than the expected income yield upon the amount invested, and may quite properly weigh the probability of principal enhancement over a term of years without departing from the most conservative viewpoint.[3]**

So if, as the theory asserts, dividends and price behavior are inextricably linked, then investors stand to maximize their total return on equities by emphasizing dividend growth in their stock selection process. Right?

To get at the answer, we started by collecting historical dividend and price information[4] for each of the 30 stocks in the Dow Jones Industrial Average (DJIA). Once in hand, the data were organized into a spreadsheet to enable a convenient analysis of each company's dividend and stock market records.[5] Stocks were then ranked according to the strength of their dividend policy for the 10-year period ended December 31, 1997.

THE ANALYTICAL FRAMEWORK

More specifically, stocks were evaluated using fairly simple, yet stringent criteria. First, we calculated the percentage change in each company's dividend payout and then we adjusted the results to reward those companies that religiously boosted their payout. Stocks with "spotty" increases (those that cut their payout) were penalized.

To understand our analytical framework, think about how it would apply to three DJIA stocks, each with a contrasting dividend profile:

* WalMart—a company that raised its dividend every year for the past decade.
* Goodyear—a company that grew its dividend some 43 percent over the period but failed to raise its payout in 2 of the last 10 years.
* General Motors—one of the few Dow stocks that slashed its dividend (20%) over the period.

As reported in Table 5-1, WalMart boosted its dividend some 800 percent over the 10-year period ended December 31, 1997. Equally impressive, WalMart enriched its payout in every year of the period—a perfect batting average. Now look at the column headed Dividend Factor.[6] Here we handicap the dividend records of the various companies according to the frequency of their rate hikes. Businesses, like WalMart, earn full credit (factor weight = 1.0). But the factor weight is *seriously* reduced should a company fail to raise its dividend on one or more occasions. Each company's dividend rank is determined by multiplying its dividend increase by its factor weight.

DIVIDENDS AND SHARE PRICES: ARE THEY LINKED?

Now, here's the big question: Is there a connection between dividend rank and stock market performance? You bet! As demonstrated even by this sample exercise, WalMart's stock price earned blue ribbon honors, appreciating from $6.50 in 1987 to $39.44 by the end of 1997—a whopping 507 percent increase.

How about the other two stocks? Here, again, market participants were discerning. Despite a 308 percent rise in the general market (as proxied by the Dow Jones Industrials), General Motors was able to eke out a 98 percent gain, finishing last. Goodyear, which twice failed to raise its dividend, was the runner-up on a price basis.

OK. So far the theory seems to hold water. But the possibility exists that we just happened to pick three companies that confirm the point. So what happens when we apply the methodology to the spectrum of Dow stocks? A back-of-the-envelope calculation confirms the classical idea that dividends count.

Each point in Figure 5-1 was determined by subjecting all the DJIA companies to these same criteria and lining up their respective dividend (vertical axis) and price appreciation (horizontal axis) rankings. When viewing the figure, remember that a rank of 30 indicates the best record, while a rank of 1 signals the worst performance. The matrix results by

TABLE 5-1
Dow Jones Industrials Dividend and Price Data, 1987–1997

	10-Year Dividend Increase (%)	Number of Years Dividend Increased	Dividend Factor	Adjusted Dividend Record	Dividend Rank	10-Year Price Increase (%)	Price Rank
WalMart	800	10	1	800	1	507	1
Goodyear	43	8	.76	32	2	112	2
GM	-20	4	0	0	3	98	3
DJIA	91	N.A.	N.A.	N.A.	N.A.	308	N.A.

FIGURE 5-1

Looking at the Dow Jones Industrials: Dividends and Prices

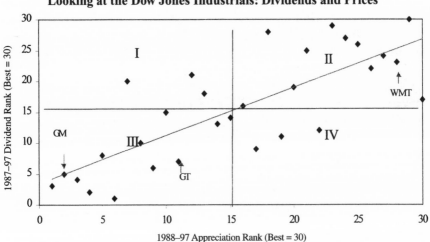

1988–97 Appreciation Rank (Best = 30)

locating a point where the dividend and appreciation ranks intersect on the graph. As an example, WalMart was among the best performers for both dividends and price appreciation. General Motors finished near the bottom of the list in both categories.

The scatter plot shows a strong, unambiguous verdict. Companies with superior dividend policies tended to outperform and vice versa. Indeed, if the exceptional test proves the rule, it's interesting to note that only four DJIA stocks ended the period with lower payouts. How did they do price-wise? All of them sunk to the bottom of the barrel, with three occupying the three worst positions.

As we discussed earlier, GM slashed its payout some 20 percent and, a raging bull market notwithstanding, managed to appreciate roughly 98 percent—and that's a 10-year price change. Only IBM—which cut its quarterly payout by an even greater percentage (65%)—suffered a worse fate, posting an anemic 35 percent price gain. Conversely, WalMart (which increased its quarterly payout from 3 to 27 cents) was the silver medalist for appreciation, rewarding shareholders with more than a five-fold increase.

Obviously, the relationship depicted in Figure 5-1 isn't perfect. If it were, all the points would fall neatly on the "best-fit line." But, as we'll see, when a portfolio is created under the dividend model, precision to the nth decimal place isn't essential. What's important is an ability to discriminate generous from stingy dividend payers. And on this basis, the methodology scores big.

Revisit Figure 5-1 and study the crosshairs. Imagine we were interested in creating a portfolio consisting of the 15 Dow stocks with the best dividend ranks (i.e., those stocks falling in Quadrants II and IV). Now notice that 12 of the issues were also among the best stock market performers in the Dow (three were "nonconformers")—suggesting that our technique offers great promise.

Many investors argue that corporate earnings—not dividends—are the stuff that counts. So it's not surprising that the investment community probably devotes more resources to estimating the outlook for this single factor than to any other variable in the mix. But that expenditure notwithstanding, the lion's share of professionally managed portfolios consistently fall short of the general market's performance, suggesting either that they failed to "get it right" or that market participants have tended to be a step ahead of them.

COUNT ON DIVIDENDS

Certainly dividends are linked to earnings. But there's a big difference. For starters, dividend policy is far easier to manage than revenues and earnings. And while corporate profits are susceptible to business cycle fluctuations and exogenous shocks (like wars, oil embargoes, severe weather patterns, and strikes), dividends are far less volatile—at least for healthy companies (see Figure 5-2). Indeed, history is replete with episodes where profits tanked, but dividends marched on.

> **Despite the wide variations in earnings which occur from year to year, the tendency is to keep cash dividends on a much more even keel.**[7]

For investors, then, dividends offer a simple way to evaluate companies. From this perspective, dividend growth says a lot about management's assessment of the company's underlying business prospects.

Figure 5-3 makes the point. Here we've recast the scatter plot presented in Figure 5-1 but this time we've compared the relationship between earnings and stock market performance. True, the general relationship is still visible. But it's a lot fuzzier. Notice that the constellation of points is more widely dispersed around the "best-fit line." What's more, the top earnings company, United Technologies, was ranked among the stock market laggards.

FIGURE 5-2
The Stability of Dividends versus Earnings

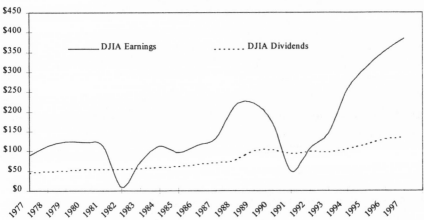

Now count the number of points appearing in Quadrants I and IV of Figure 5-3. As we mentioned earlier, these are the companies that bucked the trend. Companies in Quadrant IV, for example, ought to have been poor stock market performers based on their bottom-half earnings rank. As events unfolded, though, they proved to be superior investment choices.

FIGURE 5-3
Looking at the Dow Jones Industrials: Earnings and Prices

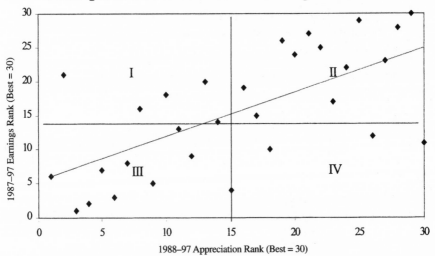

The flip side is visible in Quadrant I, which describes companies that had solid earnings records but finished on the bottom in terms of price.

Repeat the exercise using Figure 5-1. The bottom line stands clear: the dividend model, with its smaller number of "nonconformers" and tighter fit about its trend line, demonstrates superior association with stock market performance.

For investors searching for a disciplined way to build portfolios, the dividend factor has a lot going for it. Once the portfolio is constructed, dividend policy affords investors an easy-to-monitor, critical variable. When a "dividend grower" fails to raise its payout, it's a warning sign worth heeding. Dividend cuts suggest deep-rooted problems. Small wonder, then, that managements loathe slashing dividends. They know how long it will take to repair the damage.

Our point is not to make specific stock recommendations, but to provide a structure for evaluating common stocks and building portfolios. The evidence presented here strongly suggests that astute investors have long prized dividend growth and its importance to overall investment performance.

But there are wrinkles. The relationship between dividend growth and stock market performance isn't perfect. So it would be foolhardy to rely on this methodology to cherry-pick a stock or two from among the 30 Dow companies. There's slippage that must be taken into account. Fortunately, the solution is straightforward.

Remember, our analysis is not aimed at taking what the British would call a "flutter" on a single stock. Rather, our mission is to develop an effective strategy for building a portfolio, or basket, of stocks. By spreading our investment funds across a number of issues, we can compensate for any imprecision in the dividend growth model while capitalizing on the general relationship between dividends and price performance. In the event some of our selections fail to deliver superior dividend records, the idea is that other stocks in the portfolio ought to compensate for the shortfall. And there are solid reasons to think that they will.

Look at Figure 5-4. In producing this graph, we divvied up the DJIA stocks appearing in Figure 5-1 according to their dividend records and created two hypothetical portfolios. We then estimated the returns that would have accrued to both funds assuming an equal dollar amount was invested in each company.[8] The results were striking.

As shown in the graph, the Top 15 dividend growers in the Dow not only blew the doors off the competing portfolio but eclipsed the general market index as well. What's more, notice that the Bottom 14 dividend growers seriously lagged the benchmark (DJIA).

FIGURE 5-4
Does Dividend Growth Spell Portfolio Performance?

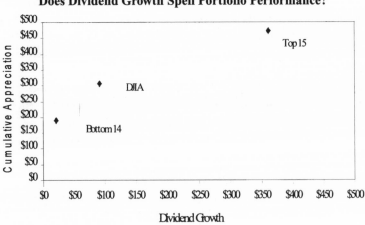

There's yet another problem. Thus far, our analysis has benefited from hindsight. That is, the results immediately above presume that the investor was able to predetermine the dividend record of the various Dow stocks. Obviously, clairvoyance isn't part of the human makeup, so it would appear that the dividend model has little, if any, merit as an investment tool. Scratch deeper, though, and you'll discover how long-term investors can overcome this objection to allow the dividend factor to play a pivital role in guiding their stock selection process.

If we are to capitalize on the association between dividends and price appreciation, we must figure a way to determine *likely* dividend outcomes. Luckily, when it comes to dividends, the empirical record offers the solution. True, historical observations don't guarantee future outcomes. But remember, we're talking about corporate policy. The weight of the evidence suggests that whatever a company's dividend policy, liberal or stingy, management tends to stick by it.

Consider General Electric (the sole surviving company in the original makeup of the DJIA). As we mentioned in Chapter 3, GE has paid a dividend forever. Better yet, the company has hiked its payout every year since 1975. If actions speak louder than words, it's probably a safe bet that General Electric's management has adopted a policy to reward shareholders via dividends. More important, the GE experience isn't an aberration.

All this adds up to a potential solution for the problem of anticipating likely "winners." If past dividend performance is a barometer of future payouts, then portfolios could be created by targeting those DJIA stocks with the best prior 10-year dividend records. Let's take a closer look by recasting the results in Figure 5-4 to eliminate the hindsight.

Figure 5-5 was created by dividing the Dow stocks into two portfolios on the basis of their past dividend record. In other words, unlike the prior simulation, we have relied solely on the historical dividend record to discriminate dividend growers from nongrowers. More specifically, we created the Top 15 portfolio by targeting those stocks that amassed the best dividend performance over the 1977–1986 investment period—information that would have been available at the time the portfolios were constructed. So how did the technique work? More than satisfactorily.

To see just how similar the results are, we superimposed Figure 5-5 on top of Figure 5-4. As shown in Figure 5-6, the hindsight-eliminated version mirrored the results presented in the earlier exercise.[9] In both instances there was little, if any, difference in portfolio appreciation. Indeed, if any disparity is visible, it favors the no-hindsight methodology.

Compare the performance differential between the two Top 15 portfolios in Figure 5-6. Notice that the hindsight-removed version delivered identical appreciation. But, impressively, it was able to accomplish this performance while generating enhanced dividend flow. The bottom line stands clear: dividend growth is critical to total return performance. Moreover, the historical dividend record is an effective way to identify the top dividend payers in the Dow.

FIGURE 5-5
Does Dividend Growth Spell Portfolio Performance?
(Hindsight Eliminated)

FIGURE 5-6

Comparing Hindsight versus No-Hindsight Portfolios

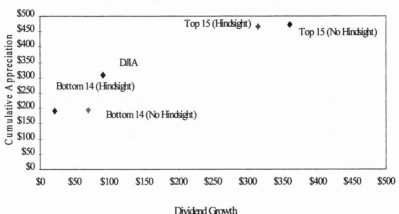

Dividend Growth

Were the results depicted in Figure 5-6 a fluke? Hardly. Table 5-2 affirms a critical point. As before, it was constructed by applying our dividend criteria (based on the prior 10-year history) to each of the DJIA companies and determining their dividend rank starting at the end of 1986. The exercise was repeated for each successive year through 1997. As even a casual examination reveals, stocks with stellar dividend records were persistently atop the rank-ordered list, while those with weaker records (ranks greater than 15) tended to remain on the bottom.

> **Given two companies in the same general position and with the same earnings power, the one paying the larger dividend will always sell at the higher price.[10]**

Let's focus a little closer on the hindsight-eliminated methodology. Imagine that an investor launched the Total Return Portfolio strategy on December 31, 1987, based on the strength of each company's dividend record over the prior 10 years. The initial portfolio would have consisted of the first 15 stocks listed in Table 5-2.

Once such a portfolio was created, the investor could ensure that funds were always exposed to those stocks with the highest prospects for dividend growth by "rebalancing" the portfolio at the conclusion of each calendar year. To do this, the investor would simply update the dividend data for the passing of another year and rerank the stocks according to the procedure detailed earlier. Portfolio holdings that failed to maintain their posi-

TABLE 5-2
Historical Dividend Rankings
(Based on Prior 10-Year Record)

	1987	1988	1989	1990	1991	1992	1993	1994	1995	1996	1997
WalMart	1	1	1	1	1	1	1	1	1	1	2
McDonald's	2	2	3	4	5	6	8	8	10	9	11
Philip Morris	3	3	2	2	2	2	2	2	2	3	3
Disney	4	8	7	12	12	13	6	10	5	5	5
Hewlett-Packard	5	5	5	5	4	4	4	4	4	2	1
Merck	6	4	4	3	3	3	3	3	3	4	4
Johnson & Johnson	7	6	6	6	6	5	5	5	6	6	6
JP Morgan	8	7	8	8	8	9	10	9	9	10	12
General Electric	9	10	9	7	7	7	9	7	8	8	9
Exxon	10	9	10	13	16	14	14	15	14	15	16
Minnesota Mining	11	11	11	10	10	11	12	11	12	14	13
Coca-Cola	12	12	12	9	9	8	7	6	7	7	7
Boeing	13	16	18	15	14	15	15	14	15	17	18
Procter & Gamble	14	13	13	11	11	12	13	12	11	11	10
Eastman Kodak	15	15	14	18	18	18	19	22	28	27	24
DuPont	16	17	16	14	15	10	11	13	13	13	14
Sears & Roebuck	17	20	23	26	23	23	22	24	24	26	26
United Technologies	18	19	19	16	17	16	17	18	18	18	17
American Express	19	14	15	17	13	17	18	16	22	21	20
Chevron	20	18	17	19	19	20	16	17	16	16	15
Allied Signal	21	21	22	25	24	25	26	27	29	25	23
IBM	22	23	25	21	20	19	28	29	27	29	29
Union Carbide	23	22	27	27	25	24	23	25	25	24	27
ALCOA	24	24	20	23	27	28	21	20	21	19	22
Goodyear	25	25	21	22	29	29	29	23	20	22	19
International Paper	26	26	24	24	21	21	20	19	19	20	21
General Motors	27	27	26	20	22	22	27	26	26	28	28
Caterpiller	28	29	29	28	26	26	25	28	17	12	8
AT&T	29	28	28	29	28	27	24	21	23	23	25
Number Of Positions Rotated:	1	0	2	1	1	0	0	0	1	1	

tion atop the list would be replaced by those sporting superior dividend records.[11]

Interestingly, trading activity would have been minimal over the 11-year period shown in Table 5-2 owing to the stability of corporate dividend policy. As indicated by the highlighted rankings in the table, only 7 positions would have been rotated over the course of all the annual rebalancings.

So how would the portfolio have performed? In a word, well. Look at Figure 5-7. Excluding dividends, every $1 exposed to the Total Return Portfolio would have ballooned to $5.84—outdistancing the cumulative return of the Bottom 14 portfolio ($3.68) and eclipsing the Dow Jones Industrial Average performance ($4.08) by a healthy margin. True, repositioning the portfolio each year does create tax events as well as increased brokerage costs. Given the stability of corporate dividend policies evidenced in Table 5-2, though, the amount of activity likely would be minimal.

THE TOTAL RETURN PORTFOLIO: HOW COST-EFFICIENT IS IT?

So far, the hypothesis that dividend growth matters is compelling. But the analysis is far from over. While the investment community competes on the basis of pretax performance numbers, investors are concerned only with the share of profit that ends up in their account. So just how efficient is the Total Return Portfolio?

Let's adjust the Top 15 portfolio returns shown in Figure 5-7 for costs and taxes. In producing Figure 5-8, we assumed that dividend income was subject to a 36 percent federal tax rate but free from state income tax. For simplicity, all capital gains were treated as the long-term variety and taxed at today's 20 percent rate. Since our portfolio strategy can be implemented without benefit of professional advice, the investment management fees associated with the Total Return Portfolio could be zero. But in an effort to be conservative, let's assume that the investor was willing to pay a small annual fee (0.25%) to have a money manager oversee the strategy. Finally, since the approach targets blue chip issues, we figured that brokerage costs (which these days hover around $20 per trade) would be of little consequence—say, 0.3 percent of the principal amount involved with each transaction.

FIGURE 5-7
Cumulative Portfolio Returns

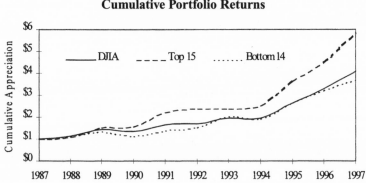

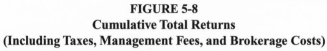

FIGURE 5-8
Cumulative Total Returns
(Including Taxes, Management Fees, and Brokerage Costs)

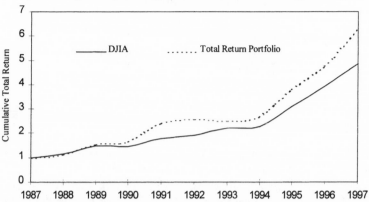

As shown in Figure 5-8, the end result was highly acceptable. Measured over the 10-year period, the Total Return Portfolio's after-tax cumulative return eclipsed the DJIA benchmark, despite increased costs and taxes.[12]

Figures 5-9 and 5-10 round out our efficiency analysis. Here we've analyzed the 10-year cumulative results of the Total Return Portfolio and the DJIA to identify how much of each ended up in the investor's pocket. To capture the entire tax bite, we assumed that both portfolios were liquidated at the end of the period, with taxes paid on any realized gains.

Notice that the Total Return Portfolio's results compared favorably with the Dow even though the dividend strategy was exposed to higher transaction costs and taxes. True, on a percentage basis, investors electing to clone the DJIA would have received a greater percentage of the overall return (81.9% vs. 77.03% for the Total Return Portfolio). But investors can't eat efficiency ratios. They spend dollars. And on this score, assuming full liquidation at the end of the period, every dollar invested in the dividend strategy was worth $5.35 against $4.19 for the Dow Jones Industrials.

There's another point about dividend flows. Appreciation potential notwithstanding, "dividend growers" are a terrific store of value. For many investors, dividend income is critical. And when you're retired and living on a fixed income, it's especially important to stay ahead of the inflation curve.

FIGURE 5-9
Total Return Portfolio: Who Got What?

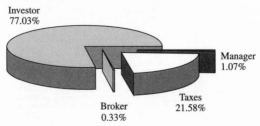

This fact is of greater moment to individual investors whose investments are made with the happiness and comfort of their children in
mind, than is usually supposed. "Safety of principal" yes—that is
the first essential. But what is "principal"—is it merely the obliga-
tion of some organization to repay a certain number of fluctuating
measures of value at a future date? What if, at the date of repay-
ment, the measure has shrunk to one-half of its present size? Has
the principal been safeguarded?[13]

Figure 5-11 contrasts the Total Return Portfolio's dividend growth with
inflation as measured by the Consumer Price Index. Once again, our strategy paid off. Notice that the portfolio's dividend growth was generally able
to keep pace with the cost of living. And let's remember that the value of all
investment returns is purchasing power.

For investors looking to fund their retirement years, the dividend factor
has a lot going for it. Imagine an investor with, say, a 30-year horizon. Let's
assume the investor purchases shares in a company currently yielding 1
percent, with a 12 percent dividend growth rate. Assuming the company

FIGURE 5-10
Dow Jones Industrials: Who Got What?

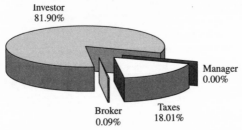

FIGURE 5-11
Keeping Abreast of Inflation

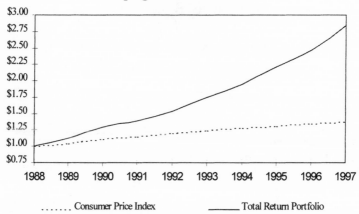

.... Consumer Price Index   _____ Total Return Portfolio

adheres to its policy, at retirement the yield on cost would approximate 30 percent—per annum. But, as we've seen, market prices aren't likely to be static. As evidenced by the Total Return Portfolio's performance record (Tables 5-3 and 5-4), they'll adjust so as to maintain the same current yield relationship with competing financial assets.

TABLE 5-3
Total Return Portfolio:
Schedule of Calendar-Year Returns*

Year	Total Return Portfolio	DJIA	Excess
1988	11.2%	14.7%	-3.50%
1989	39.5%	30.0%	9.50%
1990	5.6%	-1.9%	7.58%
1991	47.5%	22.6%	24.82%
1992	6.1%	6.2%	-0.15%
1993	-2.0%	15.7%	-17.65%
1994	5.9%	3.9%	2.00%
1995	43.3%	35.4%	7.95%
1996	25.0%	27.5%	-2.51%
1997	31.8%	23.8%	8.01%
Mean:	21.39%	17.79%	3.60%

* Net of costs and taxes

TABLE 5-4
The Total Return Portfolio:
Performance Analytics,
1988–1997*

Descriptive Statistic	Portfolio	DJIA
Median Return	18.07	19.15
Mean Return	21.39	17.79
Risk (Standard Deviation)	18.20	12.21
Return Per Unit Of Risk	1.18	1.46
Best Return	47.45	35.40
Worst Return	-1.98	-1.93
Cumulative Return Per $ Invested	6.28	4.89
Number Of Positive Returns	9	9
Mean Of Positive Returns	23.99	19.98
Number Of Negative Returns	1	1
Mean Of Negative Returns	-1.98	-1.93

*Net of management fees, brokerage costs and taxes on income and realized gains

SUMMARY

If you're the type of personality who needs to have the latest mousetrap, the electric apple peeler, the motorized hairbrush, or the like, force yourself to step out of character. When it comes to investing, you don't need that latest razzle-dazzle strategy. What we've seen in this chapter is an investment approach as old as the hills—the idea that dividend growth is the foundation of long-term stock selection.

> **Theoretically, then, the most valuable security in the world would be the one which: a. Produced the largest income in a year; b. Increased this income the most rapidly over a period of years; and c. Sustained this maximum rate of increase for the longest period of time.[14]**

Through a series of charts we've illustrated how the shares of companies with superior dividend records outperform those with stingy dividend policies. And since the dividend payout is a matter of management policy, we've shown that past performance tends to be a reliable indicator of future dividend increases. As a result, portfolio turnover is minimal, thereby keeping costs and taxes at bay.

Table 5-4 compares the simulated performance record of the Total Return Portfolio against that of the Dow Jones Industrial Average. As shown, dividends matter. The Total Return Portfolio, with its modest turnover, is tax- and cost-efficient.

FIGURE 5-12
The Total Return Portfolio Strategy:
Construction and Rebalancing Process

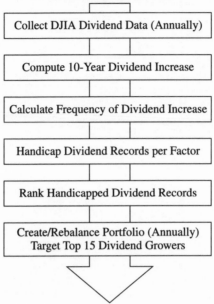

What's more, as summarized by Figure 5-12, the portfolio once constructed requires minimal annual evaluation and adjustment.

A good portfolio is one which can be given constant and complete supervision—and at most reasonable cost to each investor.[15]

CHAPTER SIX

Funding Equity Portfolios: Dynamic Hedging

> The soundness of a security purchase is determined by develop-
> ments and not by past history or statistics. But the future cannot be
> analyzed; we can seek only to anticipate it intelligently and prepare
> for it prudently. Here the past comes in . . . experience tells us that
> investment anticipations, like other business anticipations, cannot
> be sound or dependable unless they are closely related to past per-
> formance.[1]
>
> *Benjamin Graham and David L. Dodd*
> *1951*

JUST AS AIRLINE PASSENGERS expect turbulence, equity investors anticipate that volatility will grip the stock market periodically. But the timing of a downdraft can make all the difference. Obviously, wind shear is a lot easier to deal with when you're cruising at 35,000 feet than when you're 35 feet off the runway. So too, encountering a stock market "correction" just as you've exposed funds to equity risk can have a big impact.

The 1987 stock market is a case in point. Imagine the hapless investors who fully committed to the stock market at the end of September on the heels of a 30 percent run-up. Poof! Within weeks their portfolio would have shed a quarter of its value. Worse, undisciplined investors probably suffered a double whammy. Unable to withstand the psychological strain of a market crash, many bailed out—only to see the market fully recover.

Actually, infusing fresh capital into the volatile equity market is tricky business even in the best of times. You might invest the funds all at once, figuring that the "bull" run will persist. Certainly the "Roaring '90s" created an environment in which even passbook savers flocked to the stock market without hesitation. True, equity investors opting to fund their stock portfolio straightaway could reduce—if not eliminate—underperformance risk. But there's a hitch. The portfolio's exposure to principal risk has increased. Should the stock market take a sudden turn for the worse, investors wouldn't have time to fasten their seat belts let alone avert the "correction." The flip side of the problem is equally worrisome. Investors who sit on their cash can't lose money. But they don't stand to gain anything either should the market rally.

Sophisticated investors are ever mindful of the need to temper return expectations by the risk of achieving them. Not surprisingly, they prize structured ways to create stock portfolios while balancing the trade-off between absolute risk (losing principal) and relative risk (lagging a benchmark return).

Now that we've identified a viable investment strategy based on the classical idea that dividends matter, how do we go about exploiting it? Imagine giving a teenager a sports car but not driving lessons. While the youngster could undoubtedly get it started, what are the odds of backing it out of the garage without taking the doors along?

AVOID TIMING DECISIONS

The trouble with all-or-nothing trading strategies is that they boil down to "timing" bets. In effect, investors electing immediate funding strategies are gambling that a given trade date will prove to be the most opportune time to invest their money. Maybe so, but the chance of that being the case seems awfully slim. Fortunately there's an alternative, unemotional way to launch our Total Return Portfolio: dynamic hedging.

Dynamic hedging is a highly disciplined approach to coping with the challenge of funding equity portfolios. It funnels money into the market by managing two critical variables: time and volatility. To understand how dynamic hedging works requires a bit of statistics and something called a "bell-shaped curve" or "frequency distribution."

What's a bell-shaped curve? Picture a fourth-grade classroom with a couple of dozen kids. Let's say we organized them according to height and found that they averaged 48 inches. Half were taller; and two-thirds were within plus or minus 6 inches of this average. But there were exceptions. One youngster measured just over 60 inches and another a tad under 36 inches. The rest of the students were somewhere in between.

We could show all this by sorting the children according to the range of their heights (say, 30–36", 36–42", 42–48", and so on). The number (or frequency) of students falling in each "range" could be represented by drawing a bar over a horizontal axis, as shown in Figure 6-1. The height of each bar corresponds with the number of kids observed in each range, as shown on the vertical axis. For example, seven kids measured between 42" and 48" and only one was in the 30–36" range. The familiar Liberty Bell shape emerges when a curve is fitted to the tops of the resulting bars.

Armed with our distribution analysis, and assuming our sample is a representative class of fourth graders, we can draw certain inferences.[2] For example, we could reasonably conclude that the majority of fourth graders are between 42 and 54 inches tall, although occasionally (roughly a third of the time) we'd expect to encounter kids outside this range. And very rarely, we should find individuals whose height falls in the "tails" of the distribution—say, less than 36 inches or more than 60 inches.

Imagine that the stock market's monthly returns were "normally distributed" under the bell-shaped curve. Much like children's heights, the distribution of returns could guide our thinking about future outcomes. Happily the Dow's historical performance does, in fact, fit the curve.

FIGURE 6-1
Fourth-Grade Children

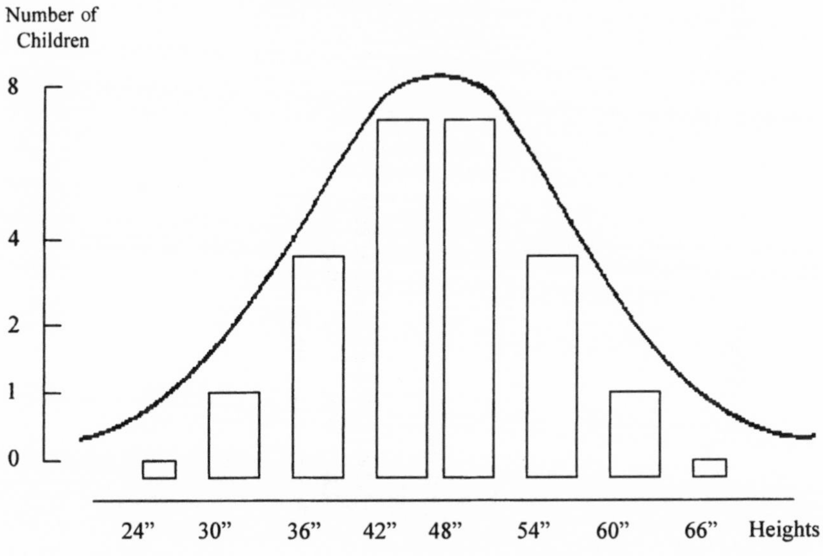

Number of Children

Figure 6-2 was constructed by sorting the DJIA's historical monthly return data into "bins." Each bin is represented by a bar on the graph and describes the frequency of outcomes falling in a given range. For convenience, we organized the Dow's returns by 2.5 percent increments. For example, as noted in Figure 6-2, some 71 of 300 monthly returns were between 0 and 2.5 percent during the 25-year period ended December 31, 1997.

A casual examination of the resulting graph confirms that the stock market has tracked the path suggested by the bell-shaped curve. In fact, as we will explore below, the Dow's historical (mean) return was a tad over 1 percent (1.19%), with roughly two-thirds of its monthly outcomes falling between −3 and +5.5 percent.[3] Even the possibility of a "crash" (à la October 1987) is contemplated by the distribution. But just like 60-inch fourth graders, the likelihood of such an event is low.

THE METHODOLOGY
All this points to a useful methodology for implementing our equity strategy. More specifically, our plan boils down to three critical steps.

Step 1: Invest Half Now.
Since nobody knows if the stock market's instant move will be up or down, prudence suggests that the smart move is to invest half the available funds straightaway. On the one hand, should the market take off, we've cut the

FIGURE 6-2
Dow Jones Industrial Average:
Monthly Appreciation, 1972–1997

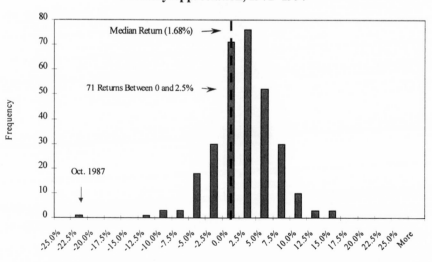

odds of missing it in half. On the other hand, if there is a "correction," at least we've exposed only half our funds. Plus, we've preserved the balance of our cash to capitalize on lower prices. What about the balance of the money?

Step 2: Manage Time.

Since there's no way of predicting the timing of monthly downturns, our funding technique must contemplate the possibility—however remote—that the stock market will enter a period void of turbulence. We apply a Time Rule whereby remaining cash balances are "averaged" into the equity market in equal, predetermined quarterly installments. Given the market's historical volatility, though, it makes sense to keep the quarterly investments to a minimum—say, 5 percent of the remaining funds—to allow ample time for a correction to occur. In other words, absent volatility, the equity portfolio would be fully funded over a 5-year interval.

Let's see how the first two steps would have worked for a hypothetical investor with $1 million earmarked for the stock market at the end of 1986. Remember, the stock market soared some 30 percent over the initial 9 months of 1987. So any funding strategy that failed to invest all the money up front would have seriously lagged the benchmark, at least through September.

FIGURE 6-3
Dynamic Hedging: Time Rule

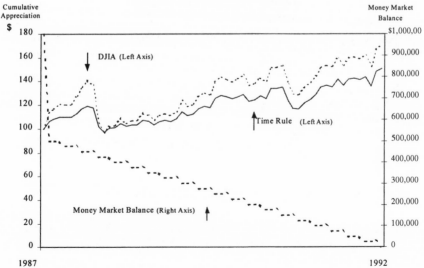

OK. Half the funds ($500,000) would be invested immediately (Step 1). Under the Time Rule, the remainder would be phased into the stock market at the end of each calendar quarter in increments of 5 percent. The Money Market line in Figure 6-3 traces the transfer of funds into the stock market until all the cash was invested (i.e., the end of 1992).

Now notice the value of the resulting portfolio (solid line) compared with the DJIA benchmark (dotted line). As we mentioned earlier, it's not surprising that the Time Rule produced inferior results given the meteoric rise in share prices witnessed during the 10-year investment period. After all, even when the market crashed in 1987, the Time Rule wouldn't have taken advantage of seriously reduced share prices. It would have adhered to the quarterly investment schedule. This is where the Performance Rule—which capitalizes on downturns—comes into play.

Step 3: Be Patient. Capitalize on Volatility.

Now dynamic hedging turns opportunistic. From our earlier discussion, we know that downturns happen; happen with regularity; and are of different magnitudes. So the idea is to be patient and wait for a dip. The Performance Rule component of dynamic hedging kicks in whenever the market suffers a negative monthly return in excess of a predetermined threshold. In other words, rather than rely on subjective opinion to trigger our funding decisions, we could allow the stock market's downside volatility (the "dynamic" underlying dynamic hedging) to identify "when" and "how much" to invest.

To envision the Performance Rule, think about the bell-shaped curve presented earlier. As we discussed in Chapter 3, the method for measuring the frequency of expected outcomes in any region under the curve has long been established—for investors a highly useful input. In our view, investors would probably be a lot more relaxed about capitalizing on a downturn if they had a "feel" for how often (and pronounced) the downdrafts were likely to be.

The calculation is straightforward and requires knowledge of two statistics discussed in Chapter 2: the Dow's "mean" return or "central tendency" and the "standard deviation," a statistical measure of the variability of returns about the mean.[4] As a side note we should mention that when it comes to expressing mathmatical values and operations, the universal language is a set of letters and symbols. In this instance, the Greek symbols μ refers to the mean value and σ denotes the standard deviation. For ease of writing, we'll use these symbols from time to time in the pages ahead.

The rule of thumb for a "normally distributed," random variable (like stock market returns) holds that roughly 68 percent of the probable outcomes will fall within ± 1 standard deviation of the mean. Given the frequency of outcomes in this range, we'll consider all such returns "normal." A bandwidth of ±2 standard deviations ought to describe 95 percent of the results, and a whopping 99.7 percent of the likely outcomes would be expected to fall within ±3 standard deviations of the average result.

Figure 6-4 illustrates the rule as it applies to the Dow Jones Industrial Average. Don't forget, the Dow's historical mean monthly return was 1.19 percent, with a standard deviation of 4.37 percent. By definition, then, the mean locates the peak of the curve such that half the probable results would fall to either side of this divide. So under the Performance Rule, two-thirds of the DJIA outcomes should lie between −3.17 and +5.57 percent. An interval of −7.54 to +9.94 percent would contain 95 percent of the expected returns, while a range of −11.91 to +14.31 percent would describe nearly all (99.7%) of the likely outcomes.

The Performance Rule is aimed at capitalizing on negative returns to trigger additional cash infusions. So we need focus only on the left-hand side of the distribution in Figure 6-4. As a starting point, we know that 50 percent of the probable outcomes are likely to fall the left of the mean (1.19%). If 34 percent of them are between −3.17 and +1.19 percent, then the "tail" of the distribution must contain the other 16 percent of probable outcomes. Over time, patience should pay off. After all, roughly 16 percent of the time we should witness a monthly decline in this region of the distribution. And, much like the pattern among our fourth graders, occasionally we would expect more pronounced downturns.

**FIGURE 6-4   The Frequency Distribution:
Dow Jones Industrial Average
(Expected Monthly Appreciation)**

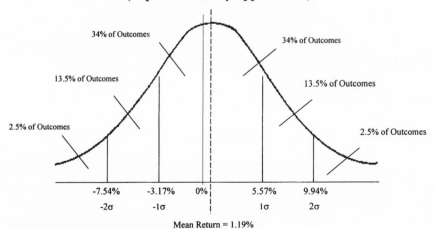

Importantly, the technique provides a dispassionate way to determine whether additional equity exposure is warranted and, if so, the amount to invest. We could, for example, estimate the frequency (or probability) of a dip greater than, say, 15 percent or any other magnitude. Naturally, should we encounter a correction of this magnitude, we would not only seize the opportunity but apportion our investment to reflect the intensity of the downturn.

For this we make an easy calculation to express the observed monthly decline in terms of standard deviations. We then refer to Table 6-1, which suggests the amount to invest according to the size of the downturn. Notice that the table lists the "buy" amounts associated with various stock market "corrections." We start with a −1 standard deviation event, since declines of less than −1 standard deviations occur relatively frequently and, as we mentioned, are more or less typical.

Notice how the investment amounts listed in Table 6-1 are related to the size of the downturn. While our methodology for determining the size of the investment is discussed below, suffice it to say that our technique is sensitive to the magnitude of negative returns. In a phrase, the bigger the correction, the bigger the buying opportunity!

TABLE 6-1
"Buy" Amount under the Performance Rule

Magnitude of Decline (Standard Deviations)	Normal Distribution Value	Performance Rule "Buy" Amount
-1.0	15.87%	0.85%
-1.1	13.57%	1.00%
-1.2	11.51%	1.17%
-1.3	9.68%	1.39%
-1.4	8.08%	1.67%
-1.5	6.68%	2.02%
-1.6	5.48%	2.46%
-1.7	4.46%	3.03%
-1.8	3.59%	3.76%
-1.9	2.87%	4.70%
-2.0	2.28%	5.93%
-2.1	1.79%	7.56%
-2.2	1.39%	9.71%
-2.3	1.07%	12.59%
-2.4	0.82%	16.47%
-2.5	0.62%	21.74%
-2.6	0.48%	28.96%
-2.7	0.35%	38.94%
-2.8	0.26%	52.83%
-2.9	0.19%	72.35%
-3.0	0.13%	100.00%

In sum, the Performance Rule funnels cash balances into the equity portfolio whenever monthly declines exceed one standard deviation. Since three standard deviation events occur infrequently, the system capitalizes on "crashes" by sweeping all remaining funds into the market.

Let's walk through a couple of examples. Imagine that the DJIA declined 7.5 percent during October 1997 in response to the so-called Asian Monetary Crisis—a 1.4 standard deviation event.[5] Now turn to the column labeled Normal Distribution Value in Table 6-1. Here we've scheduled the percentage of negative outcomes likely to exceed a decline of −1.4 standard deviations. As shown in the table, roughly 8 percent of the DJIA's monthly downturns should exceed −7.5 percent. True, a −1.4 standard deviation event is sufficient to justify additional equity exposure. But if history is a guide, bigger corrections are possible.

So how much of our cash balance ought to flow into our common stock portfolio? While there's no hard-and-fast rule, a simple formula allows us to automatically adjust the "buy amount" to reflect the size of the downturn. Since fewer than 1 percent of negative outcomes ought to exceed −11.9 percent, we started with the notion that investors should take immediate and full advantage of such opportunities. So any monthly setback equal to (or greater than) −3 standard deviations would cause all the remaining cash balance to flow into equities.

Hence our formula simply divides the normal distribution value associated with a −3 standard deviation event by the value given for the observed downturn. For the example at hand, then, investors would shift only an additional 1.67 percent of their original cash position into the equity portfolio (0.13% ÷ 8.08% = 1.67%).[6]

What about an extreme case, like the more than 20 percent crash witnessed on October 19, 1987 ("Black Monday")—a meltdown well in excess of −3 standard deviations? Under our formula, all remaining cash balances would have been swept into equities (0.13% ÷ 0.13% = 100%). Disciplined investors wouldn't have missed the opportunity to buy stocks at bargain prices.

Figure 6-5 plots the DJIA's monthly returns for the 10-year period ended December 31, 1997 as a "line graph." Even the most robust market in memory has had its share of downdrafts. Consistent with our earlier discussion, the Dow's monthly fluctuations averaged slightly over 1 percent, with a similar standard deviation.

Notice that we've superimposed various thresholds over the graph to reflect the Time and Performance Rules. As shown, the Time Rule applies as long as the monthly outcomes are greater than −3.17 percent, whereas the Performance Rule is triggered by corrections below this threshold.

FIGURE 6-5
Capitalize on Volatility

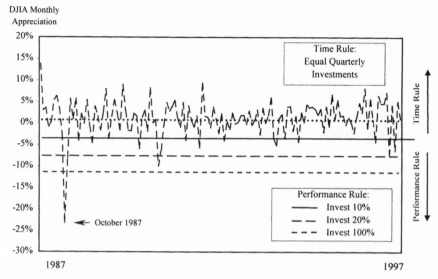

Let's continue with the 1987 simulation using the full dynamic hedging discipline in Figure 6-6. When examining the graph, keep in mind that decisions through September were driven by the Time Rule, since the big run-up in share prices was achieved without any downturns. Hence initial performance was identical to that depicted in Figure 6-3. But one month later (October 1987), things changed—radically.

FIGURE 6-6
Dynamic Hedging: Performance Rule

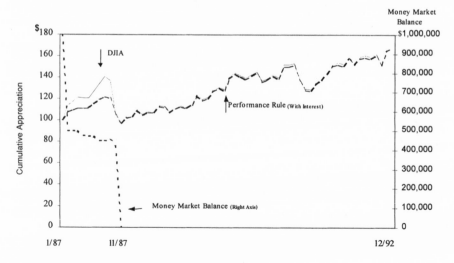

Disciplined investors waiting to capitalize on a market correction real-ized their opportunity when share prices dropped 25 percent. Under the Performance Rule, the balance of their money market funds would have flowed into the stock market by the end of November (the right axis in Fig-ure 6-6). From that point on, dynamic hedging delivered a greatly enhanced result compared with results under the Time Rule: the return on the result-ing portfolio approximated that of the DJIA.

Remember, the idea behind dynamic hedging is to capture the bench-mark return while controlling downside risk. In this ball game, success isn't a function of hitting home runs. An effective hedge occurs whenever the portfolio's performance mirrors the cumulative return of the DJIA, even though the odds of losing money have been reduced by virtue of a sizable cash position.

So far, of course, our dynamic hedging exercise describes a single inception period—one that allowed us to demonstrate how investors could have capitalized on a correction in excess of 3 standard deviations—the biggest stock market collapse in memory. How would investors have fared over a larger number of inception dates?

To get at the answer, we "back-tested" the strategy assuming a January 1st inception date for every year back to 1961. Cumulative values were cal-culated for ensuing 5-year periods and compared with the DJIA bench-mark. Not surprisingly, the methodology tended to eclipse the Dow's performance in "bear" market cycles and lag it somewhat during "bull" markets. Still, overall results proved satisfactory. Dynamic hedging pro-duced results that, on average, captured better than 99 percent of the Dow's cumulative return.

DYNAMIC HEDGING AND THE TOTAL RETURN PORTFOLIO

From the analysis presented in Chapter 5, we know that the Total Return Portfolio delivers superior performance relative to the Dow Jones Industrial Average. Interestingly, though, statistical testing reveals that the Total Return Portfolio is not immune to the ebb and flow of the general stock market (see Figure 6-7). Indeed, our analysis indicates that our dividend strategy's monthly performance is highly correlated with month-to-month fluctuations in the DJIA.[7]

For investors electing to rely on dynamic hedging to trigger their stock purchases, this finding is highly useful. Rather than constantly track the price action of 15 securities, we need only monitor the Dow. Whenever dynamic hedging signals a buying opportunity, we would invest equal dollar amounts in the constituent stocks that comprise the Total Return Portfolio.[8]

FIGURE 6-7
Monthly Appreciation Comparison

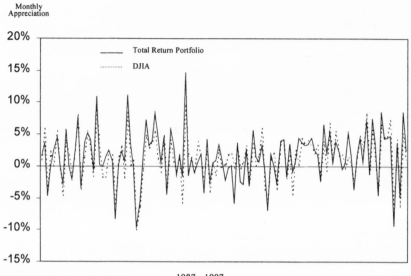

1987 - 1997

Let us now attempt to harness the dynamic hedging rules to fund the Total Return Portfolio assuming a January 1, 1988 inception date (a start date that eliminates the October 1987 crash from the performance measurement). Figure 6-8 recasts the results of implementing our dividend growth portfolio via the Time Rule (only).

So far, so good. Even the Time Rule gets us within striking distance of the benchmark return—and this during a period void of any sizable meltdowns. Still, there's a gap between the DJIA's ending value and that of the Total Return Portfolio. Add in the Performance Rule, though, and the picture brightens rather dramatically.

As shown in Figure 6-9, by being patient and allowing dynamic hedging to guide their funding strategy, investors would have emerged from the critical inception period well ahead of the benchmark—and with fewer sleepless nights. Notice too, that the general market's normal volatility caused the Performance Rule to completely migrate the money market balances into the stock market by April 1992. Thus, reliance on dynamic hedging to fund the Total Return Portfolio produced a result that eclipsed the DJIA cumulative 5-year return. As indicated by the left-hand axis of Figure 6-9, every $100 invested in our dividend strategy finished out the inception period at $190 versus $170 for the Dow Jones Industrials. Not bad, but was it a fluke? Hardly.

FIGURE 6-8
Funding the Total Return Portfolio: The Time Rule

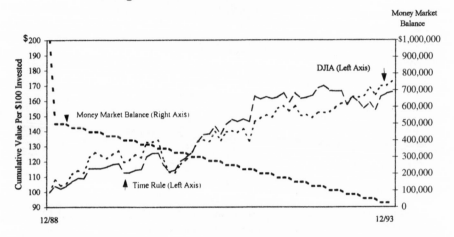

Table 6-2 lists the results of simulating the process going back to 1987. As noted, dynamic hedging failed in its mission on two occasions (1991 and 1992)—not surprising, given that this period heralded the beginning of the runaway 1995–1997 bull market. Still, overall results proved satisfactory.

FIGURE 6-9
Funding the Total Return Portfolio: Dynamic Hedging

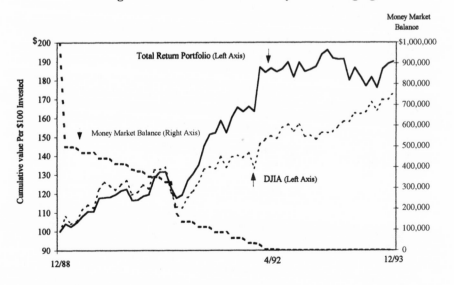

TABLE 6-2
Funding the Total Return Portfolio:
Dynamic Hedging

Inception Date (year ended)	Cumulative Value per $100 Investment (ensuing 5-year period)		
	DJIA	Portfolio*	$ Difference
1987	170	219	49
1988	173	190	17
1989	139	144	5
1990	194	200	6
1991	203	192	-11
1992	240	226	-14
Average:	187	195	8

* Includes interest on cash balances

One final point. Given the intensity and duration of the bull market run, just imagine how many investors elected to sit on the sidelines and wait for the market to come back to them. They're still waiting at the platform. So even though dynamic hedging fell short of the benchmark in 2 years out of 6, at least investors would have captured the bulk of the equity market performance.

FIGURE 6-10
Funding the Total Return Portfolio:
Dynamic Hedging Strategy

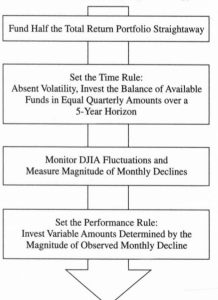

SUMMARY

Shrewd investors look before they leap. Wall Street is littered with imposters who charged ahead out of impatience, lack of foresight, or because it "just felt right." Instincts and emotions can work wonders for athletes and actors but they aren't the tools of superstar investors. The challenge in equity investing is to find reliable, disciplined ways to exploit the stock market while controlling risk.

In this chapter we've explored something called dynamic hedging—an effective way to fund equity portfolios. The approach is intuitive and (thankfully) easily implemented (see Figure 6-10). It achieves its funding objectives by avoiding "all or nothing" decisions and managing two critical variables: time and the downside volatility of the general market as proxied by the Dow Jones Industrial Average.

CHAPTER SEVEN

Strategic Asset Allocation: Diversification

> Diversification is both observed and sensible; a rule of behavior which does not imply the superiority of diversification must be rejected both as a hypothesis and as a maxim.[1]
>
> *Harry Markowitz*
> *1952*

YOU LOVE MCDONALD'S. You love the arches. You love the fries. You love the fact that it has restaurants all over the United States and is steamrolling internationally. Best of all, the kids love it. Sounds like a great stock idea and it *even* pays a dividend. So you fall in love with the stock and buy as many shares as you can afford.

Whoops! Out of nowhere comes Mad Cow disease.[2] Consumers head for Kentucky Fried Chicken and McDonald's share price tumbles—putting a big dent in your wallet despite a raging bull market (see Figure 7-1).

The mistake in this scenario was not so much buying McDonald's as buying *only* McDonald's. Think back to the cardinal rules presented in Chapter 4. Would a fiduciary expose your nest egg to nondiversified risk, even if McDonald's was the only fast-food chain around? Never. Fiduciaries worth their salt would realize that a number of factors, many beyond company control, can exact a heavy toll.

By "betting the farm" on a single issue, you end up paying a hefty price for your lack of foresight and judgment. If you had diluted the risk merely by including a few stocks from other industry groups, the fallout from this

FIGURE 7-1
Expect Market Jitters:
Even Good Companies Have Bad Luck

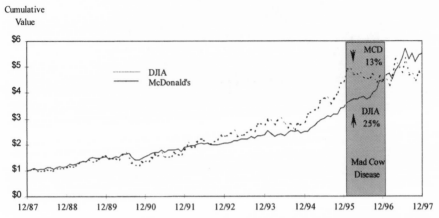

unforeseen event would have been far less costly.[3] As Harry Markowitz, dean of modern portfolio theory, put it nearly a half century ago:

> The adequacy of diversification is not thought by investors to depend solely on the number of different securities held. A portfolio with sixty different railway securities, for example, would not be as well diversified as the same size portfolio with some railroad, some public utility, mining, various sort of manufacturing, etc. The reason is that it is generally more likely for firms within the same industry to do poorly at the same time than firms in dissimilar industries.[4]

STRATEGIC ASSET ALLOCATION AND THE LONG-TERM INVESTOR

While many people fancy themselves as "long-term investors," most professionals have come to appreciate a different reality. Investors tend to be fickle. All it takes to trigger a personality change is a bit of turbulence. In up markets, it's "relative" performance that counts. In down markets, only "absolute" returns matter. Small wonder so many portfolios underperform the general market. Moving targets are hard to hit. And as we discussed in Chapter 1, failure to safeguard the investment process from human emotions is a prescription for mediocrity and possibly disaster.

> The reader must develop self-control, both to refrain from attempting to profit by the short-swing fluctuations, which are what most people endeavor to follow, and to act quickly to take advantage of the major movements, from which people fail to profit. This is because they are infatuated with prosperity or scared by panic or depression.[5]

Not surprisingly, the investment community has devised some innovative ways to take advantage of "risky securities" while protecting against unexpected downdrafts. Strategic asset allocation is one of them. To envision the technique, think about the root problem: price variability. Take a look at Figure 7-2, which traces McDonald's quarterly price movements from the end of 1994—roughly a year before the outbreak of Mad Cow disease.

Now consider the psychological strain. In the face of the biggest bull market in bovine history, MCD shares not only gyrated wildly but "tanked" in 4 of the 12 calendar quarters shown (the shaded areas in Figure 7-2). Oddly enough, despite the pain, McDonald's managed to post an annualized return of 17.7 percent over the entire 36-month interval—a pretty good result in absolute terms. Still, investors might not have been all that pleased. Simply riding out the period in a basket of Dow Jones stocks would have earned an annualized return of 27.3 percent—a rather sizable pickup for a "no-brainer" portfolio.[6]

Let's say we do some research before plunging into McDonald's stock. Since financial assets don't all move in lockstep, one worthwhile exercise is to identify a competing security that displays a countervailing trend. The underlying idea is straightforward. If we can combine McDonald's (MCD) with issues that have similar returns but "zig" when MCD "zags," we could end up with the same overall result but without having to negotiate troubled waters.

Imagine that we are looking to pocket a 10 percent return each year. One possibility, of course, is to buy a stock with an average return of 10 percent and pray for consistency. But given stock market realities, the odds

FIGURE 7-2
Riding the Wave: Is It Worth It?

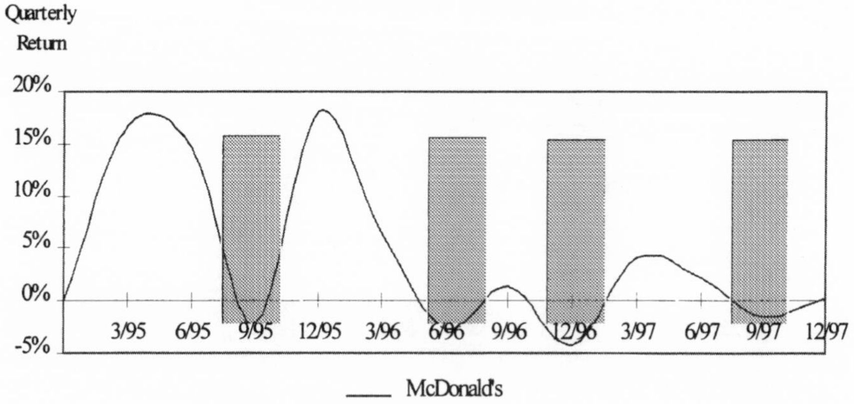

Quarterly
Return

_____ McDonald's

of achieving smooth annual results are necessarily slim. Now consider the benefit of combing two "noncorrelated" (or even "negatively correlated") assets.[7] We ought to achieve our goal more regularly and with fewer scary trading sessions. In a year when Company A's return slumps to zero, for instance, Company B could come through with a 20 percent performance. The net results would be 10 percent. We're happy. If Company B suffered a reversal in a subsequent year, Company A's return might rebound to save the day.

Actually, given the vagaries of financial markets, creating a counter-balanced portfolio is usually doable, at least to some extent. Even a glance at Figure 7-3 suggests an easy move. Notice how McDonald's cumulative return snaked around the Dow Jones Industrial Average. Over the course of the 10-year investment cycle, MCD underperformed the Dow half the time. If we spread our risk by allocating, say, 50 percent of our money to the basket of Dow stocks, we could survive Mad Cow disease without the heartburn.

Take a closer look. In Figure 7-3 the DJIA's quarterly performance is superimposed on McDonald's. While it's not a perfect illustration of what we're talking about, it is remarkable. Upon inspection we observe that the two securities moved in opposite directions fairly often (5 of 12 quarters). How did the two assets behave during the tough times? They were never simultaneously negative. Notice that when the amplitude of McDonald's price swings was extreme, the Dow was relatively calm. Over the second half of the interval, the opposite was true. The price movements of the two components canceled out, preserving our return objective.

FIGURE 7-3
Diversification: The Key to Taming Volatility

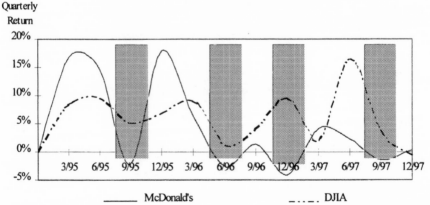

The Dow, of course, is a diversified portfolio in its own right. For the very reasons we've been talking about, it's no fluke that a basket of 30 stocks suffered only one subzero outcome compared with McDonald's four. And remember, the eleventh commandment for investors is don't lose money. The twelfth is don't forget the eleventh.

The foregoing analysis underscores the benefits of modulating price oscillation via asset allocation. Figure 7-4 shows the happy result. When McDonald's stock is "cocktailed" with an equal dollar amount of the DJIA, the volatility of the resulting portfolio is lowered significantly. More specifically, as measured by the standard deviation statistic, the risk factor associated with the diversified portfolio is one-third less than McDonald's.[8]

There's more good news. Since the Dow's trend line performance was superior to McDonald's, the diversified portfolio was not only less volatile but its quarterly returns were consistently better too. As shown in Figure 7-5, the portfolio capitalized on McDonald's big years while largely averting its downturns (shaded areas). As a result, the portfolio's annualized return was 22.7 percent, a 28 percent improvement over McDonald's.[9]

Here's another angle. Notice from the shaded area in Figure 7-6 that McDonald's started losing ground to the DJIA just prior to the halfway point in the cycle. In fact, the cumulative value of every dollar invested in MCD shares topped $1.64 by the end of March 1996. Then MCD stagnated. A positive stock market environment notwithstanding, MCD's cumulative value at the end of 1997 was a tad less ($1.63). Had we maintained a nondiversified portfolio, the psychological pressure would have

FIGURE 7-4
Diversified Portfolio Results

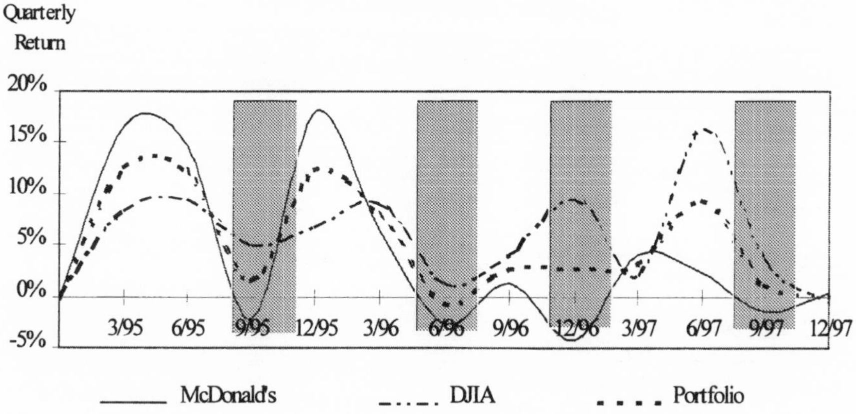

FIGURE 7-5
Comparing Quarterly Returns

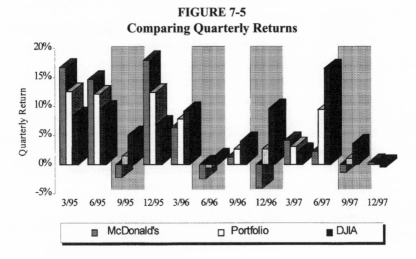

been building. Chances are that we would have abandoned course and bailed out. That's precisely how inefficient portfolios are usually born.

Don't forget that there are brokerage commissions and taxes to worry about when unwinding stock positions, assuming the portfolio isn't held in an IRA or other tax-advantaged account. As shown in Figure 7-6, over the same interval every dollar invested in the DJIA would have more than doubled, to $2.06. That leaves us with the problem of having to redeploy our tax-depleted funds in a significantly appreciated stock market. The lesson: proper prior preparation prevents poor performance. A well-diversified portfolio wouldn't be susceptible to such problems.

FIGURE 7-6
Comparing Cumulative Returns

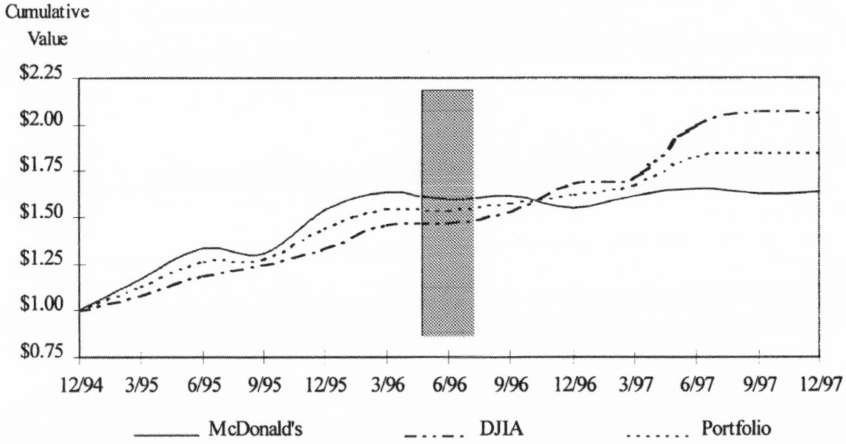

The bottom line is that even a naïve diversification strategy that relied on the DJIA to enhance overall performance would have accomplished the task. For McDonald's shareholders the result would have been nothing short of nirvana. Vis-à-vis the original plan, this "middle of the road" portfolio would have afforded more resilience to unanticipated shocks. Importantly, relieved of the pressure, our ability to stand by our long-range plan would have improved dramatically.

CORRELATION COEFFICIENTS: THE DIVERSIFICATION SEARCH ENGINE

The Dow Jones Industrial Average, of course, isn't the only diversification agent in the spectrum of financial assets. Even if we offset all the ups and downs associated with McDonald's,[10] per se, our portfolio would still be exposed to the ebb and flow of the general stock market.[11] Just try to identify a stock that circumnavigated the 1987 crash. To dampen this exposure, we'll have to consider spreading our investment dollars across other asset classes and possibly geographical boundaries.

Even though competing investments have different return profiles, in combination they may allow investors to shape portfolio performance. The key is to understand how the returns on the alternative investments match up or "correlate" with the portfolio. The value of so-called correlation coefficients lies in their ability to tell us something about the directional relationship between assets—a critical ingredient to the strategic asset allocation process. Correlation coefficients can range from a value of "minus 1" (for assets that always fluctuate in the opposite direction of the portfolio) to "plus 1" (for vehicles that consistently move in lockstep). A reading at or around 0 indicates little, if any, correlation between the returns.

Sticking with our McDonald's example, if the price of MCD shares declines 10 percent, we can expect an asset that is negatively correlated (−1) to move up. The correlation statistic doesn't tell us if the counterweight will perfectly offset potential losses in our McDonald's position. But at least we have reason to believe that any downturns will be mitigated to some extent.

Given the importance of correlation to asset allocation, it's worth repeating the central point. The objective behind strategic asset allocation is to exploit risky assets while mollifying the portfolio's volatility. For this purpose, positively correlated assets (say, those with a correlation coefficient approaching +1) are of less interest. Why? Because whenever McDonald's headed south, so would the diversification agent.

As it turned out for the 36-month period illustrated in Figure 7-6, when McDonald's share price hit the skids, the portion of the portfolio invested in the Dow Industrials didn't follow suit. Measured over the period, the correlation coefficient between MCD and the DJIA was fairly low (0.29). Hence the improvements shown along the dotted line in Figure 7-6.

Here's the general rule: the lower the correlation between variables, the more effective the diversification. But how do we calculate the correlation coefficient? Well, not everyone wants to know. But if you do, we've already presented the bulk of the methodology in Chapter 4. All we need is another column in our spreadsheet and a few extra steps.[12] If you don't need to know how the clock works, we recommend that you fast-forward to "No Risk, No Glory" below.

Table 7-1 repeats the data set from Chapter 4 (Table 4-4) for two competing companies with quite different return profiles but identical mean returns. Company B, you'll recall, was a nightmare. Notice that we've inserted a column to show that the observed correlation between the two return series is nearly zero (0.139). In an instant, the correlation coefficient enables us to identify potential diversification agents. Assuming we owned stock in Company B, there's solid reason to believe that a more consistent, possibly enhanced, result could be achieved by shifting a portion of our portfolio to Company A.

The correlation recipe isn't actually all that complicated. First, multiply Company A's annual deviations by Company B's. As shown, the year 1 outcome of this initial step is -30 ($-2 \cdot 15 = -30$). Next we sum all the annual results (25) and divide by the number of years in the series ($25 \div 5 = 5$). The result of the math at this point is known as the "covariance." Finally, multiply the "variance" for Company A by that for Company B ($2 \cdot 650 = 1,300$).

TABLE 7-1
Calculating the Correlation Coefficient

	Company A			Company B			Correlation
	Return	Deviation	Deviation (Sq)	Return	Deviation	Deviation (Sq)	Dev(A)*Dev(B)
Year 1	8.00	-2.00	4.00	25.00	15.00	225.00	-30
Year 2	9.00	-1.00	1.00	-25.00	-35.00	1225.00	35
Year 3	10.00	0.00	0.00	0.00	-10.00	100.00	0
Year 4	11.00	1.00	1.00	50.00	40.00	1600.00	40
Year 5	12.00	2.00	4.00	0.00	-10.00	100.00	-20
		Sum:	10.00			3250.00	25
		Variance:	2.00			650.00	
	Standard Deviation:		1.58			28.50	
	Mean Return:		10.00			10.00	
	Return Per Unit Of Risk:		6.32				

Covariance: 5.00

Variance (A) multiplied by Variance (B):   1300

Correlation Coefficient: 0.139

The correlation coefficient is found by simply dividing the covariance by the square root of 1,300 ($5 \div \sqrt{1,300} = 0.139$).

As with our McDonald's exercise, the proof of the pudding is in the results. As shown in Figure 7-7, Company B shareholders would have improved their lot by allocating a portion of their holdings to Company A. Consistency and the magic of compounding would have added up to enhanced performance, even though the portfolio's mean return was identical to Company B's. More specifically, a dollar invested in Company B's shares alone would have been worth $1.41, whereas every dollar invested in the diversified portfolio would have appreciated to $1.56—a "pickup" of 10.6 percent.

NO RISK, NO GLORY

Over a market cycle, there's a reason the return on equity investments ought to exceed that on bonds and bond returns should beat the interest earned on "cash equivalents." It's a nasty little four-letter word: risk.

Think about it. Cash equivalents (like Treasury bills) enjoy a unique property: zero downside risk.[13] But it would be a mistake to think that liquid assets are risk-free. What about relative risk? True, over the decade ending December 31, 1997, investors who elected to protect principal by rolling over 3-month Treasury bills never lost a penny. But they would have underperformed the Dow in 9 of 10 years, earning a paltry annualized return of 5.5 percent versus 18.6 for the DJIA.

FIGURE 7-7
Correlation and Diversification

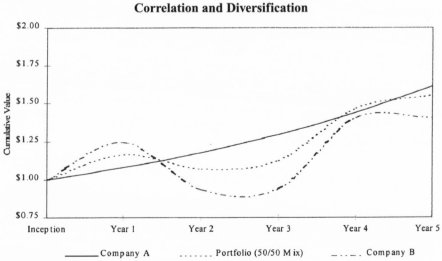

Plus, there's some volatility, albeit modest relative to stocks and bonds. Inflation, taxes, and other variables buffet T-bill yields. More precisely, the volatility of "riskless" assets as captured by the standard deviation of calendar-year average T-bill returns was 1.7 percent compared with 18.6 percent for the Dow.

The flip side of the absolute/relative risk trade-off also holds. If we define the Dow Jones Industrial Average as the "stock market," the odds that the DJIA will underperform itself are, obviously, zero. So the relative risk associated with the Dow is nil but the odds that it will suffer a negative return in any given year are fairly high.[14] The Dow finished in negative territory 9 of the last 35 years—roughly 25 percent of the time.

Figure 7-8 puts it all together and shows the multidimensional risk/return relationship for the three principal asset classes: cash, bonds, and stocks. Creating the graph was a snap. We simply drew two axes and scaled them in order to pair up each investment vehicle's historical return with its corresponding risk factor (standard deviation). Look at the point marked T-bills, for instance. As we mentioned earlier, the return on this riskless asset was 5.5 percent with a standard deviation of 1.7 percent. Locating a position for T-bills in the graph was accomplished by finding the point that lines up these values on the appropriate axes. The procedure was repeated for stocks and bonds.

FIGURE 7-8
Understanding Risk/Reward Trade-Offs
(1988–1997)

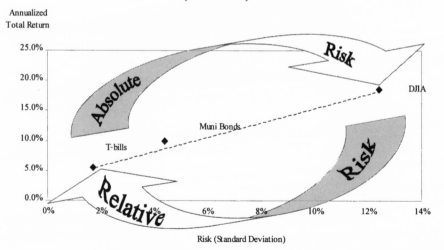

As you see, the adage holds. Increased volatility was rewarded with ever-higher returns (the diagonal line in Figure 7-8). And maybe you've guessed from the arrows superimposed over the graph that there are some other interesting nuances. Remember from our previous discussion that the chance of losing money in any given year (absolute risk) increases as you move from T-bills toward equities. Conversely, relative risk (the probability of underperforming the general stock market) increases as you descend the curve.

Investing isn't a game of chance. By the same token, it's not a science either. Nothing is guaranteed. In many respects, decisions are a matter of probability. And effective diversification strategies recognize that time frames factor into the probability calculation.

Imagine that a casino offered gamblers the opportunity to double their money each time they rolled a 6 with a single die. Going in, the house knows that the odds of a player coming up with a 6 on a single attempt are 1 in 6, or 16.6 percent—unless the game is fixed. So the casino knows full well that it stands a fair chance of losing money on a given player in single try. Much like an investor, then, the house diversifies this risk by spreading it across a large number of players and encouraging "winners" to stay at the table. After all, the longer the game, the better the chance of pocketing the "pigeon's" cash, since the odds of getting a 6 rapidly approach zero with each successive roll.[15]

Note that we qualified our statement about losing money in the stock market by saying "in any given year." As we've already noted, the Dow posted red ink in 9 of the last 35 years. But if we extend the time frame to, say, 2-year intervals, the chances of losing money on a cumulative basis drop off. What's more, the longer the time horizon, the lower the frequency of unhappy outcomes. Over 20-year spans, equity investors have not only enjoyed healthy returns but never lost a dime of their principal.[16] Figure 7-9 illustrates how the frequency of negative stock market returns diminishes as the investment horizon lengthens.

The important point here is that the diversification mix, in part, is linked to the time frame. While generalizations are dangerous, equity allocations for portfolios with relatively short investment horizons ought to be remarkably different from those with life spans of 20 years or more. This isn't to say that equity investments should be avoided. The idea is that investors who are counting on cashing in their nest egg in a year or two could be unlucky.

There's another point. Diversification is a dynamic process. Think about a portfolio with a 30-year outlook. As time passes, the relative performance of the various assets causes the allocation to go out of alignment.

FIGURE 7-9
Losing Money in the Stock Market: A Matter of Time Horizon

Outcomes

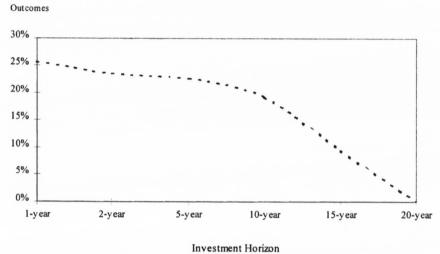

Investment Horizon

So the portfolio needs to be rebalanced periodically. Also, as time elapses, a portion of the equity allocation may have to shift toward fixed income and riskless assets as the distribution years approach.

DIVERSIFYING "RISKY" ASSETS

OK. Let's go back to the McDonald's example using Figure 7-10 as our framework for analysis.[17] As before, the graph was constructed by locating a point where the values on the vertical and horizontal axes intersect. The resulting graph allows us to develop a mental picture of how alternative securities are likely to alter risk/return trade-offs.

From our earlier discussion we appreciate the need to avoid a concentrated position. Thankfully, there are a lot of options. Certainly we could cut our exposure to company-specific (and industry-specific) problems like Mad Cow disease by "cocktailing" McDonald's with stocks selected from a variety of diverse industries.[18] And, as we've seen, targeting the DJIA stocks is a convenient way to go. But imagine the possibilities if we substituted the Total Return Portfolio with its demonstrated ability to outperform the general market index (see Chapter 5).

Look at the point labeled McDonald's in Figure 7-10. As is immediately apparent, there's little if any justification for holding it as a stand-alone portfolio. Notice that the Total Return Portfolio earned a significantly higher return (21.1% vs. 16.9%) with less risk (18.3% vs. 21.6%). Don't forget that

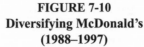

FIGURE 7-10
Diversifying McDonald's
(1988–1997)

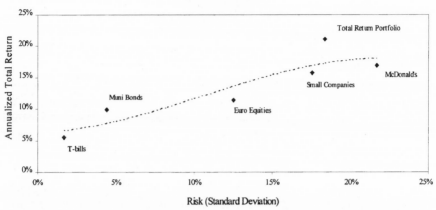

McDonald's, with its stellar dividend record, is among the issues that comprise the Total Return Portfolio.[19] Just by owning this blue chip portfolio (15 stocks), we would be well along the road to diversification. For the balance of this discussion, then, we'll assume that the Total Return Portfolio forms the "core" portfolio.

As we've already mentioned, financial markets don't march to the same drummer. So we've included some competing asset classes in our analysis. Even then, there could be a problem. What if the U.S. economy faltered, triggering a panic on Wall Street? The best portfolios wouldn't be immune. Depending on the size of our portfolio, diversification across geographical borders could make sense.

> **Each class of investment has its useful purpose and its proper place in any investment plan. A clearer understanding of their differing attributes may help to determine the relative proportion . . . which will best serve the investment requirements and purposes of each investor.**[20]

Now let's surf the curve. Observe how returns diminish and volatility subsides as we travel down the dotted line toward bonds and T-bills, allowing the pivotal question to be addressed: What allocation mix would allow us to satisfy our growth and income needs while balancing risk factors?

Investment goals vary from investor to investor of course. Since no single asset allocation fits all investors, we made a few assumptions. First we set aside 5 percent in Treasuries in the event an extraordinary investment opportunity pops up—or simply for a rainy day. To satisfy income needs,

we decided to allocate 10 percent of the portfolio to municipal bonds, figuring that the account was fully taxable and subject to maximum state and
federal tax rates. Since both of these allocations were born of prudence and
lifestyle requirements, they are a constant in our exercise.

Not surprisingly, the correlation between the Total Return Portfolio and
Treasuries was low (0.177). Municipal bonds also profiled with a fairly modest 0.28 correlation coefficient (see Table 7-2). So our allocation to these
asset classes should generate income sufficient to our needs while knocking
down the volatility of the consolidated portfolio. Small company shares are a
different story. Relative to the Total Return Portfolio, "small caps" had a third
less return with roughly the same risk factor. Plus, the correlation coefficient
of their quarterly returns was fairly high anyway (0.61).[21]

So what about the balance of the portfolio? Should we go for "all the
marbles" and target the Total Return Portfolio with its superior growth and
income properties? To get at the answer, we calculated the risk/return profile for a number of diversified portfolios, starting with what might be
labeled the "benchmark"—a blend of cash (5%), municipal bonds (10%),
and the Total Return Portfolio (85%). As with all the investment vehicles
shown in Figure 7-11, we assumed that the benchmark portfolio (Option A)
was launched on December 31, 1987 and that the portfolio allocation was
"rebalanced" quarterly in order to maintain the original mix.

All things considered, Option A turns out to be a nifty solution for
a host of reasons. Vis-à-vis a nondiversified position in McDonald's,

TABLE 7-2
Total Return Performance Summary: Annual Data, 1988–1997

	MCD	Total Return Portfolio*	Small Cos.	Euro Stocks	Muni Bonds	T-Bills	Diversification Options		
							A	B	C
Mean Return	18.6%	22.3%	16.9%	12.1%	10.0%	5.5%	20.2%	18.5%	14.3%
Median Return	14.3%	19.0%	18.3%	15.7%	11.0%	5.3%	17.2%	15.9%	12.7%
Annualized Return	16.9%	21.1%	15.7%	11.4%	9.9%	5.5%	19.3%	17.4%	14.0%
Standard Deviation	21.6%	18.3%	17.5%	12.5%	4.4%	1.7%	15.8%	14.0%	9.6%
Return Per Unit of Risk	0.78	1.15	0.90	0.91	2.25	3.24	1.22	1.24	1.46
Number of Negative Years	1	1	2	2	0	0	0	0	0
Number Of Underperforming Years**	6	3	5	9	8	9	2	2	6
Cumulative Return Per $ Invested	4.75	6.77	4.28	2.94	2.57	1.70	5.84	5.14	3.70
Correlation Coefficient***	0.638	na	0.610	0.503	0.282	0.177	nm	nm	nm

Strategic Asset Allocation									
McDonald's							0	0	0
Total Return Portfolio*							85%	75%	50%
Municipal Bonds							10%	10%	10%
Treasury Bills							5%	5%	5%
Euro Stocks							0	10%	35%

* Includes McDonald's   ** Relative To DJIA   *** With Total Return Portfolio Quarterly Returns

FIGURE 7-11

Strategic Asset Allocation: The Key to Capital Creation and Preservation

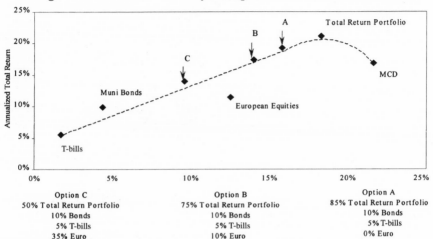

Option C	Option B	Option A
50% Total Return Portfolio	75% Total Return Portfolio	85% Total Return Portfolio
10% Bonds	10% Bonds	10% Bonds
5% T-bills	5% T-bills	5% T-bills
35% Euro	10% Euro	0% Euro

Option A would have earned an enhanced annualized return (19.3% vs. 16.9%). Moreover, investors would have enjoyed higher returns with less risk (15.8% vs. 21.6%). So far, so good.

Targeting municipal bonds satisfies our income needs. The cash buffer affords a bit of safety. And the Total Return Portfolio protects against underperformance risk. As summarized in Table 7-2, Option A not only earned enhanced returns over McDonald's but produced across-the-board, meaningful risk reduction. Also note that Option A's return per unit of risk (i.e., return divided by standard deviation) increased from 0.78 to 1.22 percent—a 56 percent improvement.

Options B and C repeat the exercise. But this time we've allowed European stocks to play a role in order to make a point. At first glance, an international exposure promises to lower the volatility of the benchmark portfolio (Option A). But the potential drag on performance looks rather uninviting (see Table 7-2). Don't be overly swayed, though.[22] Some investors may be well advised to opt for, say, a 5 to 10 percent international equity exposure. Keep in mind that the exercise presented here describes a discrete 10-year investment period—one in which U.S. equity markets prospered relative to their foreign counterparts. Down the line, international markets could have their day in the sun.

If adversity is the test of theory, let's replay the Mad Cow disease cycle we presented in Figure 7-6 to see how well Option A would have weathered the crisis. As shown in Figure 7-12, the simulation produced a

FIGURE 7-12
Bull Markets, Tax-Advantaged Income: The Benefits of Diversification

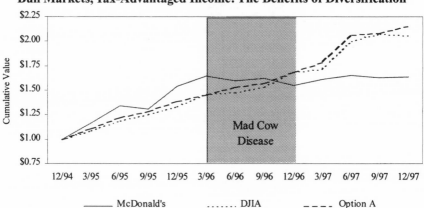

rather striking, although not unexpected, result. Not only did the diversified portfolio avert the problem but its cumulative value outpaced the Dow Jones Industrial Average—all of this while generating enhanced, tax-advantaged income.

Actually, when you think about it, Option A's performance was even more impressive than Figure 7-12 suggests. Keep in mind that these were jubilee years for equity investors. Over the course of 36 months, the Dow's annualized return (excluding dividends) was a whopping 27.3 percent. So Option A achieved a superior result despite a serious drag from its cash buffer (5%) and muni bond component (10%).

SUMMARY

As the pundits are quick to point out in bull market environments, over the long haul, equities are the place to be. But, as we've seen time and again, the history of equity markets includes long-lived cycles during which even the best stock pickers would have done just as well rolling their assets over in unexciting, riskless Treasury bills. So it would be a mistake to allow such numbers to drive investment decisions. In this arena, no single game plan is appropriate to all investors or even to the same individual at different stages of life.

In sum, strategic asset allocation is a vital component of every long-term investment program. Importantly, it's not a "static" concept. As time frames, risk tolerances, income needs, and other factors change, the diversification mix should be reevaluated (see Figure 7-13).

FIGURE 7-13
Strategic Asset Allocation: Diversification

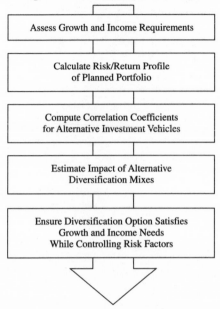

Diversification, although a useful technique for reducing risks, should never be thought of as a simple and complete answer to the problem of risk. . . . The gravest risks are from war, monetary disruptions, and technological changes, and they have to be borne or at best met through such foresight and judgement as experience and education make possible.[23]

CHAPTER EIGHT

Tactical Asset Allocation: Controlling Short-Term Risk

> We have not touched upon the opportunities to investment management at different stages of shorter economic cycles, through shifting from common stocks . . . into maturing obligations and thereafter returning to common stocks. Such opportunities have existed in the past and have been in many instances defined with sufficient clarity to be used to the material advantage of funds under informed investment management.[1]
>
> *Edgar Lawrence Smith*
> *1926*

O K. SO YOU'RE A LONG-TERM INVESTOR with your emotions in check. You've decided to fund the Total Return Portfolio and have settled on a strategic asset allocation plan tailored to your risk tolerance and income requirements. You're all set, right? Probably. At least that's the overarching answer.

But imagine this. You live in Hurricane Alley and hear that a tropical disturbance is brewing in the Caribbean. Do you rush to sell your North Carolina beach house on the chance that something more threatening may develop and come ashore at your doorstep? Not likely. On the other hand, given the possibilities, do you pay no attention or take no action? Doubtful. People who understand such risks aren't prone to cavalier behavior. It's a matter of prudence and proper prior preparation.

In large measure, investment management boils down to stretches of boredom with bursts of terror. Tactical asset allocation (TAA) is responsive to the problem. It's purpose is to dampen the impact of temporary setbacks so that they don't inflict disproportionate damage. In a nutshell, TAA is to Wall Street what batteries and plywood are to hurricane country.

The underlying idea is simple enough. Whenever equity markets appear "overvalued," investors should protect their assets by shifting some of the equity portfolio to cash equivalents, mindful of taxes and transaction costs. Now here's the tough bit. How can investors detect "pricey" markets? If the barometric pressure does fall, what protective measures can be taken short of unwinding the portfolio?

THE PRICE-TO-ECONOMY RATIO: DETERMINING THE STOCK MARKET'S INTRINSIC VALUE

The focus of this discussion is to build a valuation approach that enables us to detect *extreme* stock market valuations. While others have tried (and failed) to fashion forecasting models for the purpose of "pinpointing" year-to-year stock market fluctuations, we're looking for a way to anticipate anemic, possibly negative, stock market environments without worrying about precision.

Among other techniques, security analysts have long relied on the price-to-earnings (P/E) ratio when evaluating an individual company's stock price. The ratio (or capitalization rate) is found by dividing a company's share price by its earnings. For example, a company with $1 per share in earnings that sells for $20 would have a P/E ratio of 20. Given our operating assumption that the past is a useful indicator of future outcomes, a perspective emerges when the current ratio is interpreted in comparison with its historical norm. In their penetrating 1934 discussion of "intrinsic value," Graham and Dodd were clear about a critical point:

> Security analysis does not seek to determine exactly what is the intrinsic value of a given security. It needs only to establish either that the value is adequate . . . or else that the value is considerably higher or considerably lower than the market price. For such purposes an indefinite and approximate measure of the intrinsic value may be sufficient. To use a homely simile, it is quite possible to decide by inspection that a woman is old enough to vote without knowing her age, or that a man is heavier than he should be without knowing his exact weight.[2]

The concept of intrinsic value is central to tactical asset allocation as it relates to the general stock market. As Graham and Dodd put it nearly 50 years ago:

> Market prices periodically tend to exceed and fall below investment value based on the longer term considerations, and it appears safe to

assume that in the future, as in the past, a deviation will sooner or later be followed by corrective action that will in turn go beyond reasonable limits. So long, therefore, as investment value can be determined with some measure of assurance, these changes in market sentiment should offer attractive investment opportunities.[3]

Think back to our discussion of the economy and its relationship to equity markets (Chapter 2). Given the linkages (Gross Domestic Product spells corporate profits and dividends—prime determinants of stock market returns), it's convenient to think of the stock market as the price of the economy. From this perspective, the stock market's aggregate capitalization (total shares outstanding multiplied by their respective share prices) directly reflects market participants' assessment of the corporations that produced it.

By substituting the capitalization of the New York Stock Exchange for P in the ratio and nominal GDP for E, we can derive the price-to-economy (P/Ec) ratio—a macroindication of the overall market's intrinsic value or capitalization rate.[4] Measured over the 35-year interval ended in December 1997, the P/Ec ratio averaged roughly 58 percent, with two-thirds of the measurements ranging between 42 and 73 percent (i.e., the mean plus and minus a standard deviation).

Don't lose sight of our mission. We're searching for what Graham and Dodd might have labeled an *indefinite and approximate measure* of the stock market's intrinsic value. So, in this context, let's see how well the P/Ec has performed in its intended role.

Table 8-1 organizes historical ratio values according to broad ranges and contrasts the stock market's average performance during the ensuing 12-month period. On balance, the data confirm the P/Ec's ability to provide an unbiased, objective way to discriminate between under and overvalued

TABLE 8-1
Stock Market Valuations and the Price-to-Economy Ratio:
Establishing the Danger Zone

P/Ec Range	Number of Years	DJIA Ensuing-Year Performance*		
		Mean Return	Median Return	Risk **
0 - 100%	35	12.5	15.52	15.28
0 - 50%	16	16.7	21.28	14.57
50 - 100%	19	9.0	9.58	15.33

* Total Return (1962-97). ** As measured by standard deviation.

stock markets. And while there were exceptions to the rule, detailed examination of the data reveals that the stock market's prospects diminish as the
P/Ec ratio moves even higher.

So when the P/Ec closed at a value of 50 percent or less, the market's
mean return in the following year was 16.7 percent and its median return
was 21.28 percent. But when the ratio exceeded 50 percent, stocks didn't
perform nearly as well during the ensuing year.

For our purposes, then, the P/Ec ratio offers promise as a general market indicator—a signal that we could allow to play a role in determining the
size of the cash component of our diversified portfolio. More specifically,
when the odds of a subpar stock market increase, we could shift a small
fraction of our equity money into riskless assets and then reverse the action
when the danger subsides.

Let's apply this logic to the diversified portfolio described in Chapter 7
as Option A. You will recall that the strategic asset allocation plan called for
a fixed 5 percent cash position with 10 percent of the funds allocated to
municipal bonds for income purposes and the balance devoted to equities
via the Total Return Portfolio strategy. Now imagine we allowed the size
of the cash component to vary from, say, 5 to 15 percent. Since family
expenses are ever present, the muni portfolio allocation must remain constant in our exercise. Obviously, the equity commitment would have to
decline whenever the cash allocation increases.

While tactical asset allocation would allow the size of the cash position
to vary, keep in mind that, on balance, the strategy is to allow the power of
dividend growth to shape overall portfolio results over the long haul. While
some flexibility might be warranted, we would want to constrain the upper
limit of the cash exposure. For discussion purposes, then, we've assumed
that the cash buffer will be allowed to range from 5 to 15 percent in any
given year. So how can investors harness the P/Ec ratio in determining their
cash/equity allocations?

One convenient way to set the cash allocation is simply to multiply the
maximum allowable cash position (15 percent in this example) by the P/Ec
ratio value. Over the 35-year interval at hand, for instance, the P/Ec ratio
reached an all-time low at the end of 1974 (34%). So the 1975 cash position would have been 5.25 percent (15% · 34% = 5.25%). At the other end
of the spectrum, the P/Ec ratio closed out 1996 at a record high (95%).
Under our methodology, the 1997 cash commitment would have been a
smidgen over 14 percent (15% · 95% = 14.25%).

It's always possible, of course, that the multiplication process could
result in a cash allocation outside our predetermined boundaries (5% and
15%). In this case, we'd simply constrain the outcome to be no less than 5

percent and no more than 15 percent. So far, so good. But further refinements are possible.

BE WARY OF INVERTED YIELD CURVES

If interest rates are forward-looking and reflect market expectations of risk, inflation, and taxes, then we ought to be able to capture the information embedded in credit market prices to good advantage.[5] Radical credit market swings suggest changing expectations. And few events are more radical than "inverted yield curves."

What's a yield curve? It's a simple graph that depicts the rate of interest (or yields) paid on fixed income obligations of varied maturity dates.[6] Conventionally the curve is drawn using Treasury securities and is found in the credit market section of most financial dailies. By using Treasuries, we can eliminate (at least for practical purposes) any differentials in credit worthiness that might otherwise creep into the analysis.

Figure 8-1 presents the Treasury yield curve at the end of 1996. Notice how the curve slopes upward. It only makes intuitive sense that the rate of interest should increase as "durations" stretch from 1 to 30 years. After all, the odds of encountering an unforeseen negative event are a lot higher over a 30-year span than they are for 12 months.[7] To lend a bit more perspective, a snapshot of Treasury yields at the end of each calendar year produced a similar positively sloped curve in 26 of the last 35 years. But what about the other 9 years?

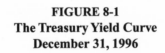

FIGURE 8-1
The Treasury Yield Curve
December 31, 1996

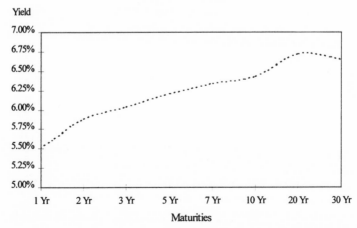

It's a strange market indeed that compensates investors less for risking long-term loans to the federal government—say, in a 10-year Treasury note—than it does those willing to stick their necks out for 12 months in a Treasury bill. But that's exactly what happens when the yield curve becomes inverted. To see the point, we've plotted the Treasury yield as of the end of 1980, the last time the market encountered a negatively sloped yield curve (see Figure 8-2).

While any number of explanations for inverted yield curves exist, our primary interest lies with the fact that they occur and with their implication for stock market performance. Still, since downward-sweeping yield curves are the exception and not the rule, a few words seem appropriate.

One plausible explanation rests on Irving Fisher's hypothesis (Chapter 2) that the price of credit (interest rates) reflects market expectations of inflation, taxes and credit risk *over the term of the instrument.* Since statutory tax rates change infrequently and the credit risk associated with Treasuries is miniscule, inflation expectations loom as the driving force behind credit market fluctuations. In a phrase, different terms to maturity have different outlooks. And the pricing of fixed income obligations ought to vary so as to preserve risk-adjusted real returns. Remember, the value of any investment return is its purchasing power. From this perspective, then, it's entirely possible that investors could be worried about the near-term economy but sanguine about its long-term prospects. If so, inverted yield curves could be a warning sign that the near-term inflation environment has deteriorated. Let's take a closer look.

FIGURE 8-2
The Inverted Yield Curve
December 31, 1980

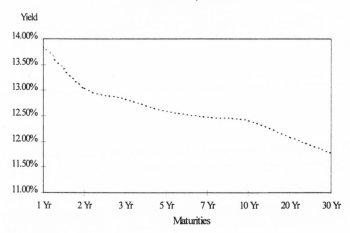

The initial step, of course, is to identify all the inverted yield curves. To ease the job, we simply subtracted the yield on 1-year Treasury bills from that on 10-year notes at the close of each calendar year. Whenever this yield "spread" was negative, we considered the curve inverted.

Figure 8-3 compares year-end closing spreads with the ensuing year's change in the Consumer Price Index for All Urban Consumers (CPI-U). Notice how inflation accelerated as the spread narrowed and vice versa. Now look at what happened when the slope of the yield curve turned negative; that is, the solid line in the graph slumped below zero. Inflation in the following year tended to spike—bad news for investors.

As we pointed out earlier, if Fisher's formula holds, then these extreme interest rate movements ought to tell us something about the stock market's prospects. Few observers would expect equity prices to remain unaffected if interest rates doubled, for example. So the next step is to see if forward-looking credit market prices tell us anything about the stock market outlook when the yield spread turns negative.

Let's continue with our 1980 example. As shown in Table 8-2, the 1-year Treasury bill closed at a stunning 13.86 percent yield, while the 10-year note was priced to yield 12.42 percent. Hence the spread was negative (−1.44%). How did the stock market perform over the ensuing 12-month period? Including dividends, it lost 2.9 percent.

The year 1980 wasn't an isolated incident. As shown in Table 8-2, the Dow's performance immediately following inverted yield curves was paltry compared with its average performance for the full interval. There were two

FIGURE 8-3
Inverted Yield Curves and Inflation

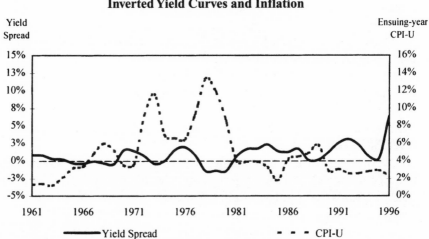

TABLE 8-2
Are Inverted Yield Curves a Warning Sign?

	Closing Treasury Yields		Yield	DJIA
	1-Year Bill	10-Year Note	Spread	Performance*
1965	4.96%	4.65%	-0.31%	-14.9%
1966	5.00%	4.64%	-0.36%	18.5%
1967	5.76%	5.70%	-0.06%	7.6%
1968	6.46%	6.16%	-0.30%	-11.0%
1969	8.32%	7.88%	-0.44%	8.6%
1973	7.30%	6.90%	-0.40%	-21.5%
1978	10.57%	9.15%	-1.42%	10.3%
1979	11.70%	10.33%	-1.37%	20.6%
1980	13.86%	12.42%	-1.44%	-2.9%

The Dow Jones Performance Scoreboard

	All Years	Post Inverted
	1962 - 97	Yield Curves
Mean Return:	12.5%	1.7%
Median Return:	15.5%	7.6%

* Ensuing-year Total Return.

notable exceptions (1966 and 1979). If the exceptional test proves the rule, it should be noted that, over the entire 35-year interval, the Dow Jones Industrial Average posted negative returns on only 7 occasions. Of these, 4 were preceded by inverted yield curves.

Again, our objective seeks to develop an unbiased way to determine our cash allocation. From the foregoing discussion, it seems that we could have established a simple decision rule: keep cash to a minimum setting (5%) whenever the yield curve remains "normal"—that is, positively sloped. But whenever the spread between the short and long rates turns negative, raise cash to the upper limit (15%).

Clearly, overall portfolio results wouldn't be immune to anemic markets. After all, the lion's share of our capital would have remained exposed to equity risk. Still, by increasing the cash buffer in response to an inverted yield curve, we could have enhanced performance.

THE TAA MODEL: COMBINING THE P/EC RATIO AND INTEREST RATE SIGNALS

We're now ready to assemble our decision rules into a tactical asset allocation (TAA) model. Here's the procedure. Recall from Chapter 5 that we need to "rebalance" the Total Return Portfolio at the start of each calendar year so as to ensure that its constituent stocks profile with the strongest dividend records. At the same time, we could reexamine our cash allocation decision for the upcoming year via a three-step process.

Step 1: Calculate the Price-to-Economy Ratio.

Express the market capitalization of the New York Stock Exchange as a percent of nominal GDP.[8] Then multiply the maximum cash limit (15% in this example) by the P/Ec ratio as described earlier. A P/Ec value of 75 percent, for instance, would imply a cash amount of 11.5 percent (15% · 75% = 11.5%.).

Step 2: Calculate the Yield Spread Between Treasury Bills and 10-Year Notes.

Whenever the yield spread is negative, the interest rate cash signal would be 15 percent. Otherwise it's the minimum amount (5%).

Step 3: Average the Signals.

For example, assuming a negative yield spread and a P/Ec ratio of 75 percent, the cash allocation would be set at 13.125 percent for the upcoming year. In the case of our diversified portfolio, then, the allocations would be 13.125 percent cash, 10 percent municipal bonds, and 76.875 percent equities. Again, given the math involved, it's possible for the combined model to indicate a cash amount outside our limits—that is, less than 5 percent or more than 15 percent. But this is easily handled by simply constraining the answer to the appropriate limit.

Sure, no methodology is foolproof—including ours. But a simple backtest confirms an ability to provide a useful input. Historically, the cash allocation generated by our TAA model would have ranged from 5 to 14.7 percent. To understand the effectiveness of these decisions, we organized the cash signals into "bins" and paired them up with the ensuing-year's DJIA performance. If the methodology has merit, then the Dow's performance ought to vary inversely with the size of the cash allocation. In other words, modest cash positions should presage better-than-average stock market returns. As the size of the cash component increases (and the equity exposure declines), the Dow's returns ought to show signs of sloughing off.

Take a look at Table 8-3. Here we've sorted the historical cash signals by 2.5 percent increments. Now note the DJIA's performance, remembering that the Dow's mean return measured over the entire 1962–1997 period was 12.5 percent. Unambiguously, small cash allocations were associated with robust stock markets while high cash periods preceded poor markets.

A stringent test illustrates the potential impact of these market/cash decisions on investment returns. Obviously, with the size of the cash com-

TABLE 8-3
The Tactical Asset Allocation Model

Indicated Cash Amount	Number of Observations	Ensuing-Year Return*	
		Mean	Median
5.0 - 7.5%	25	15.9%	17.7%
7.6 - 10.0%	6	5.6%	9.4%
10.1 - 12.5%	0	na	na
12.6 - 15%	3	-6.1%	-11.0%

* DJIA Total Return.

ponent constrained to be no less than 5 percent or more than 15 percent the differences in performance (even if the TAA signal worked perfectly) would be relatively imperceptible. To see what's going on, we'll need to expand the size of our cash band, at least for the sake of analysis.

So imagine we removed all constraints on the size of the cash component. There's a real possibility that the entire portfolio could be devoted to Treasury bills or the Dow Jones Industrial Average depending on the strength of the TAA signal. We could then calculate the cumulative value of the resulting portfolio and compare it with a fully invested equity portfolio. Under this extreme-case simulation, the portfolio would suffer (big time) should the methodology fail.

When viewing Figure 8-4, keep in mind that the stock component of the portfolio stands no chance of outperforming the overall market. After all, the equity vehicle involved is the Dow itself. Excess returns are attainable only if we succeed in preserving assets via T-bills during market slumps.

TAA NOT A "MARKET TIMING DEVICE"

Achieving superior performance over market cycles by systematically "timing" the market's ups and downs is an idea long since rejected by the investment community. And while many have tried, we're unaware of any techniques that have demonstrated an ability to routinely avert downturns and exploit the rebounds. It's probably not all that surprising. After all, in our view, market timing requires omniscience.

Still, critics may argue that, at root, our TAA model is a "market timing device." In a way, there's a kernel of truth in such assertions. But don't forget, all investment decisions—however they are born—involve an element of "timing." Imagine the mutual fund manager who elects to sell IBM in favor of Gillette on the basis of recommendations from the research depart-

FIGURE 8-4
The Tactical Asset Allocation Model: A Stringent Test

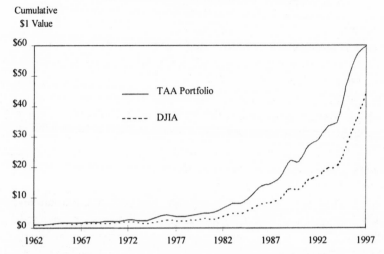

ment. Nobody would "pigeonhole" the manager as a "market timer." Yet, by definition, it must have been *the time* to make the trade. If there were a moment's doubt that it wasn't, would the fund manager do so? Of course not. The difference is that the decision reflects the manager's best judgment of the intrinsic value of the stocks involved relative to their current price.

The TAA methodology described here is advanced in this context. The model makes no attempt to capitalize on periodic ups and downs in the stock market. Indeed, "time" is a constant, since the model is estimated at the end of each calendar year for the purpose of determining cash allocations within prescribed limits. All future trade dates are known today.

There's always the possibility that a tactical decision will prove "faulty." So what are the likely consequences of an incorrect signal? During investment periods when the cash component is at its upper limit and the stock market booms, we would still make money. It's just that we stand to make less than we otherwise would have earned with a full equity exposure. Don't forget, the portfolio would earn interest on the cash equivalents and most of our assets would still be invested in equities. On the flip side, if our cash position was low (5%) and the market slumped, at least we didn't have 100 percent of our assets exposed to equity risk.

On the other hand, if cash was at the max and the market turned choppy, investors might sleep a little better knowing that more of their money is safe. Plus, they would be in a position to redeploy their cash at more favorable price levels in the stock market. During minimum cash periods, if the market boomed, they'd be smiling all the way to the bank.

SUMMARY

Tactical asset allocation seeks to safeguard portfolios against the possibility of a short-term stock market decline by shifting a portion of the equity component to cash equivalents. The strategy discussed here is highly disciplined and relies on two factors to anticipate potential inflection points in the stock market cycle: namely, the ratio of the NYSE's total market capitalization to nominal GDP and the Treasury yield spread. Still, it bears repeating that long-term investors with their emotions in check and a well-designed, diversified portfolio ought to be able to weather the stock market's turbulence without worrying about a TAA overlay.

The technique is objective. It relies on unbiased, unemotional price and quantity data to signal extreme stock market valuations, at least by historical standards. More specifically, the approach starts by estimating the price-to-economy (P/Ec) ratio—a measure of the general stock market's intrinsic value. The methodology is hinged on a basic tenet: the stock market is the price of the economy. More specifically, the P/Ec ratio recognizes the linkage between economic activity, corporate profits, and in turn equity prices. In short, by comparing the current ratio value relative to its historical norm, investors may identify periods when the stock market has crossed into virgin territory.

The ratio is easily calculated by dividing the nation's Gross Domestic Product (the total dollar value of all goods and services produced within our borders) by the total market capitalization of the New York Stock Exchange.[9] The P/Ec ratio cash signal is determined by multiplying the maximum cash level by the ratio value, but constrained to be within a predetermined minimum and maximum range.

The second step in the process is to take account of the interest rate environment. Here the technique monitors the relationship between short- and long-term interest rates in order to detect any abnormalities in the pricing of credit (i.e., negative yield curves), which could also be a warning sign of a weak, possibly negative, stock market performance in the year ahead. Indeed, back-testing and real-time experience reveal that negative yield curves are a reliable barometer of anemic stock market environments.

In calculating the yield spread, at each calendar year end, investors need only subtract the yield on 1-year Treasury bills from that on 10-year Treasury notes. Whenever the resulting figure is positive, the interest rate signal implies that the cash position should be set to the minimum amount.

FIGURE 8-5
Tactical Asset Allocation:
Controlling Short-Term Risk

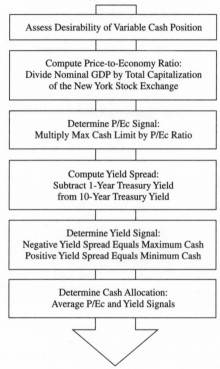

Negative yield spreads are a danger sign that warrants a maximum cash buffer.

In its final form, the TAA model sets the cash allocation equal to the average of both factors (see Figure 8-5). Assuming a prescribed minimum cash position of 5 percent with an upper limit of 15 percent, the portfolio's cash component would be 7.5 percent if the P/Ec ratio called for a 10 percent cash allocation and the yield curve was positive.

Coping with Concentrated Equity Portfolios: A Disciplined Approach to Diversifying Single-Stock Positions

> Purchase of a single stock [is] not an investment.[1]
>
> *Benjamin Graham and David L. Dodd*
> *1934*

ONSIDER THE MICROSOFT MILLIONAIRE: perhaps a 10-year engineer who joined the company fresh out of college, whose compensation through the years has included stock options, and who finds herself fabulously wealthy by virtue of a sizable holding of Microsoft shares. It's nice to be young and rich. But our millionaire has a problem. If she wants to increase her odds of remaining wealthy, she'll need to reduce her dependency on Microsoft. Concentrated equity positions are a hazard, even for the best of issues.

Prudent investors expect the unexpected whenever they embrace equities. They waste no time in protecting capital from stock-specific risk by spreading their investment dollars across a spectrum of competing assets. Still, even though they realize instinctively that overreliance on a single stock is dangerous, a growing number of people endure excessive risk levels as a consequence of corporate benefit programs, the sale of family businesses, or fortuitous events.[2] Often the problem is traceable to ignorance of the risk/return trade-offs associated with their holdings.

UNDERSTAND HISTORY

As with any carefully orchestrated investment strategy, diversification starts by understanding the price performance of what you own. And while past results are no guarantee of future outcomes, those who ignore the empirical record do so at their peril.[3] With this in mind, let's revisit the Microsoft Millionaire's situation. There's no disputing that MSFT is the blue ribbon champ among Wall Street's all-time "winners." Every dollar invested in the company's shares at the end of 1987 soared to $42.89 by the close of 1997, eclipsing the Dow's cumulative return ($4.08) by a mind-boggling margin.

But even Microsoft's impressive stock market performance was accompanied by a fair degree of volatility. Figure 9-1 plots the month-to-month price change for MSFT shares relative to the Dow. As is immediately apparent, Microsoft is significantly more volatile than the overall market.

All of which brings us to an important point. As our discussion unfolds, remember that our goal is to exploit Microsoft's return potential while controlling risk—quite a different objective from realizing the biggest bang for the buck. Sure, megareturns are always welcome. But investors holding a significant portion of their family wealth in a single issue—even Microsoft—ought to be worried. An unanticipated downturn in the company's fortunes could spell disaster.

FIGURE 9-1
Measuring the Volatility of Microsoft's Share Price
(Monthly, 1988–1997)

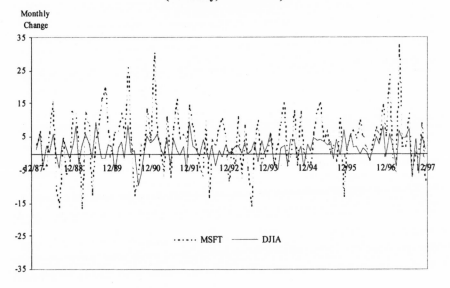

Such fears are understandable even though the idea that Microsoft could stumble may sound far-fetched. Don't forget, not too long ago IBM was held in the same esteem. Yet ironically, had Big Blue not misjudged the personal computer market, Bill Gates might have earned his Harvard degree rather than the countless billions he amassed building computer operating systems and software.

As we discussed more fully in Chapter 3, investors can develop a "feel" for the risk associated with a given stock by measuring the dispersion of its returns around its historical average (mean) via the standard deviation statistic. Once the calculation is in hand, a much-needed input is derived by applying an age-old empirical rule.[4] If history's a guide, 68 percent of expected returns will be within plus or minus one standard deviation of the stock's average return and 95 percent of the likely outcomes ought to be within two standard deviations. In a nutshell, the bigger the standard deviation, the greater the volatility. And for investors, volatility equals risk.

OK. Let's apply the rule to Microsoft. As shown in Table 9-1, MSFT's average (mean) return was an awesome 50.6 percent versus 15.7 percent for the general market. Small wonder that Microsoft shareholders are smiling. But it would be a mistake to allow a single statistic to dominate our thinking. Notice that the risk factor (standard deviation) for MSFT was also 3 times that of the DJIA (40 vs. 12.3). So, over the 10-year period summarized in the table, two-thirds of Microsoft's returns ranged between 10 and 90 percent. That's volatility. Is it worth riding the roller coaster?

TABLE 9-1
Statistical Summary
(Annual Data, 1988–1997)

Statistic*	MSFT	Portfolio (75/25 Mix)	DJIA
Years Of Observation	10	10	10
Cumulative Value Per $ Invested	42.89	26.48	4.08
Median Return	54.0	44.5	17.0
Mean Return	50.6	41.9	15.7
Standard Deviation	40	30.9	12.3
Return Per Unit of Risk	1.26	1.36	1.28
Minimum Return	-5.6	-0.7	-4.3
Maximum Return	121.8	96.4	33.5
Frequency Of Negative Returns	2	1	1
Mean Of Negative Returns	-2.2	-0.7	-4.3
Frequency Of Positive Returns	8	9	9
Mean Of Positive Returns	64.1	46.6	17.9

* Excludes Dividends

Here's how you get at the answer. Look at the return per unit of risk in Table 9-1. While there are a number of ways to calculate this statistic, the shortcut is simply to divide the mean return by the standard deviation. In this case, the calculation is 50.6 ÷ 40 = 1.26. Since only the uninitiated expose themselves to risk without compensation, at a minimum the return per unit of risk associated with our Microsoft position ought to be higher than the DJIA.

Beyond prudence considerations, the numbers indicate the need for (at least some) diversification. Microsoft's return per unit of risk (1.26) is slightly lower than the Dow's (1.28). Now look at the middle column. Had our Microsoft Millionaire elected to reallocate 25 percent of her MSFT position to the basket of DJIA stocks, the resulting portfolio would have captured the lion's share of Microsoft's cumulative return with a 23 percent reduction in volatility. What's more, the portfolio's return per unit of risk improved.

Other statistics hint at the wisdom of diversification. The picture presented in Table 9-1 is distorted somewhat by one supernormal year (a problem we discussed in Chapter 4 at "What Return"). Microsoft shares appreciated 121 percent in 1991. If we exclude 1991 from the calculations, MSFT's cumulative return falls from nearly $43 to $10.43.

THE "RISK/RETURN FRONTIER"
So how much diversification is warranted? The answer hinges on the individual investor's familiarity with the company, tolerance for risk, and investment horizon as well as other factors. Calculating something called the "risk/return frontier" provides the critical information necessary to reconcile each investor's circumstances.

Constructing the "frontier" is easily done. Here's how. First, create horizontal and vertical axes to represent the values for mean returns and standard deviations. We've placed the dotted lines in Figure 9-2 to help illustrate the procedure. First, draw a dotted line across the graph from the tick mark on the vertical axis representing MSFT's mean return (50.6%). Next, draw another dotted line straight up from the vertical axis over 40 (Microsoft's standard deviation) and place a "marker" where the two lines intersect. The resulting point neatly describes the risk/return characteristics associated with Microsoft. Repeat this process for the Dow Jones Industrials.

We rounded out the curve in Figure 9-2 by calculating the risk/return profiles accruing to various diversification mixes and locating a marker to describe the various results. For example, assuming our hypothetical investor had maintained a 75/25 allocation between Microsoft and the

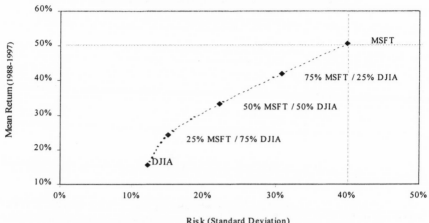

FIGURE 9-2
The Risk/Return Frontier:
Microsoft and the Dow Jones Industrial Average
(Rebalanced Annually, Excludes Dividends)

DJIA each year, the resulting portfolio would have achieved a mean return of 41.9 percent with a standard deviation of 30.9 percent (see Table 9-2). The familiar risk/return frontier emerges when the markers are connected.

Investors aren't created equal of course. Each has diverse return expectations, risk tolerances, and other specific needs. Effective diversification techniques must enable each individual to temper expected returns by the risk of achieving them. Importantly, the risk/return frontier doesn't lead to a single "right" answer. Its value lies in the perspective it delivers.

For a variety of reasons, some investors may elect to diversify 25 percent of their concentrated equity position. Still others may opt for some other mix consistent with their personal needs and circumstances. Look at the 50/50 mix. Not a bad trade-off, really. As revealed by the frontier, the portfolio's mean return declined by 35 percent but volatility was reduced by more than a commensurate amount (45%).

TABLE 9-2
Calculating Portfolio Returns

	1988	1989	1990	1991	1992	1993	1994	1995	1996	1997	Mean
MSFT	-1.8%	63.4%	73.0%	121.8%	15.1%	-5.6%	51.6%	43.6%	88.3%	56.4%	50.6%
DJIA	11.8%	27.0%	-4.3%	20.3%	4.2%	13.7%	2.1%	33.5%	26.0%	22.6%	15.7%
75/25 Mix*	1.6%	54.3%	53.7%	96.4%	12.4%	-0.7%	39.3%	41.0%	72.7%	48.0%	41.9%

* Derived by blending the appropriate percentage of MSFT and DJIA returns.

FIGURE 9-3
Microsoft and the Dow Jones Industrial Average:
Cumulative Return Comparisons

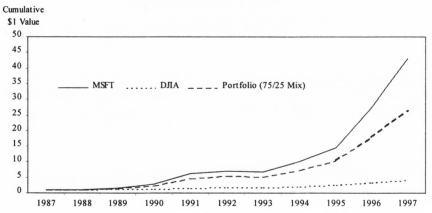

For the sake of discussion, we've elected to focus our attention on the 75/25 portfolio mix. As shown in Figure 9-3, this portfolio would have delivered an enhanced 10-year cumulative return over the DJIA ($26.48 vs. $4.08). But, as we've already mentioned, the risk attached to this diversified portfolio was a lot less than for Microsoft (standard deviation of 30.9 vs. 40). The result: solid performance, fewer sleepless nights.

Risk/return analysis offers investors a convenient way to evaluate risk and return trade-offs and provides a quantifiable basis for diversification. While the methodology offers a valued perspective, there's a hitch. The analysis is easier said than done, especially in a world of taxes and transaction costs. Understanding where you are and where you want to be is essential. Getting there is the challenge. Here's where something called the "frequency distribution" and statistical inference come into play.[5]

THE DYNAMIC IMPLEMENTATION RULES[6]
Rule 1: Collect Data.
Diversification requires the selling and buying of securities. So the price movements of the single stock and whatever an investor intends to use to diversify a portfolio (such as an index fund, an actively managed equity portfolio, bonds, or cash equivalents) must be tracked simultaneously.

To understand this point, imagine that every dollar invested in Microsoft ballooned to $1.25 in a single month—a "once in a blue moon" event. Should our Microsoft Millionaire diversify her concentrated equity position in one fell swoop? Not necessarily. What if the DJIA—the portfolio she's looking to buy—increased by 30 percent? Sure, our hypothetical investor would be celebrating over the sale price. But it would take that money and more to buy the higher-priced Dow. In the end, she would be worse off.

The solution is to monitor *relative* performance by creating a new return series. For the example at hand, just divide MSFT's price change by that of the DJIA. Had Microsoft and the Dow both moved up in unison—say, by 25 percent—there would be no relative price change and the calculation would yield a value of 1 ($1.25 ÷ $1.25 = 1). Values above 1 denote periods when the stock's relative return was positive and vice versa. Diversification opportunities arise whenever the calculation indicates positive relative performance. In the example at hand, the relative return value was less than 1, indicating a negative relative return ($1.25 ÷ $1.30 = 0.96). No diversification moves would be implemented.

Rule 2: Monitor Cumulative Return.

The aim of our Dynamic Implementation Rules is to take action only when there's a significant chance that doing so will enhance overall investment performance. So we've imposed some stringent criteria to increase the odds. First, we require the cumulative relative return of the single stock (from the time we launch our diversification strategy) to be positive. Even if other conditions warrant a transaction, no trading activity would be triggered as long as the cumulative (relative) return remained in negative territory.[7]

Rule 3: Capitalize on Volatility.

Just as with dynamic hedging (Chapter 6), the Dynamic Implementation Rules seek to capitalize on volatility. And, as we've already seen, Microsoft fits the bill. When it comes to measuring volatility, the time period for analysis (or "periodicity") is important. Turbulence tends to come in bursts. Consider the 1987 stock market. Anyone unaware of the October crash probably wouldn't detect it from annual price changes. The Dow's calendar-year return, though anemic, remained positive (2.3%). Switch to monthly data and a different picture emerges. On the heels of a 35 percent run-up over the initial 9 months, the DJIA "corrected" 23 percent in October.

By converting MSFT's monthly returns in the fashion described under Rule 1, we find that Microsoft's average (*relative*) monthly return was 1.02.[8] In other words, on average Microsoft's monthly performance beat the Dow by 2 percent. Now think about the opportunity for diversification presented by a month when the stock outperformed the DJIA by, say, 30 percent. Investors looking to reallocate their portfolio would realize that excess returns of this magnitude are worth capitalizing on.

FIGURE 9-4
XYZ Corporation: Frequency Distribution of Relative Returns

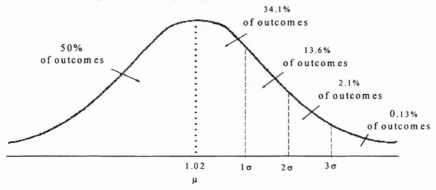

Expected Relative Return

Figure 9-4 depicts the frequency distribution of Microsoft's monthly relative returns. (The Greek symbol μ stands for mean value; σ represents the standard deviation.) By definition, the mean (1.02) locates the zenith (or midpoint) of the curve, with half the expected observations falling to either side. Knowledge of the standard deviation of relative returns (in this case, 0.08) enables us to measure the frequency (or probability) of any particular return, using the Empirical Rule:

μ ± 1σ contains 68% of the probable outcomes
μ ± 2σ contains 95% of the probable outcomes
μ ± 3σ contains 99.7% of the probable outcomes

A quick check of Microsoft's actual performance relative to the DJIA confirms that the pattern of monthly returns is consistent with the frequency distribution above. In creating Figure 9-5, we've allowed the computer to determine the "trend line" that best describes the frequency distribution. The idea is to see if there's any visual confirmation of a normal curve. Voilà. Despite ideal stock market conditions, MSFT shares displayed sufficient volatility to drive our diversification decisions. Patience should be rewarded.

So how would it work? Assuming the cumulative return is positive, trading would occur whenever Microsoft's monthly (relative) return exceeded its central tendency (0.2%). The amount to be reallocated depends upon the size of the monthly change expressed in terms of standard deviations, as shown in Table 9-3.[9] Note from the table that a 3 standard deviation (3σ) event would justify selling any remaining balance of the single stock. Why? Because 3σ events occur so infrequently that you'll

FIGURE 9-5
Measuring Monthly Relative Returns
(Microsoft ÷ DJIA Returns)

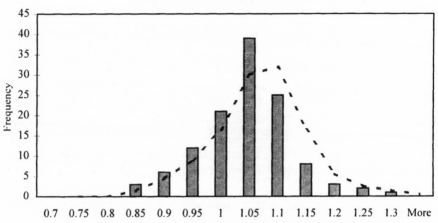

need to take advantage of them. Bigger monthly fluctuations are possible, of course, but the odds of experiencing them are sufficiently remote as to justify setting the 100 percent diversification parameter at 3σ.

Here's an example drawn from Table 9-3. Imagine that every dollar invested in Microsoft appreciated to $1.50 in a given month. Had the same dollar been invested in the DJIA, it would have increased to $1.20. The relative performance factor would be 1.25 ($1.50 ÷ $1.20 = 1.25). Relative to its mean (1.02), the excess return would be 0.23 percent, or approximately

TABLE 9-3
Normal Distribution Values and Diversification

Standard Deviation	Normal Distribution Value	Diversification Amount	Standard Deviation	Normal Distribution Value	Diversification Amount	Standard Deviation	Normal Distribution Value	Diversification Amount
0.0	0.5000	0.26%	1.0	0.1587	0.82%	2.0	0.0228	5.70%
0.1	0.4602	0.28%	1.1	0.1357	0.96%	2.1	0.0179	7.26%
0.2	0.4207	0.31%	1.2	0.1151	1.13%	2.1	0.0139	9.35%
0.3	0.3821	0.34%	1.3	0.0968	1.34%	2.3	0.0107	12.15%
0.4	0.3446	0.38%	1.4	0.0808	1.61%	2.4	0.0082	15.85%
0.5	0.3085	0.42%	1.5	0.0668	1.95%	2.5	0.0062	20.97%
0.6	0.2743	0.47%	1.6	0.0548	2.37%	2.6	0.0047	27.66%
0.7	0.2420	0.54%	1.7	0.0446	2.91%	2.7	0.0035	37.14%
0.8	0.2119	0.61%	1.8	0.0359	3.62%	2.8	0.0026	50.00%
0.9	0.1841	0.71%	1.9	0.0287	4.53%	2.9	0.0019	68.42%
						3.0	0.0013	100.00%

2.9 standard deviations (0.23 ÷ 0.08 = 2.9). How much diversification is called for? Exactly 68.42 percent.[10]

Before moving on to the balance of our Dynamic Implementation Rules, let's review a bit. Figure 9-6 presents a graphic illustration of the methodology thus far. Here we've depicted a single stock's price change relative to the DJIA. Points A through D represent month-to-month price fluctuations, while the curve traces the cumulative change of the company's share price from the time we launched our diversification strategy. Notice that both of these data series are calculated relative to average performance.

How much (if any) diversification movement would be triggered at Point A? None. Even though the company's share price experience a nifty increase on a relative basis, its cumulative performance (from the time we initiated the strategy) is underwater. Clearly Point B wouldn't present a diversification opportunity either, since both criteria (monthly and cumulative price change) are negative. In this example, only points C and D would satisfy the requirements for initiating securities transactions. The amount of diversification would be determined by expressing the observed return in terms of standard deviations and referring to the data in Table 9-3.

Rule 4: Set the Time Clock (Default).
The foregoing discussion notwithstanding, the possibility exists that equity markets could become too calm to provide an opportunity to diversify. What then? Average out of the stock according to a set timetable.

FIGURE 9-6
The Dynamic Implementation Rules

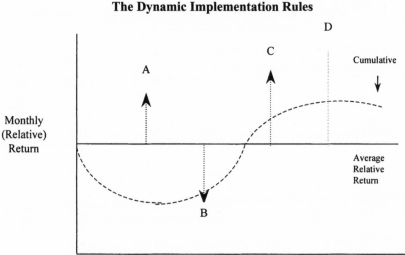

As a rule, the quicker the sale of the concentrated position, the higher the tax impact. After all, the sooner you pay taxes, the less time and money you have to earn investment returns. On the other hand, slow implementation leaves you exposed to the risk of a sudden, unexpected downturn in the company's fortunes. You can manage this problem by setting a timetable for diversification. And research indicates that a 5-year time horizon is more than adequate.

The plan works this way: assuming the volatility factor was insufficient to trigger any diversification moves, one-twentieth of the single-stock position you're trying to move out of would be committed to the diversification process at the end of each fiscal quarter. This guarantees that diversification targets will be met within the predetermined timetable.

Rule 5: Differentiate "Winners" from "Losers."

Glance back at Figure 9-2. Microsoft is clearly a "winner." Starting from the point labeled DJIA, every increment up the line is rewarded with increased return. So our hypothetical investor would want to keep a portion of the original MSFT holding in the portfolio. Just observing the positive slope of the line would immediately signal this. The diversification rules would be implemented as we've already explained.

To see just how quickly we can identify diversification options, let's take a quick peek at another risk/return frontier in Figure 9-7. While it's not a superstar like Microsoft, Chevron is a "winner" nonetheless. Excluding dividends, there's precious little difference between Chevron's return and the Dow (the left axis of Figure 9-7).[11] But what about risk? Notice from the horizontal axis in the graph that the standard deviation associated with a 50/50 portfolio mix was 12.1 percent versus 15.4 percent Chevron. That's a 21 percent reduction in volatility.

If the analysis has merit, then investors with a top-heavy Chevron portfolio ought to pocket the same returns with a diversified portfolio (50/50 mix). And, as shown in Figure 9-8, to maintain a concentrated position is to accept added risk without compensation.

What about "losers"? Are there any distinctions in the implementation rules? No. While the rules are the same, "losers" require a jump start. After all, if a stock is destined to be a laggard (or worse), the sooner diversification is accomplished the better. So once the desired amount of diversification has been decided, the process starts with an immediate sale. (Up to 50 percent of the single stock could be reallocated straightaway, keeping taxes and transaction costs in mind.) The balance of the position would be handled in the normal fashion.

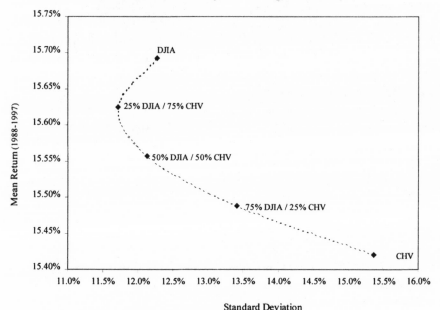

FIGURE 9-7
The Risk/Return Frontier:
Chevron and the Dow Jones Industrial Average
(Rebalanced Annually, Excluding Dividends)

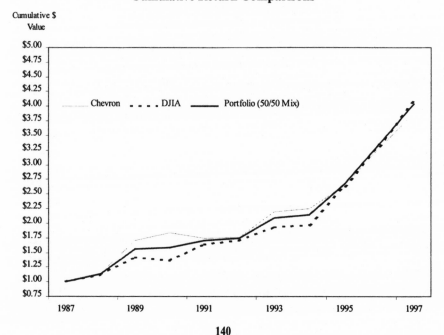

FIGURE 9-8
Chevron and the Dow Jones Industrial Average:
Cumulative Return Comparisons

Just as "winners" are instantly identified from the slope of the risk/return frontier, so too are "losers." Figure 9-9 shows the frontier for another household name, Polaroid. Notice that the risk/return frontier runs in the opposite direction from Microsoft. In short, every ounce of diversification results in increased return and lower risk.

With performance like this, it's likely that investors holding an inordinate fraction of their personal wealth in PRD wouldn't require much convincing to diversify. Still, assuming a low cost basis, there are taxes to worry about. So we'll assume that PRD shareholders opted for a 50/50 portfolio mix and simulate the resulting portfolio's performance. How would they have fared?

As shown in Figure 9-10, the long and short of it is that investors electing to maintain their nondiversified holding of PRD stock were kicked to death by a rabbit. Sadly, the unsuspecting may not have realized the problem, since the stock delivered a positive 10-year return. Investors should have been more sensitive.

Relative to the general market average, Polaroid seriously underperformed. Sure, every $1 invested in the company's shares more than doubled (to $2.44). But the opportunity cost associated with the concentrated equity position was huge. Had investors opted to diversify by even 50 percent,

FIGURE 9-9
The Risk/Return Frontier: Polaroid and the Dow Jones Industrial Average
(Rebalanced Annually, Excluding Dividends)

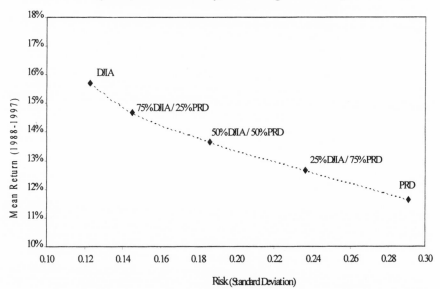

Risk (Standard Deviation)

their cumulative return would have quadrupled (to $4.02). And don't forget, all this occurred during the biggest bull market in generations. So failure to diversify, in this instance, was a squandered opportunity of major proportion.

DYNAMIC IMPLEMENTATION: THE RESULTS
OK. Our Microsoft Millionaire has performed her "due diligence" and has determined that the 25/75 diversification mix is sensible. With the decision made, should she move quickly to address the vulnerability of her single-stock portfolio or remain calm and disciplined? The hallmark of an effective diversification strategy is its ability to capture an enhanced overall result while managing risk and taxes.

Figure 9-11 depicts the results for a December 31, 1992 simulation.[12] In order to capture the full tax effect, we assumed that all portfolios were liquidated at the end of 1997 and taxes paid on any remaining unrealized capital gains. As indicated, the dynamic diversification strategy paid off. While the difference may not seem all that striking, remember that we diversified only 25 percent of the original position.

FIGURE 9-10
Polaroid and the Dow Jones Industrial Average:
Cumulative Return Comparisons

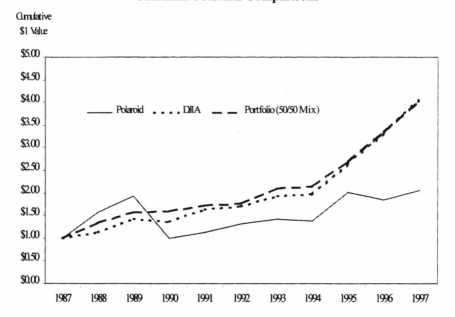

Notice that we added a third result in Figure 9-11. Thus far, our discussion has focused on diversifying a concentrated equity position by mixing it with a passive investment vehicle, the Dow Jones Industrial Average. This option is not only available to investors, but is convenient given the invention of something called Diamonds—a listed American Stock Exchange security designed to track the DJIA.[13]

But here's a thought. If an index fund produces satisfactory results, imagine the possibilities if we used an actively managed portfolio with a demonstrated ability to outperform the Dow. So we recast the dynamic diversification strategy, this time substituting the Total Return Portfolio discussed in Chapter 5. Not surprisingly, as depicted in Figure 9-11, the Total Return Portfolio produced a superior outcome.

SUMMARY

Turbulence can grab the stock market in an instant. So it pays to be nimble. Of necessity, the research presented here relies on monthly data. But investors looking to diversify a concentrated equity position should be alert for daily price changes. Should the conditions warrant action on an intra-month basis, it's advisable to follow the Dynamic Implementation Rules and time-weight the indicated transaction amount (see Figure 9-12).

FIGURE 9-11
Coping with Concentrated Equity Positions:
Dynamic Implementation versus Immediate Diversification

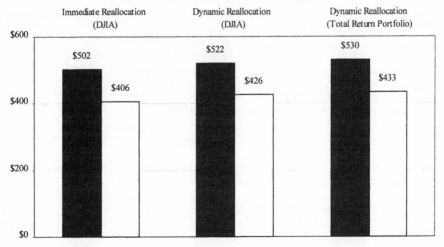

■ Before Unrealized Gains Tax   □ After Unrealized Gains Tax

FIGURE 9-12
Coping with Concentrated Equity Positions:
Dynamic Diversification

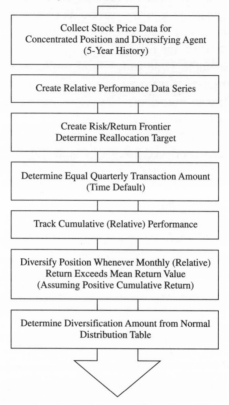

Imagine, for example, that a sale of 400 shares was signaled after only a week into the cycle. Under the methodology, 100 shares would be sold and the proceeds swept into the market basket. If the market recovered, the move would be vindicated. If the market continued to slide, we would re-estimate the model at month's end and implement the strategy for the indicated amount less any month-to-date transactions.

Diversification in the portfolio is insurance against errors in judgement. Ten sails get more wind than five sails—twenty more than ten.[14]

CHAPTER TEN

Tidbits: New Dogs, Old Tricks

> It is easy and safe to prophesy . . . that a period of high interest
> rates will lead to a sharp decline in the market.[1]
>
> *Benjamin Graham and David L. Dodd*
> *1934*

WITHIN THE INVESTMENT COMMUNITY, there's an old story about Einstein's arrival at heaven's gate. Owing to a sudden influx of newcomers, only semiprivate rooms were available. But in deference to his earthly achievements, Einstein was allowed to pick his roommate. The first candidate produced a résumé sporting an IQ of 180. Einstein was elated. Maybe his research days weren't over after all. The second candidate looked promising too, although his IQ was only 120. Still, Einstein thought, here was an opportunity to indulge his curiosity about the arts. The final candidate announced an IQ of 60 and Einstein responded: "So what's the stock market outlook, anyway?"

WHERE'S THE STOCK MARKET HEADED?
The allegory underscores just how humbling the forecasting business can be. Actually, since omniscience isn't part of the human makeup, the odds that anyone can systematically anticipate the events destined to shape the financial markets are necessarily slim. Still, given their track records, it is surprising that we continue to press Wall Street's gurus for guidance.

As we discussed in Chapter 2, the linking of interest rate fluctuations and equity market returns is an old idea.[2] To see the point, just imagine that interest rates doubled. Few observers would expect the stock market to remain unaffected. A deteriorated credit market environment would be expected to undercut Wall Street prices. And a simple test confirms the hypothesis.

Table 10-1 sorts the DJIA's performance data using a simple criterion: calendar years when interest rates moved higher and years when they moved lower. If the theory has merit, then there ought to be clear-cut evidence that lower rates spell robust stock markets and vice versa.[3] There is.

While there are exceptions, the results summarized in Table 10-1 are far from ambiguous. During years when rates declined, Wall Street celebrated. On average, the DJIA appreciated some 16 percent. But when rates moved higher, the Dow was hard pressed to keep its head above water, suffering negative performances in 8 of 19 years and earning a mean return of only 2.6 percent.

TABLE 10-1
Are Interest Rates Linked to Stock Market Performance?

Falling Interest Rate Periods			Rising Interest Rate Periods		
	Year-over-year Change			Year-over-year Change	
	T-Bill Yield*	DJIA**		T-Bill Yield*	DJIA**
1967	-0.56	15.2	1963	0.38	17.0
1970	-0.27	4.8	1964	0.39	14.6
1971	-2.06	6.1	1965	0.40	10.9
1972	-0.27	14.6	1966	0.90	-18.9
1975	-2.06	38.3	1968	1.04	4.3
1976	-0.81	17.9	1969	1.33	-15.2
1982	-3.43	19.6	1973	2.98	-16.6
1983	-1.99	20.3	1974	0.81	-27.6
1985	-2.07	27.7	1977	0.28	-17.3
1986	-1.50	22.6	1978	1.92	-3.1
1987	-0.19	2.3	1979	2.88	4.2
1990	-0.61	-4.3	1980	1.41	14.9
1991	-2.12	20.3	1981	2.57	-9.2
1992	-1.94	4.2	1984	0.92	-3.7
1993	-0.44	13.7	1988	0.89	11.8
1996	-0.48	26.0	1989	1.44	27.0
			1994	1.26	2.1
			1995	1.24	33.5
			1997	0.06	22.6
Median:	16.530				4.190
Mean:	15.573				2.695
Standard deviation:	10.959				17.121
Best:	38.324				33.451
Worst:	-4.342				-27.574
Negative Years:	1				8
Positive Years:	15				11

* Average 3-month T-bill yield   ** Excluding dividends.

Importantly, this performance differential wasn't attributed to a few exceptional years. Compared with its historical average return (8.6 percent excluding dividends), the Dow posted subpar rounds in 10 of 19 years when interest rates inched higher. But in 16 years when rates declined, only 5 returns were less than the historical norm. Finally, look at the difference in volatility as measured by the standard deviation of returns.

Given the importance of interest rate fluctuation to stock market performance, it's no wonder Wall Streeters hang on Fed Chairman Greenspan's every word. So now we arrive at a problem. How can investors anticipate if interest rates are headed up or down?

WHITHER INTEREST RATES?

Fortunately there's an objective way to assess the interest rate outlook. Implicit forecasts can be derived from unbiased, unemotional futures market quotations. Futures contracts for 3-month Treasury bills have traded on the International Monetary Market (a division of the Chicago Mercantile Exchange) since January of 1976.[4] Participants can purchase, today, a contract for a 91-day T-bill up to 2 years in advance.

While there'll be winners and losers, the process dictates efficient pricing born of the collective wisdom of the market. Such wisdom doesn't imply that futures market players always "get it right." But you can bet that every scrap of information comes into play. After all, it's difficult to imagine that anybody would risk cash today expecting to lose it tomorrow. So though futures contracts don't always hit the bull's eye, there's an important reason to trust in the market's general forecasting ability.

How would you go about estimating the upcoming year's average Treasury bill yield?[5] Simply add up the previous year-end quotations for the March, June, and September futures contracts along with the December 31 "spot" yield and divide by 4. Table 10-2 details the calculation.

As shown in Figure 10-1, the ability of the futures market to foresee the path of interest rates has been impressive. Historically, this simple technique was within half a percent of the actual outcome some 12 months in advance. What's more, the ability of market forces to correctly anticipate the upcoming year's interest rate outlook compares favorably with the consensus estimates produced by the nation's top economists. For investors already subscribing to the daily financial press, there's an added bonus—these estimates are free!

WHAT ABOUT INFLATION?

As we discussed earlier, few economic theorems have withstood the test of time. One survivor is Irving Fisher's turn-of-the-century observation that

TABLE 10-2

Calendar-Year T-Bill Yields: The Implicit Market Forecast

Previous-year Closing T-bill Quotations

	Spot	Futures Market			Implicit	Actual	Root
	Yield	March	June	September	Forecast	Average Yield	Error
1987	5.7%	5.4%	5.3%	5.4%	5.4%	5.8%	0.3%
1988	5.7%	6.0%	6.3%	6.7%	6.2%	6.7%	0.5%
1989	8.1%	8.1%	8.1%	8.1%	8.1%	8.1%	0.0%
1990	7.6%	6.9%	6.7%	6.7%	7.0%	7.5%	0.5%
1991	6.4%	6.0%	5.9%	6.0%	6.1%	5.4%	0.7%
1992	3.9%	3.7%	3.7%	3.9%	3.8%	3.4%	0.4%
1993	3.1%	3.2%	3.5%	3.9%	3.4%	3.0%	0.4%
1994	3.0%	3.2%	3.5%	3.8%	3.4%	4.3%	0.9%
1995	5.5%	6.6%	7.3%	7.7%	6.8%	5.5%	1.3%
1996	5.0%	4.9%	4.6%	4.6%	4.8%	5.0%	0.2%
1997	5.1%	5.0%	5.2%	5.3%	5.1%	5.1%	0.1%
1998	5.2%	5.0%	5.1%	5.0%	5.1%	n.a.	n.a.

Mean Error:	0.5%
Median Error:	0.4%
Biggest Error:	1.3%
Smallest Error:	0.0%

the market rate of interest reflects a "real" rate—born of creditworthiness and other loan-related considerations—plus "expected" inflation. If so, interest rate forecasts should tell us something about inflation. And make no mistake. As we detailed in Chapter 5, inflation is an insidious tax.

A quick test confirms Fisher's point. For starters, to the extent that creditworthiness enters the picture, we can minimize our exposure to this

FIGURE 10-1

Divining interest rates

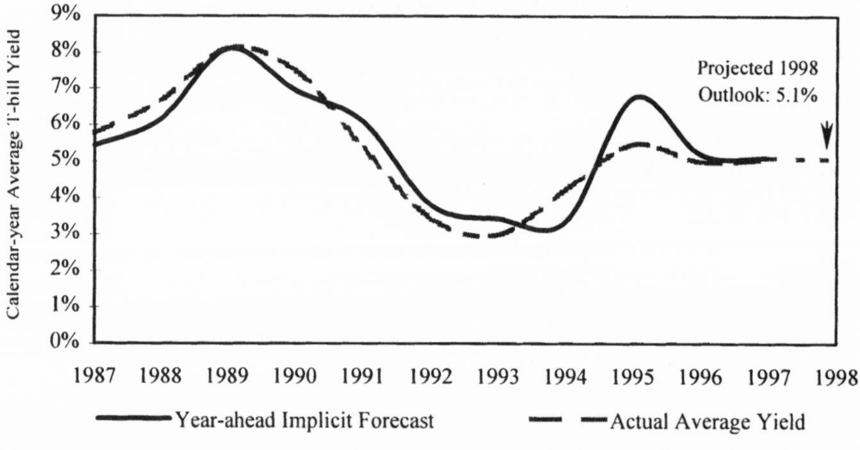

Projected 1998
Outlook: 5.1%

——— Year-ahead Implicit Forecast   ━━ ━━Actual Average Yield

FIGURE 10-2
Will Inflation Heat Up?

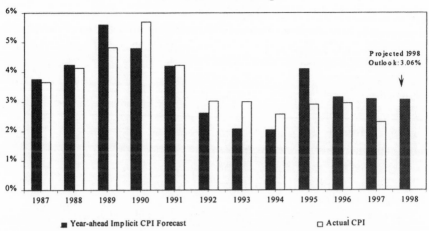

■ Year-ahead Implicit CPI Forecast   □ Actual CPI

variable by sticking with Treasury bills as our proxy for short-term interest rates. Then there's the question of taxes. While we don't know precisely what marginal tax rate clears the market, we've elected to use the highest tax bracket (currently 39.6%), since we're really not worried about the pinpoint accuracy of our implicit forecasts.

In constructing Figure 10-2, we simply subtracted this assumed tax rate from 1 and multiplied the projected calendar-year T-bill yield (Table 10-2) by this reciprocal to derive a rough estimate of the upcoming year's inflation outlook.

If Fisher's theory holds, this ballpark estimate ought to show some indication of "getting it right." So how did these implicit inflation forecasts work out? Fairly well, considering that we're leaning on our imperfect interest rate projections and making a gross assumption about tax rates. For the period shown in Figure 10-2, the estimates were roughly within half a percentage point of predicting the actual change in the Consumer Price Index. What's more, notice that inflation tended to heat up whenever interest rates were forecasted to move higher and subsided when yields were projected to fall.

INTEREST RATES AND THE ECONOMY: WHAT'S THE RELATIONSHIP?

Another widely accepted maxim is that interest rates are a prime determinant of economic activity. It's hard to imagine that anyone would expect economic boom times if rates soared. A dramatic improvement in credit terms ought to spawn robust economies. We don't quibble with the premise that interest rates are inextricably linked to the health of the economy. But the relationship is far from straightforward.

To begin with, the contemporaneous relationship between interest rates and GDP growth is not what you might expect. Examination of the raw data reveals that year-over-year fluctuations in both series run in the same direction, especially at turning points in the business cycle. Did you get that? Higher interest rates coincide with robust economies and lower rates correspond with anemic growth.

Look carefully at Figure 10-3, particularly at 1982, which marked the worst calendar-year economy in postwar history (real GDP growth was −2.1%). What happened to rates? They collapsed. Whereas the 1-year Treasury bill closed out 1981 at 13.4 percent, by the end of 1982 its yield was down to 8.68 percent—a drop of 4.72 percentage points as shown in the graph. That's a staggering 35 percent cut in the price of credit.

Now focus on the bust-to-boom periods, particularly the 1983 recovery. As shown in Figure 10-3, Gross Domestic Product growth rebounded to 4.1 percent. Which way did rates move? Higher, a lot higher. By the close of 1983, the spot yield on 1-year Treasuries had increased by 1.4 percentage points, pushing rates back up into double-digit territory (from 8.68% to 10.1%).

While recessions are the exceptional periods, they aren't conveniently organized by calendar years. Indeed, popular wisdom defines a recession as

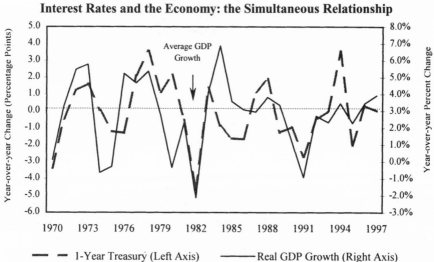

FIGURE 10-3
Interest Rates and the Economy: the Simultaneous Relationship

two back-to-back calendar quarters of negative real GDP growth. In fact, the Bureau of Economic Analysis keeps track of recessions by month, from the start to the finish. So if interest rate fluctuations and economic growth move in the same direction, then recessions ought to provide a valuable test.

Table 10-3 identifies all the official economic downturns since the end of 1969 and confirms that the 1982 episode was no fluke. Without exception, recessions coincided with a drop in interest rates. So what's the plausible explanation?

Think about the price of shirts and ask a simple question: What happens to shirt prices during recessions when nobody's buying? Faced with evaporating sales, it's probably a safe bet that retailers would slash prices. Now think about interest as being the price of credit. Which way are prices likely to go when the economy becomes mired in recession and credit demand shrivels up? Down. At some point, though, an improved credit market environment works its magic. Just as supertankers don't turn on a dime, so the economy takes a while to respond. At a price, though, people buy shirts and demand for credit perks up.

The bottom line is that interest rates are a sensitive barometer of what's really churning under the economy's hood. By the time the bad news grips Main Street and becomes the lead story on the evening news, you can bet that forward-looking financial market prices are already discounting the recovery.

THE PRICE-TO-ECONOMY RATIO: AN EARLY-WARNING INDICATOR

As we presented more fully in Chapter 8, at root the stock market is the price of the economy. By expressing the market's total capitalization as a percent of GDP, we can "normalize" its value over time and determine (at least in a general way) whether or not the stock market is "pricey" (see Fig-

TABLE 10-3
Do Lower Interest Rates Defeat Recessions?

Recession Period		Treasury Bill Yield*		
Start	End	Start	End	Change
Jul-90	Mar-91	7.7	6.3	-1.44
Jul-81	Nov-82	16.1	9.4	-6.74
Jan-80	Jul-80	12.4	9.4	-3.04
Nov-73	May-75	7.3	6.1	-1.20
Dec-69	Nov-70	8.3	5.1	-3.26

* 1-Year Treasury bills.

ure 10-4). Armed with this perspective, we can review our portfolio's asset allocation to ensure its ability to survive possible corrections.

Not surprisingly, there are a number of ways to view the price-to-economy (P/Ec) ratio. In our earlier discussion, we simply contrasted the current ratio values relative to its historical range. More specifically, we calculated the P/Ec ratio's historical mean and standard deviation. If history is a guide, we know that two-thirds of the likely outcomes ought to fall within ±1 standard deviation of the average ratio value.[6]

Figure 10-4 presents the P/Ec ratio in historical context.[7] Here we can clearly see that the 1995–1997 bull market succeeded in pushing stock market valuations into virgin territory. At year-end 1997, the total market capitalization of the New York Stock Exchange (all the listed shares multiplied by their respective price) was some $9.4 trillion, or 1.14 percent of nominal GDP. Since GDP growth is far less volatile than share prices, the implication is that the stock market would have to surrender roughly a quarter of its value in order to get the ratio value back into its normal range.

Notice that we used the word "roughly" in describing the size of a potential stock market correction. We were careful with our language for a couple of reasons. To begin with, we're not seeking to determine the stock market's exact intrinsic value at any point in time. For our purposes, "an indefinite and approximate measure of the intrinsic value [is] sufficient". After all, in developing a feel for the vulnerability of share prices, what's

FIGURE 10-4
The Price-to-Economy Ratio: Fixed Bandwidth

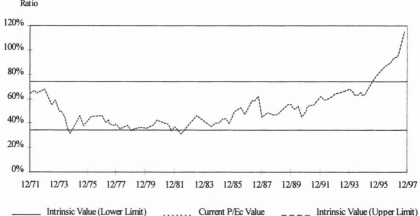

Price-To-Economy Ratio

_____ Intrinsic Value (Lower Limit)   .... Current P/Ec Value   _ _ _ _ Intrinsic Value (Upper Limit)

important is whether or not stock market valuations are "adequate . . . or considerably higher or considerably lower" than normal.[8]

So far, so good. But there are some problems. Think about the construction process used to create Figure 10-4. When the mean and standard deviations used to establish the bandwidth are calculated, recent-year data (which may be more descriptive of the current market environment) have a small influence on determining the acceptable boundaries of intrinsic value. True, a bit of data would be added with every passing year. But when you divide the sum of all the years in the data set to create the mean value, a single year's outcome simply can't alter the result all that much. So you may want to view the data from a slightly different angle.

Over time, the complexion of the world economy changes. Just think about the last quarter century. We've witnessed any number of unprecedented events, including the birth of the information age, personal computers, oil embargoes, and radical tax reform. So it may be appropriate to introduce a dynamic into our process that will allow the P/Ec ratio to be more sensitive to recent experience.

The solution is to contrast current P/Ec values (calculated in the usual fashion) relative to their 10-year rolling average, plus and minus a standard deviation. As you view the results in Figure 10-5, remember that the value of the technique lies in its ability to signal extreme market valuations. From this perspective, P/Ec values that fall above the upper band are in a danger zone.

Compare the 1987 stock market experience in Figures 10-4 and 10-5. With fixed bands, there wasn't even a hint of a potential downturn. Even if

FIGURE 10-5
The Price-to-Economy Ratio in Perspective: Variable Bandwidth

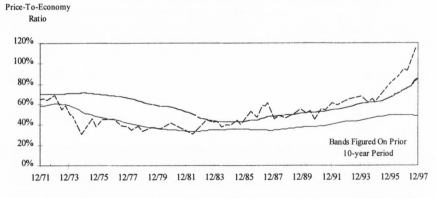

Price-To-Economy Ratio

Intrinsic Value (Lower Limit)   .... Current P/Ec Value   _ _ _ _ Intrinsic Value (Upper Limit)

we recast the plot to use only the data that would have been available at the end of 1986, the stock market's valuation would have remained within the band. But with variable bandwidths, the danger signal is visible.

The 1987 experience isn't the only example of an overvalued stock market that corrected itself during the ensuing years. Notice how the excesses of the 1991–1993 market disappeared in 1994—a year when the Dow eked out a paltry 2 percent return. Even though the timing of a "correction" is always a mystery, both methodologies suggest that the stock market crossed into uncharted waters during the 1995–1998 "bull" market. Of equal interest, the magnitude of a potential downturn suggested by the variable calculation would be less severe than that indicated by the fixed bandwidth. Either way, caution is warranted. And while the Total Return Portfolio presented in Chapter 5 isn't immune to sudden downdrafts, the strength of its dividend profile, in combination with the other *Secrets of the Masters,* should enable investors to weather any storm.

WHEN TAX-ADVANTAGED ACCOUNTS AREN'T
In Chapter 5 we presented a disciplined, tax-efficient way to build an equity portfolio based on the classical idea that dividends count. The strategy sought to achieve superior total returns by targeting those companies in the Dow Jones Industrial Average with the strongest dividend policies. A simulation of the strategy, using only information that would have been available to investors at the time of their decisions, produced enviable returns and proved stingy on brokerage costs, management fees, and taxes owing to a modest turnover rate.

For readers contemplating the advantages of the dividend growth model, another issue is bound to pop up. Is the Total Return Portfolio well suited for tax-advantaged accounts such as Individual Retirement Accounts or should it be held in a fully taxable account? We recommend the taxable account.[9]

The issue of positioning equity portfolios in tax-deferred accounts has been hotly debated ever since IRAs were introduced in the early 1970s. The central issue is fairly simple. Since Individual Retirement Accounts are allowed to compound free of taxes until time of withdrawal, investors have more of their money working for them than they otherwise would be. So the gross value of the portfolio would be higher at retirement. Plus, as the argument goes, investors are better off deferring the tax bite on dividends and capital gains, since their tax rates during retirement are likely to be lower than those they face during their working years. Maybe.

First of all, who's to say what the tax code will look like down the road? Few things are more politically charged than tax policy. Still, for the sake of discussion, we'll assume that today's environment will prevail. Now let's imagine that we funded the strategy within a tax-advantaged account. Certainly the benefits of compounding pretax income (both gains and income) would add up to a higher cumulative return. But there are off-sets—major ones.

For starters, IRA distributions are subject to ordinary income tax rates. But in a taxable account, assuming the position was held for more than a year, the appreciation would be taxed at the long-term capital gains tax rate (20%). Investors anticipating a 36 or 39.6 percent federal income tax rate during their retirement years could easily chew up more in taxes than they gained in the compounding process. There are other nasty surprises with IRAs. At age 70½ required annual distributions kick in—forcing tax liabilities on the investor. Worse, if investors happen to die holding IRAs, there's no "step-up" in the cost basis of their stock holdings to pass along to heirs. Distributions to beneficiaries would be required, with income taxes payable at ordinary income tax rates.

Got the picture? By electing to implement our tax-efficient, dividend growth strategy in a tax-deferred account, the investor would effectively convert capital gains to ordinary income. The result would likely be a stiffer tax bill compared with the fully taxable account. But we haven't finished. There's still more tax to pay. Once the income taxes have been paid, federal estate taxes (currently 55 cents on the dollar) would apply to the remaining balance. Assuming a beneficiary was already in the top marginal income tax bracket (39.6%), the effective federal tax rate on the IRA portfolio could exceed 70 percent (that is, when income and estate tax rates are combined). Toss in state taxes and somebody's got a problem.

Given the Total Return Portfolio's expected low turnover, any realized capital gains subject to taxation would be minimal and, as we've already mentioned, would be of the long-term variety. Also, with the taxable account there wouldn't be any pressure from Uncle Sam to liquidate any of the portfolio positions. Investors would have more control over their tax liabilities.

As we said earlier, taxable accounts wouldn't be exempt from estate taxes. But unlike the tax-deferred accounts there wouldn't be any income taxes due. Here's a big point. If you paid $3 for General Electric in 1977 and it grew to $73 in 1987 (the year of your demise), the cost basis for your beneficiary would be "stepped up" to $73.[10] Your beneficiary would be subject only to capital gains tax on any future appreciation beyond $73. So all the profits you've amassed in the portfolio could be passed along to future generations. That's tax efficiency.

PENNY WISE, POUND FOOLISH

While we're on the topic of tax-advantaged accounts, think back to the problem of concentrated equity positions in Chapter 9. Our Microsoft Millionaire, you'll recall, had the bulk of her assets tied up in MSFT shares. Assuming the lion's share of this position was held in a profit-sharing or 401(k) salary savings plan, she could have made a costly error if she had left the company and rolled her highly appreciated stock into an Individual Retirement Account.

Ironically, popular wisdom suggests that's exactly the right move, especially for distributions before age 59½—which, in most instances, are subject to both income taxes and a 10 percent penalty for early withdrawal. The IRA Rollover option avoids all this and keeps the tax-deferral aspect of her account alive. So why would anyone opt for a taxable distribution? Simple, a potential tax arbitrage.

Imagine our investor (now age 35) holds 100,000 shares of Microsoft stock in her plan at a cost basis of $1 and that it ballooned up to $100 by the end of 1997. Sure, if she left the company and shifted her stock position into a taxable brokerage account, she'd incur a tax liability plus the penalty. But here's the big point: both the tax and penalty would be figured on her cost basis—that is, $1 per share or $100,000 in this example. No tax would be assessed on the $9 million gain, the so-called net unrealized appreciation (NUA), until the stock was sold. Down the road, if she sold her Microsoft shares, a capital gains tax rate (20%) would apply—not the higher income tax rate. On the other hand, had she gone for the IRA Rollover, the existing capital gains as well as any future gains would be subject to ordinary income tax rates. And this tax differential could easily swamp the tax-deferral advantage.

Table 10-4 compares the two options. To demonstrate the arbitrage opportunity, we've assumed that both accounts are liquidated at retirement in the year 2022, with all taxes paid. We've also allowed for the fact that multimillionaires are likely to face the highest marginal income tax rate even though they spend their days on the golf course.

As shown in the table, at the outset the IRA Rollover had an extra $50,000 by virtue of avoiding the 1997 tax and penalty. Compounding over a 25-year period widens the spread to $537,401. But if we cashed out both

TABLE 10-4
Rolling Over Company Stock:
Tax-Deferred Accounts Can Be Costly

	Taxable Account	IRA Rollover
Number of Shares:	100,000	100,000
Cost Basis	$100,000	$100,000
Pretax Value (1997)	10,000,000	10,000,000
Less:		
Tax Liability (1997)	39,600	0
Tax Penalty (1997)	10,000	0
Equals:		
Adjusted Value (1997)	9,950,400	10,000,000
Plus:		
Cumulative Return (1998-2022)	97,859,258	98,347,059
Equals:		
Pretax Value (2022)	107,809,658	108,347,059
Less:		
Income Tax (2022)	0	42,905,436
Capital Gains Tax (2022)	19,571,852	0
Equals:		
After-tax Value (2022)	$88,237,806	$65,441,624

Assumptions:
1998-2022 Annualized Return: 10%
Tax rates: 39.6% on ordinary income and 20% on capital gains

accounts and paid the tax liabilities, the after-tax picture is dramatically different. There are estate-planning issues to consider as well. As noted in the preceding section, if our Microsoft Millionaire happened to die holding MSFT in the IRA Rollover, her beneficiaries would owe income tax on the entire account, plus estate taxes.

With the taxable account, estate taxes would apply on the entire account and a capital gains tax would be assessed on the 1997 NUA. But all the appreciation amassed during the 1998–2022 period ($97,859,258) would step up in basis and pass along to the next generation tax-free. Her beneficiaries would be subject to a capital gains tax on any appreciation *beyond their stepped-up basis* when (or if) they decided to sell their MSFT shares. It's an enormous benefit.

The lesson here is clear. If anyone, including the IRS, seems to be offering a "deal," take a firm grip on your wallet. Don't assume that terms like "tax-advantaged" and "tax-deferred" imply "tax efficiency." Sometimes incurring an up-front tax and penalty could be the prudent choice, for you and your loved ones who stand to inherit your hard-earned nest egg.

SUMMARY

The bottom line is that forward-looking market prices contain valuable information. And even though the identity of market participants is hidden, there's an important reason we ought to trust their collective opinion as expressed through price: implicit forecasts are backed with cash.

Between every individual and his tomorrow a veil is drawn. There are ways by which this veil can be penetrated to some extent.[11]

The Dow Jones Industrial Average

RACKING THE UPS AND DOWNS of the stock market wouldn't be nearly as convenient, and absolutely not as much fun, were it not for the inventiveness of two 19th century icons, Charles Henry Dow and Edward D. Jones.

Charles Dow was a journalist who worked at newspapers in Springfield, Massachusetts and Providence, Rhode Island, where he met Edward Jones in 1875. The two worked together for the Providence *Morning Star* and *Evening Press* until Dow moved to the Providence *Journal* in 1877. Two years later Dow and Jones departed Providence to join the Kiernan News Agency in New York, and in 1882 they struck out to form Dow Jones & Company, a firm that gathered daily financial news and price data for distribution via messenger across the financial district.

Charles Dow set to work compiling an index of market prices that reflected the dominance of railroad stocks in his day. Railroads were national and, although America was still in the horse-and-buggy era, rail was the preferred means of transport for moving people and goods coast to coast. Dow's first market barometer was comprised of 11 stocks—9 railroad issues plus 2 industrials: Pacific Mail Steamship and Western Union. On July 3, 1884—the first day Dow reported his new stock market indicator—the index closed at 69.93. Initially, the index was published in a daily, two-page bulletin known as the *Customer's Afternoon Letter,* which evolved into the *Wall Street Journal.* Dow commercialized this initial market indicator for about 12 years.

By the late 1800s the industrial age was in full swing across America and on May 26, 1896 the Dow Jones Industrial Average was introduced (see Table A-1). The original index consisted of a dozen companies whose names at the time were synonymous with America's burgeoning industrial complex.

Through his "average movement of prices," Dow devised a system that enabled investors to determine if the U.S. stock market had advanced or declined. Daily trading volume at the time was about 250,000 shares with more than 35 issues actively traded. In addition, there were hundreds of smaller publicly held companies that were thinly traded but offered promise to grow into much larger operations.

Dow calculated his average as the simple mean of 12 stock prices. So when the Dow Jones Industrial Average closed at 40.94 on May 26, 1896, the index was quickly determined by summing up the dozen stock prices on his short list and figuring the average ($491.28 \div 12 = 40.94$).

Dow, who was 44 when he created the Industrial Average in 1896, died in 1902. Fortunately for the investors who followed, the *Wall Street Journal* (of which he had been editor-in-chief) continued to publish the index. In 1916 the number of companies included in the index was expanded to 20 and subsequently bumped up to 30 stocks (the current number) in 1928.

It was also in 1928 that the editors of the *Wall Street Journal,* who select the companies that comprise the list, began adjusting the average with a special "divisor." The idea was to maintain the continuity of the index by preventing irregularities that crop up when the companies "split" their shares or when a stock in the Dow is replaced. More often than not, the divisor changes because of stock splits rather than a substitution in the index's constituent stocks. In this regard, the daily average is simply a number that, when compared with the previous day's closing figure, helps establish a trend line indicating whether the market is rising or falling. Though not really a simple "average" any longer, the label remained.[1]

At the time of this writing, the most recent change in the list occurred in 1991 when USX Corp., a giant steel and oil company, was replaced by

TABLE A-1
The Dow Jones Industrial Average
(May 1896)

American Cotton Oil	Laclede Gas
American Sugar Refining Co.	National Lead
American Tobacco	North American Co.
Chicago Gas	Tennessee Coal, Iron & Railroad Co.
Distilling & Cattle Feeding Co.	U.S. Leather (preferred)
General Electric	U.S. Rubber Co.

entertainment giant Walt Disney Company. Over the years, though, there have been a number of roster changes through mergers, acquisitions, and bankruptcies. For example, General Electric (the only member of the original 12-company list in today's index) was removed in 1898, restored in 1899, taken off again in 1901, and reinstated in 1907; it has remained there ever since.

Following the names that have come and gone from the Dow industrials during the decades is like following the evolution of the U.S. economy. Companies such as Standard Rope & Twine, Continental Tobacco, International Paper, and Colorado Fuel & Iron appeared during the early part of the century, followed by other American giants such as Woolworth, Bethlehem Steel, and International Harvester.

Through the years other stock market indexes have come along, notably the Standard & Poor's 500, the Russell 2000, and the Nasdaq Composite. Still, the Dow Jones Industrial Average with its 30 blue chip companies remains the most widely quoted market indicator (see Table A-2).

Because the Dow has climbed above the 11,000 level, its largest single-day point fluctuations have occurred during the 1980s and 1990s. With only a few exceptions, such as October 19, 1987, when the Dow experienced its greatest one-day percentage decline (−22.61%), most of the big percentage moves took place during the first half of the 20th century. Eight of the top ten largest percentage declines occurred before 1938 and nine of the ten biggest percentage gains took place before 1933.[2]

TABLE A-2
The Dow Jones Industrial Average
(December 1998)

Allied Signal Inc.	Hewlett-Packard Co.
Aluminum Co. of America	International Business Machines Corp.
American Express Co.	International Paper Co.
AT&T Corp.	J.P. Morgan & Co.
Boeing Co.	Johnson & Johnson
Caterpillar Inc.	McDonald's Corp.
Chevron Corp.	Merck & Co.
Citigroup	Minnesota Mining & Manufacturing Co.
Coca-Cola Co.	Philip Morris Cos.
DuPont Co.	Procter & Gamble Co.
Eastman Kodak Co.	Sears, Roebuck & Co.
Exxon Corp.	Union Carbide Corp.
General Electric Co.	United Technologies Corp.
General Motors Corp.	WalMart Stores Inc.
Goodyear Tire & Rubber Co.	Walt Disney Co.

The popularity of the Dow Jones Industrial Average was demonstrated on January 10, 1998, with the introduction of something called Dow Jones Diamonds—a listed American Stock Exchange security that trades under the ticker symbol DIA.[3] On the initial day of trading, about 1.7 million units changed hands. That topped the previous single-day AMEX volume record for a new equity product, a distinction held since 1993 by Standard & Poor's Depository Receipts.[4]

More precisely, Diamonds are units of beneficial interest in the Diamonds Trust, an investment trust with a portfolio of common stocks that mimic the price and dividend performance of the Dow Jones Industrial Average. An efficient alternative to building a well-diversified portfolio, Diamonds enable investors to trade a "basket" of the 30 Dow companies as conveniently as dealing in a single stock.

Diamonds differ from an index mutual fund, however, because they trade throughout the day just like shares of common stock. Most mutual fund transactions, on the other hand, are based on the daily closing prices and a calculation of "net asset value."

APPENDIX B

Historical Data

TABLE B-1
The Dow Jones Industrials Historical Price Record

		1977	1978	1979	1980	1981	1982	1983	1984	1985	1986
AA	ALCOA	11.66	11.94	13.72	14.91	12.81	15.50	22.44	18.50	19.25	16.94
ALD	Allied Signal	7.37	4.71	8.19	8.92	7.31	5.40	9.29	8.63	11.69	10.03
AXP	American Express	8.97	7.28	7.47	10.06	11.03	16.06	16.31	18.81	26.50	28.31
T	AT&T	60.50	60.50	52.13	47.88	58.75	59.38	61.50	19.50	25.00	25.00
BA	Boeing	1.85	4.70	5.00	6.54	3.33	5.02	6.48	8.39	11.61	11.36
CAT	Caterpillar	13.72	14.69	13.50	14.50	13.88	10.03	11.81	7.75	10.50	10.03
CHV	Chevron	9.72	11.72	14.09	24.88	21.44	16.00	17.31	15.63	19.06	22.69
KO	Coca-Cola	1.55	1.83	1.44	1.39	1.45	2.17	2.23	2.60	3.52	4.72
DIS	Disney	2.50	2.51	2.80	3.20	3.27	3.95	3.29	3.74	7.05	10.78
DD	DuPont	6.69	7.00	6.73	7.00	6.21	5.98	8.67	8.25	11.31	14.00
EK	Eastman Kodak	22.72	26.06	21.39	31.00	31.61	38.22	33.83	31.94	33.75	45.75
XON	Exxon	6.02	6.14	6.89	10.08	7.81	7.44	9.34	11.25	13.78	17.53
GE	General Electric	3.12	2.95	3.16	3.83	3.59	5.93	7.33	7.08	9.09	10.75
GM	General Motors	31.44	26.88	25.00	22.50	19.25	31.19	37.19	39.19	35.19	33.00
GT	Goodyear	8.63	8.06	6.44	8.00	9.50	17.50	15.19	13.00	15.63	20.94
HWP	Hewlett-Packard	2.29	2.81	3.70	5.59	4.95	9.13	10.59	8.47	9.19	10.47
IBM	IBM	34.19	37.31	32.19	33.94	28.44	48.13	61.00	61.56	77.75	60.00
IP	Int'l Paper	10.94	9.13	9.25	10.50	9.78	12.09	14.75	13.47	12.69	18.78
JNJ	JNJ	3.20	3.07	3.30	4.16	4.64	6.20	5.11	4.52	6.58	8.20
MCD	McDonald's	2.54	2.28	2.14	2.41	3.23	4.47	5.22	5.74	8.99	10.15
MRK	Merck	3.08	3.76	4.01	4.71	4.71	4.70	5.02	5.22	7.61	13.76
MMM	MMM	12.13	15.78	12.56	14.75	13.63	18.75	20.63	19.66	22.44	29.16
JPM	JP Morgan	10.75	11.34	11.56	12.91	13.44	16.88	16.84	19.63	32.06	41.25
MO	Philip Morris	1.29	1.47	1.50	1.80	2.03	2.50	2.99	3.36	3.68	5.99
PG	Procter & Gamble	5.37	5.55	4.64	4.30	5.02	7.39	7.11	7.13	8.72	9.55
S	Sears & Roebuck	28.00	19.75	18.00	15.25	16.13	30.13	37.13	31.75	39.00	39.75
TRV	Travelers Group	n.a.	n.a.	n.a.	n.a.	n.a.	n.a.	n.a.	n.a.	n.a.	3.42
UK	Union Carbide	13.67	11.33	14.00	16.75	17.13	17.63	20.92	12.25	23.63	22.50
UTX	United Technologies	8.97	9.72	10.75	15.25	10.44	14.16	18.13	18.13	21.88	23.00
WMT	WalMart	0.16	0.18	0.27	0.47	0.66	1.56	2.44	2.37	3.98	5.81
	DJIA	831.2	805	838.7	964	875	1047	1259	1212	1547	1896

TABLE B-1   (*Continued*)

		1987	1988	1989	1990	1991	1992	1993	1994	1995	1996	1997
AA	ALCOA	23.38	28.00	37.50	28.81	32.19	35.81	34.69	43.31	52.88	63.75	70.38
ALD	Allied Signal	7.06	8.13	8.72	6.75	10.97	15.13	19.75	17.00	23.75	33.50	38.81
AXP	American Express	22.88	26.63	34.88	20.63	20.50	24.88	30.88	29.50	41.38	56.50	89.25
T	AT&T	27.00	28.75	45.50	30.13	39.13	51.00	52.50	50.25	64.75	43.38	61.31
BA	Boeing	8.22	13.47	19.79	22.69	23.88	20.06	21.63	23.50	39.19	53.25	48.94
CAT	Caterpillar	15.50	15.91	14.47	11.75	10.97	13.41	22.25	27.56	29.38	37.63	48.50
CHV	Chevron	19.81	22.88	33.88	36.31	34.50	34.75	43.56	44.63	52.38	65.00	77.00
KO	Coca-Cola	4.77	5.58	9.66	11.63	20.06	20.94	22.31	25.75	37.13	52.63	66.69
DIS	Disney	14.81	16.44	28.00	25.38	28.63	43.00	42.63	46.00	58.88	69.75	99.00
DD	DuPont	14.56	14.71	20.50	18.38	23.31	23.56	24.13	28.06	34.94	47.06	60.06
EK	Eastman Kodak	49.00	45.13	41.13	41.63	48.25	40.50	56.25	47.75	67.00	80.25	60.56
XON	Exxon	19.06	22.00	25.00	25.88	30.44	30.56	31.56	30.38	40.25	49.00	61.19
GE	General Electric	11.03	11.19	16.13	14.34	19.13	21.38	26.22	25.50	36.00	49.44	73.38
GM	General Motors	30.69	41.75	42.25	34.38	28.88	32.25	54.88	42.13	52.88	55.75	60.75
GT	Goodyear	30.00	25.56	21.75	9.44	26.75	34.19	45.75	33.63	45.38	51.38	63.63
HWP	Hewlett-Packard	14.56	13.31	11.81	7.97	14.25	17.47	19.75	24.97	41.88	50.25	62.38
IBM	IBM	57.75	60.94	47.06	56.50	44.50	25.19	28.25	36.75	45.69	75.75	104.63
IP	Int'l Paper	21.13	23.19	28.25	26.75	35.38	33.31	33.88	37.69	37.88	40.50	43.13
JNJ	JNJ	9.36	10.64	14.84	17.94	28.63	25.25	22.44	27.38	42.75	49.75	65.88
MCD	McDonald's	11.00	12.03	17.25	14.56	19.00	24.38	28.50	29.25	45.13	45.38	47.75
MRK	Merck	17.61	19.25	25.83	29.96	55.50	43.38	34.38	38.13	65.63	79.63	106.00
MMM	MMM	32.19	31.00	39.81	42.88	47.63	50.31	54.38	53.38	66.38	83.00	82.06
JPM	JP Morgan	36.25	34.88	44.00	44.38	68.63	65.75	69.38	56.13	80.25	97.63	112.88
MO	Philip Morris	7.11/	8.49	13.88	17.25	26.75	25.71	18.54	19.17	30.08	37.67	45.25
PG	Procter & Gamble	10.67	10.88	17.56	21.66	23.47	26.81	28.50	31.00	41.50	53.81	79.81
S	Sears & Roebuck	33.50	40.88	38.13	25.38	37.88	45.50	52.88	46.00	39.00	46.00	45.25
TRV	Travelers Group	3.73	3.63	4.75	3.81	6.56	8.06	12.96	10.79	20.88	30.25	53.88
UK	Union Carbide	21.75	25.63	23.25	16.38	20.25	16.63	22.38	29.38	37.50	40.88	42.94
UTX	United Technologies	16.94	20.56	27.13	23.94	27.13	24.06	31.00	31.44	47.44	66.25	72.81
WMT	WalMart	6.50	7.84	11.22	15.13	29.44	32.00	25.00	21.25	22.25	22.75	39.44
	DJIA	1939	2169	2753	2634	3169	3301	3754	3834	5117	6448	7908

TABLE B-2
The Dow Jones Industrials Historical Dividend Data

		1977	1978	1979	1980	1981	1982	1983	1984	1985	1986
AA	ALCOA	0.42	0.48	0.65	0.80	0.90	0.83	0.60	0.60	0.60	0.60
ALD	Allied Signal	0.31	0.33	0.33	0.36	0.39	0.40	0.40	0.44	0.45	0.45
AXP	American Express	0.39	0.39	0.45	0.50	0.38	0.55	0.78	0.64	0.66	0.69
T	AT&T	4.20	4.60	5.00	5.00	5.40	5.40	5.85	1.20	1.20	1.20
BA	Boeing	0.06	0.13	0.21	0.21	0.21	0.21	0.21	0.21	0.23	0.27
CAT	Caterpillar	0.39	0.47	0.53	0.58	0.60	0.60	0.38	0.31	0.13	0.13
CHV	Chevron	0.59	0.64	0.73	0.90	1.10	1.20	1.20	1.20	1.20	1.20
KO	Coca-Cola	0.06	0.07	0.08	0.09	0.10	0.10	0.11	0.11	0.12	0.13
DIS	Disney	0.01	0.02	0.02	0.05	0.06	0.08	0.06	0.09	0.08	0.08
DD	DuPont	0.32	0.40	0.46	0.46	0.46	0.40	0.42	0.48	0.50	0.51
EK	Eastman Kodak	0.93	1.04	1.29	1.42	1.56	1.58	1.58	1.60	1.62	1.63
XON	Exxon	0.37	0.41	0.49	0.68	0.75	0.75	0.78	0.84	0.86	0.90
GE	General Electric	0.13	0.16	0.17	0.18	0.20	0.21	0.23	0.26	0.28	0.30
GM	General Motors	3.40	3.00	2.65	1.48	1.20	1.20	1.40	2.38	2.50	2.50
GT	Goodyear	0.60	0.65	0.65	0.65	0.65	0.70	0.70	0.75	0.80	0.80
HWP	Hewlett-Packard	0.01	0.02	0.02	0.03	0.03	0.03	0.04	0.05	0.06	0.06
IBM	IBM	1.25	1.44	1.72	1.72	1.72	1.72	1.86	2.05	2.20	2.20
IP	International Paper	0.50	0.50	0.55	0.60	0.60	0.60	0.60	0.60	0.60	0.60
JNJ	Johnson&Johnson	0.06	0.07	0.08	0.09	0.11	0.12	0.13	0.15	0.16	0.17
MCD	McDonald's	0.01	0.02	0.03	0.04	0.05	0.06	0.07	0.08	0.10	0.11
MRK	Merck	0.09	0.10	0.11	0.13	0.15	0.16	0.16	0.17	0.18	0.22
MMM	Minnesota Mining	0.43	0.50	0.60	0.70	0.75	0.80	0.83	0.85	0.88	0.90
JPM	JP Morgan	0.51	0.57	0.64	0.72	0.79	0.87	0.94	1.03	1.13	1.26
MO	Philip Morris	0.03	0.04	0.05	0.07	0.08	0.10	0.12	0.14	0.17	0.21
PG	Procter & Gamble	0.16	0.17	0.19	0.21	0.24	0.26	0.28	0.30	0.33	0.33
S	Sears & Roebuck	1.08	1.27	1.28	1.36	1.36	1.36	1.52	1.76	1.76	1.76
TRV	Travelers Group	n.a	n.a	n.a	n.a	n.a	n.a	n.a	n.a	n.a	0.01
UK	Union Carbide	0.93	0.93	0.97	1.03	1.10	1.13	1.13	1.13	1.13	1.50
UTX	United Technologies	0.41	0.50	0.55	0.55	0.60	0.60	0.64	0.69	0.70	0.70
WMT	WalMart	0.00	0.00	0.00	0.00	0.00	0.01	0.01	0.01	0.02	0.02
DJIA	DowJones	45.84	48.51	50.97	54.36	55.65	54.12	56.34	60.63	62.04	67.08

TABLE B-2   (*Continued*)

		1987	1988	1989	1990	1991	1992	1993	1994	1995	1996	1997
AA	ALCOA	0.60	0.65	1.36	1.53	0.89	0.80	0.80	0.80	0.90	1.33	0.98
ALD	Allied Signal	0.45	0.45	0.45	0.45	0.40	0.25	0.29	0.34	0.39	0.45	0.52
AXP	American Express	0.57	0.97	0.86	0.92	0.96	0.75	1.00	1.18	0.68	1.13	0.90
T	AT&T	1.20	1.20	1.20	1.32	1.32	1.32	1.32	1.32	1.32	1.32	1.32
BA	Boeing	0.31	0.34	0.39	0.48	0.50	0.50	0.50	0.50	0.50	0.54	0.56
CAT	Caterpillar	0.13	0.19	0.30	0.30	0.30	0.15	0.15	0.23	0.60	0.75	0.90
CHV	Chevron	1.20	1.28	1.40	1.48	1.63	1.65	1.75	1.85	1.93	2.08	2.28
KO	Coca-Cola	0.14	0.15	0.17	0.20	0.24	0.28	0.34	0.39	0.44	0.50	0.56
DIS	Disney	0.08	0.07	0.11	0.13	0.16	0.19	0.23	0.28	0.33	0.40	0.49
DD	DuPont	0.55	0.62	0.73	0.81	0.84	0.87	0.88	0.91	1.02	1.12	1.23
EK	Eastman Kodak	1.71	1.90	2.00	2.00	2.00	2.00	2.00	1.60	1.60	1.60	1.76
XON	Exxon	0.95	1.08	1.15	1.24	1.34	1.42	1.44	1.46	1.50	1.56	1.63
GE	General Electric	0.33	0.37	0.43	0.48	0.52	0.58	0.65	0.75	0.85	0.95	1.08
GM	General Motors	2.50	2.50	3.00	3.00	1.60	1.40	0.80	0.80	1.10	1.60	2.00
GT	Goodyear	0.80	0.85	0.90	0.90	0.20	0.28	0.58	0.75	0.95	1.03	1.14
HWP	Hewlett-Packard	0.06	0.07	0.09	0.11	0.12	0.18	0.23	0.28	0.35	0.44	0.52
IBM	IBM	2.20	2.20	2.37	2.42	2.42	2.42	0.79	0.50	0.50	0.65	0.78
IP	International Paper	0.61	0.64	0.77	0.84	0.84	0.84	0.84	0.84	0.92	1.00	1.00
JNJ	Johnson&Johnson	0.20	0.24	0.28	0.33	0.39	0.45	0.50	0.56	0.64	0.74	0.85
MCD	McDonald's	0.12	0.14	0.15	0.17	0.18	0.20	0.21	0.23	0.26	0.29	0.32
MRK	Merck	0.30	0.46	0.57	0.67	0.79	0.96	1.06	1.16	1.28	1.48	1.74
MMM	Minnesota Mining	0.93	1.06	1.30	1.46	1.56	1.60	1.66	1.76	1.88	1.92	2.12
JPM	JP Morgan	1.40	1.54	1.70	1.86	2.03	2.24	2.48	2.79	3.06	3.31	3.59
MO	Philip Morris	0.26	0.34	0.42	0.52	0.64	0.78	0.87	1.01	1.22	1.47	1.60
PG	Procter & Gamble	0.34	0.34	0.38	0.44	0.49	0.51	0.55	0.62	0.70	0.80	0.90
S	Sears & Roebuck	2.00	2.00	2.00	2.00	2.00	2.00	1.60	1.60	1.26	0.92	0.92
TRV	Travelers Group	0.04	0.05	0.05	0.06	0.08	0.12	0.16	0.19	0.27	0.30	0.40
UK	Union Carbide	1.50	1.15	1.00	1.00	1.00	0.88	0.75	0.75	0.75	0.75	0.79
UTX	United Technologies	0.70	0.77	0.80	0.90	0.90	0.95	0.90	0.95	1.03	1.10	1.24
WMT	WalMart	0.03	0.04	0.06	0.07	0.09	0.11	0.13	0.17	0.20	0.21	0.27
DJIA	DowJones	71.22	79.56	102.99	103.71	95.19	100.71	99.66	105.66	116.55	131.16	136.10

TABLE B-3
Historical Economic and Market Capitalization Data

Period Ended	GDP ($Nominal)*	NYSE Capitalization*	Price-To-Economy Ratio
Q1 60	527.3	287.4	0.545
Q2 60	526.1	298.1	0.567
Q3 60	529	283.3	0.536
Q4 60	523.9	307.0	0.586
Q1 61	528.1	347.6	0.658
Q2 61	538.9	348.9	0.647
Q3 61	549.6	361.1	0.657
Q4 61	562.6	387.4	0.689
Q1 62	575.3	381.4	0.663
Q2 62	582.8	299.0	0.513
Q3 62	589.9	308.4	0.523
Q4 62	592.9	345.8	0.583
Q1 63	602.2	365.9	0.608
Q2 63	610.9	382.0	0.625
Q3 63	623.7	396.2	0.635
Q4 63	632.8	411.3	0.650
Q1 64	649.4	436.8	0.673
Q2 64	658.4	455.0	0.691
Q3 64	669.2	472.0	0.705
Q4 64	675.1	474.3	0.703
Q1 65	695.6	490.2	0.705
Q2 65	708.2	478.8	0.676
Q3 65	725	517.7	0.714
Q4 65	747.7	537.5	0.719
Q1 66	770.5	523.9	0.680
Q2 66	780	502.4	0.644
Q3 66	793.6	454.9	0.573
Q4 66	807.1	482.5	0.598
Q1 67	816.9	549.5	0.673
Q2 67	823	559.5	0.680
Q3 67	838.9	600.9	0.716
Q4 67	855.6	605.8	0.708
Q1 68	880.6	568.5	0.646
Q2 68	904.7	641.0	0.709
Q3 68	919.7	668.4	0.727
Q4 68	937.3	692.3	0.739
Q1 69	959.9	672.6	0.701
Q2 69	973.7	650.5	0.668
Q3 69	993.3	627.5	0.632
Q4 69	1002	629.5	0.628

* $billions

TABLE B-3   (Continued)

Period Ended	GDP ($Nominal)*	NYSE Capitalization*	Price-To-Economy Ratio
Q1 70	1014	615.4	0.607
Q2 70	1029	491.2	0.477
Q3 70	1047.2	579.7	0.554
Q4 70	1052.3	636.4	0.605
Q1 71	1096.7	709.3	0.647
Q2 71	1116.8	709.6	0.635
Q3 71	1137.1	709.0	0.624
Q4 71	1150.9	741.8	0.645
Q1 72	1190.1	790.2	0.664
Q2 72	1223.5	793.2	0.648
Q3 72	1247.6	816.2	0.654
Q4 72	1287.9	871.5	0.677
Q1 73	1337.2	809.8	0.606
Q2 73	1367.7	752.6	0.550
Q3 73	1390.5	807.2	0.581
Q4 73	1435.3	721.0	0.502
Q1 74	1446.6	701.2	0.485
Q2 74	1480.2	628.5	0.425
Q3 74	1510.9	472.6	0.313
Q4 74	1549.7	511.0	0.330
Q1 75	1559.6	626.2	0.402
Q2 75	1596.4	723.0	0.453
Q3 75	1657.3	636.9	0.384
Q4 75	1709.1	685.1	0.401
Q1 76	1767.4	791.8	0.448
Q2 76	1797.1	809.2	0.450
Q3 76	1830.5	827.1	0.452
Q4 76	1880.8	858.3	0.456
Q1 77	1933.4	795.8	0.412
Q2 77	2005.3	828.5	0.413
Q3 77	2067.5	799.0	0.386
Q4 77	2101.2	796.6	0.379
Q1 78	2144.4	760.3	0.355
Q2 78	2274.6	818.9	0.360
Q3 78	2334.8	883.9	0.379
Q4 78	2411.7	822.8	0.341
Q1 79	2464.9	877.9	0.356
Q2 79	2522.4	901.6	0.357
Q3 79	2592.6	961.3	0.371
Q4 79	2650.1	960.6	0.362

* $billions

TABLE B-3
Historical Economic and Market Capitalization Data *(Continued)*

Period Ended	GDP ($Nominal)*	NYSE Capitalization*	Price-To-Economy Ratio
Q1 80	2722.9	989.8	0.364
Q2 80	2719.4	1027.1	0.378
Q3 80	2783.2	1147.6	0.412
Q4 80	2911.6	1242.8	0.427
Q1 81	3043.2	1248.9	0.410
Q2 81	3073.3	1224.7	0.398
Q3 81	3163.2	1080.6	0.342
Q4 81	3183.9	1143.8	0.359
Q1 82	3179.6	1036.9	0.326
Q2 82	3234.7	1017.5	0.315
Q3 82	3258.5	1120.3	0.344
Q4 82	3295.5	1305.4	0.396
Q1 83	3359.5	1431.6	0.426
Q2 83	3469.4	1604.0	0.462
Q3 83	3563.8	1591.4	0.447
Q4 83	3665.4	1584.2	0.432
Q1 84	3792.8	1525.6	0.402
Q2 84	3879.2	1463.3	0.377
Q3 84	3943.3	1585.2	0.402
Q4 84	3994.4	1586.1	0.397
Q1 85	4080.3	1716.2	0.421
Q2 85	4135.4	1812.4	0.438
Q3 85	4221.9	1702.8	0.403
Q4 85	4285.1	1950.3	0.455
Q1 86	4358.2	2204.1	0.506
Q2 86	4386.7	2289.3	0.522
Q3 86	4442.4	2127.3	0.479
Q4 86	4501.4	2199.3	0.489
Q1 87	4565.6	2628.7	0.576
Q2 87	4644.9	2718.5	0.585
Q3 87	4722.6	2885.1	0.611
Q4 87	4836.2	2216.3	0.458
Q1 88	4898.5	2346.2	0.479
Q2 88	5000.5	2456.5	0.491
Q3 88	5094.5	2440.0	0.479
Q4 88	5204.9	2457.5	0.472
Q1 89	5316.9	2591.6	0.487
Q2 89	5413.1	2771.5	0.512
Q3 89	5486.8	3008.8	0.548
Q4 89	5537.9	3029.6	0.547

* $billions

TABLE B-3   (*Continued*)

Period Ended	GDP ($Nominal)*	NYSE Capitalization*	Price-To-Economy Ratio
Q1 90	5660.4	2904.1	0.513
Q2 90	5751	3045.5	0.530
Q3 90	5782.4	2617.5	0.453
Q4 90	5781.5	2819.8	0.488
Q1 91	5822.1	3209.9	0.551
Q2 91	5892.3	3216.2	0.546
Q3 91	5950	3400.3	0.571
Q4 91	6002.3	3712.8	0.619
Q1 92	6121.8	3654.9	0.597
Q2 92	6201.2	3712.8	0.599
Q3 92	6271.7	3840.6	0.612
Q4 92	6383.1	4035.1	0.632
Q1 93	6444.5	4249.0	0.659
Q2 93	6509.1	4291.1	0.659
Q3 93	6574.6	4410.4	0.671
Q4 93	6704.2	4545.4	0.678
Q1 94	6794.3	4392.6	0.647
Q2 94	6911.4	4375.8	0.633
Q3 94	6986.5	4548.7	0.651
Q4 94	7095.7	4448.3	0.627
Q1 95	7170.8	4879.6	0.680
Q2 95	7210.9	5269.1	0.731
Q3 95	7304.8	5665.0	0.776
Q4 95	7391.9	6014.0	0.814
Q1 96	7495.3	6262.7	0.836
Q2 96	7629.2	6647.9	0.871
Q3 96	7703.4	6823.3	0.886
Q4 96	7818.4	7301.6	0.934
Q1 97	7955	7452.6	0.937
Q2 97	8063.4	8184.9	1.015
Q3 97	8170.8	9329.5	1.142
Q4 97	8254.5	9415	1.141

* $billions

TABLE B-4
U.S. Treasury Yields
(Secondary Market—Constant Maturities)

Year-end Close	1-Year Bills	10-Year Bonds	Yield Spread
1965	4.96	4.65	-0.31
1966	5.00	4.64	-0.36
1967	5.76	5.70	-0.06
1968	6.46	6.16	-0.30
1969	8.32	7.88	-0.44
1970	4.94	6.50	1.56
1971	4.46	5.89	1.43
1972	5.68	6.41	0.73
1973	7.30	6.90	-0.40
1974	7.35	7.40	0.05
1975	6.16	7.76	1.60
1976	4.86	6.81	1.95
1977	6.98	7.78	0.80
1978	10.57	9.15	-1.42
1979	11.70	10.33	-1.37
1980	13.86	12.43	-1.43
1981	13.35	13.98	0.63
1982	8.68	10.36	1.68
1983	10.08	11.82	1.74
1984	9.22	11.55	2.33
1985	7.60	9.00	1.40
1986	5.95	7.23	1.28
1987	7.10	8.83	1.73
1988	9.02	9.14	0.12
1989	7.76	7.93	0.17
1990	6.82	8.08	1.26
1991	4.12	6.71	2.59
1992	3.61	6.70	3.09
1993	3.63	5.83	2.20
1994	7.20	7.84	0.64
1995	5.18	5.58	0.40
1996	5.51	6.43	0.92
1997	5.51	5.75	0.24

Handy Web Sites

SECRETS OF THE MASTERS—STRATEGY UPDATES
www.TopTheDow.com

ECONOMIC & INTEREST RATE DATA
www.fedstats.gov
www.bea.doc.gov
www.bog.frb.fed.us
www.stats.bls.gov
www.census.gov
www.fedworld.gov
www.dismal.com

SECURITIES MARKET DATA
www.sec.gov
www.nasd.com
www.nyse.com
www.amex.com
www.nasdaq.com
www.dowjones.com
www.russell.com/indexes/
www.dri.mcgrawhill.com
www.mafh.org
http://cbsmarketwatch.com

BUSINESS NEWS
www.forbes.com
www.businessweek.com/today.htm
www.wsj.com
www.abcnews.com
www.bloomberg.com
www.quicken.com
www.reuters.com
www.moneynet.com
www.cnnfn.com/markets/
www.yahoo.com/headlines/business/bs/
www.smartmoney.com/

Biographical Sketches

BABSON, ROGER WARD (1875–1967)

Educated at the Massachusetts Institute of Technology (1898), Roger Babson entered the business world as an investment banker in Boston and, later, in New York. In 1900 he relocated to Wellesley, Massachusetts and, a year later, was diagnosed with tuberculosis.

He and his wife, Grace, founded Babson's Statistical Organization (now called Babson's Reports) in 1904 and, within a decade or so, amassed a fortune. In collaboration with MIT Professor of Engineering George Swain, he introduced the Babsonchart of economic indicators for the purpose of assessing current and future business conditions. Interestingly, Babson is distinguished as being one of a handful of investment professionals to anticipate the 1929 stock market crash. Roger Babson was a prolific writer, authoring some 47 books over a 33-year span. From 1910 into the early 1920s, he was a columnist for the *Saturday Evening Post* as well as a contributor to the *New York Times*.

In 1919, gathering an enrollment of fewer than 30 students, Roger Babson founded the Babson Institute (renamed Babson College in 1969) for the purpose of providing business education.

DEMOIVRE, ABRAHAM (1667–1754)

A noted French mathematician, Abraham DeMoivre settled in London, England in 1685. Despite his genius, DeMoivre had difficulty finding work and supported himself as a mathematics tutor and adviser to insurance companies and gamblers on problems involving mortality statistics and probability theory. If the exceptional test proves the rule, DeMoive demonstrated the credibility of his theories by predicting (*correctly*) the day of his death.

Among his other scientific contributions, DeMoivre is recognized as a pioneer in the theory of probability. He is credited with developing the con- cept of the "normal" or "bell-shaped" curve to describe how random obser- vations cluster around their average value. Importantly, he introduced a statistical tool for measuring the number of the observed observations that would fall within specified regions under the curve—a device known to today's practitioners as the "standard deviation."

DeMoivre authored a number of important works, including *The Doc- trine of Chances, or a Method of Calculating the Probabilities of Events at Play* (1718). Sponsored by Sir Isaac Newton and the British astronomer Edmund Halley, he became a fellow of the Royal Society of London, under whose auspices he published numerous scholarly papers.

DODD, DAVID L. (1895–1988)

Graduated from the University of Pennsylvania, David Dodd earned his master's and doctorate from Columbia. He joined the Columbia faculty in 1922 and was elevated to full professorship in 1947. From 1948 to 1952 he was associate dean of the Graduate School of Business. In 1934, Professor Dodd and his colleague **Benjamin Graham** authored *Security Analysis,* a work that was published in five editions and sold more than a quarter of a million copies.[1]

FISHER, IRVING (1867–1947)

Irving Fisher earned his doctorate at Yale University in 1891. Fisher joined the Yale faculty in 1890, serving first as professor of mathematics until 1897 and then as professor of political economy until 1935.

In his seminal work as an economist, *The Rate of Interest* (1907), Fisher made the distinction between the "nominal" rate of interest (the mar- ket rate before adjustment for loss of purchasing power from inflation) and the "real" rate (the inflation-adjusted rate). Fisher was also one of the first to apply statistical methods to economic analysis and was especially con- cerned about speculation in the stock market.

Fisher developed several stock market indexes, but his reputation as a market expert was damaged when his forecasts failed to anticipate the 1929 crash and its aftershocks. Still, his contributions in the field of economics have not been overshadowed by these errant predictions.

GRAHAM, BENJAMIN (1894–1976)

Known as the "Dean of Wall Street," Benjamin Graham was a partner in an investment banking firm and suffered ruinous losses during the 1929 stock market crash. As a part-time finance professor at Columbia University, he mentored a number of notables, including Warren Buffett, and in 1934 authored his famous *Security Analysis* with another of his students, **David L. Dodd.** This work achieved national prominence and, even today, is considered the bible of "value investing." Graham later taught at UCLA and was president of the Graham-Newman Corporation, an investment fund.

KEYNES, JOHN MAYNARD (1883–1946)

Educated at Eton and Cambridge in England, John Maynard Keynes is regarded as Great Britain's most influential modern economist. From 1906 to 1908 he worked in the India Office, after which he returned to lecture in economics at Cambridge. In 1936 Keynes authored his acclaimed *General Theory of Employment, Interest, and Money,* in which he argued the income and employment depend on private and public expenditure—a concept at odds with the classical economic thought, shaped by **Adam Smith,** that had guided economic policy for well over a century.

Keynes' new economics was firmly held in Britain as well as the United States. In 1941 he was made a director of the Bank of England and headed the British delegation to the United Nations Monetary and Financial Conference at Bretton Woods, New Hampshire in 1944. He was appointed a governor of both the International Monetary Fund and the International Bank (World Bank) just before his death.

LAPLACE, PIERRE SIMON DE (1749–1827)

Considered the "Isaac Newton of France," Pierre Laplace studied mathematics at the Academy of Beaumont, becoming professor of mathematics at the Ecole Militaire in 1767. His work on probability theory, *Théorie Analytique des Probabilités* (1812), received wide recognition and addressed approximations to various expressions occurring in probability theory. Like many of his contemporaries, Laplace was a brilliant astronomer and, through mathematics, made many predictions that were later confirmed through powerful telescopes. In recognition of his contributions to the field, a lunar feature is named Promontorium Laplace.

Laplace was elected adjunct member (1773), and later member (1785), of the Academy of Sciences. After serving on the faculties of numerous institutions of higher learning, he was appointed Minister of the Interior (1799) by Napoleon Bonaparte—a position that was short lived owing to his "conducting the government on the principles of infinitesimal calculus." As a consolation, he was awarded a seat in the Senate, where he became its vice president and, in 1803, its chancellor. Upon the establishment of the French empire, he became a Count of the Empire (1806) and subsequently a marquis at the hands of the monarchy in 1817.

Laplace was admitted to the Académie Francaise and was elected its president in 1817.

MARKOWITZ, HARRY M. (1927–)

Considered the father of modern portfolio theory, Harry Markowitz is a product of the University of Chicago. In 1952 he joined the RAND Corporation and, in that same year, published his famous paper "Portfolio Selection" in the *Journal of Finance.* In recognition of his pioneering work in developing his "efficient frontier" (a device that allows investors to determine the maximum expected portfolio return for a given level of risk), he was awarded the 1990 Nobel Prize—a distinction he shared with Merton Miller and William F. Sharpe.

In his autobiography, Markowitz acknowledges that the writings of **John Burr Williams,** particularly *The Theory of Investment Value* (1938), influenced his thinking on the basic concepts of portfolio theory.

MASLOW, ABRAHAM H. (1908–1970)

Born and raised in Brooklyn, New York, Abraham Maslow was a professor at Brooklyn College from 1937 to 1951 and at Brandeis University from 1951 until 1961.

One of the leading psychologists of the 20th century, Maslow is considered the founder of humanistic psychology. He was a prolific writer on the topic of organizational behavior and motivation and human behavior. In 1954 his groundbreaking work *Motivation and Personality* introduced such concepts as the "need hierarchy" and "self-actualization." According to Maslow, human beings are motivated by a hierarchy that begins with the most basic human needs of air, food, water, and sex, followed by safety and then social needs. At the top of his ladder were the self-actualizing needs, in which humans have a desire to reach their potential as individuals.

SAMUELSON, PAUL A. (1915–)

A Nobel laureate in economics, an adviser to presidents, and a professor emeritus at the Massachusetts Institute of Technology, Paul Samuelson literally wrote the book on economics. There are more than 3 million copies of his text *Economics,* first published in 1948, which has become fundamental reading for any serious economics student. Samuelson has long been an advocate of the economic theories of **John Maynard Keynes,** and his book was the first to explain Keynesian principles to beginning students.[2]

Samuelson received his undergraduate degree from the University of Chicago. He earned his master's and doctorate at Harvard. In 1970 Samuelson became the first American to win the Nobel Prize in Economics, for his scientific work "through which he has developed static and dynamic economic theory" and for "raising the level of scientific analysis in economic theory."

An adviser to Presidents Kennedy and Carter, Samuelson also made Richard Nixon's "enemies list," along with several other MIT professors, for his criticism of Nixon's economic policies.

SLOAN, LAURENCE H. (1889–1949)

Born in 1889, Laurence Sloan was a man of letters. He received his bachelor of arts degree from DePauw University in 1912 and was a member of the first graduating class of Columbia's School of Journalism (1913).

In the early days of his career, Sloan was an editor for a number of New York newspapers before assuming his position as assistant economist for the National City Bank of New York. In 1921 he became vice president of Standard Statistics Co. and oversaw the merger of that business with Poor Corporation. Later he was appointed executive vice president and director of the newly combined firm, known today as Standard & Poor's, a division of the McGraw-Hill Corporation.

Sloan authored four books dealing with business cycles, corporate profits, and the equity markets. Of these, *Everyman and His Common Stocks—A Study of Long Term Investment Policy* (1931) identifies and illuminates the basic investing principles essential to the viability of any long-term investment program.

SMITH, ADAM (1723–1790)

Adam Smith, the Scottish economist and philosopher, was borne in Kirkcaldy, Fife, Scotland and studied at the University of Glasgow and at Oxford. He was appointed a professor of logic at Glasgow in 1751 and soon thereafter became the chair of moral philosophy.

In matters of content and style, his lectures on rhetoric, the political economy, and ethics were held in high esteem. After a long residence in France, Smith returned to Scotland in 1766 and led a life of retirement for 10 years. During this period, he devoted his energies to the strict study of economic activity. The output of these inquiries was his famous *Inquiry into the Nature and Causes of the Wealth of Nations* (1776)—a work that dealt with the importance of economic freedom to economic growth and that, to this date, is cited as the precursor of the modern science of political economy. Smith also examined the role of self-interest, the function of markets, and the implications of a free market economy.

SMITH, EDGAR LAWRENCE (1882–1971)

A graduate of Harvard College (1905) and life member of the Royal Economic Society, Edgar Smith was a New York money manager and financial analyst in the 1920s. In 1924 he authored *Common Stocks As Long-Term Investments,* an analysis that other notables of the period found especially worthy and that continues to enjoy favor with today's practitioners.

Smith was a leading proponent of equity investing, advocating that a diversified portfolio of stocks would provide a greater return than fixed income securities. In particular, he held that even if an investor was unfortunate enough to buy stocks at their peak, there was only a 6 percent likelihood that the investor would have to wait as much as 6 to 15 years before being able to liquidate without a loss. His book, published just as the stock market was reaching record levels in the late 1920s, was praised by investment professionals and academics alike, including Yale University's **Irving Fisher.**

Not surprisingly, in the aftermath of the 1929 stock market crash, Smith's observations that equity investments were capable of delivering superior returns over bonds fell out of vogue. But in the mid-1960s, his ideas were rediscovered as a way to accumulate wealth.

TCHEBYSHEV, PAFNUTY LVOVICH (1821–1894)

P. L. Tchebyshev was a preeminent Russian mathematician known for his contributions to the scientific inquiries into the fields of algebra, probability analysis, and applied mathematics. He was appointed to the University of St. Petersburg in 1847 and became an associate of the Institut de France in 1874 and elected to the Royal Society of London in 1877.

In 1874 Tchebyshev published "Sur les Valeurs Limites des Integrales" in the *Journal des Mathématiques.* Here he set forth Tchebyshev's Inequality, a general methodology for measuring the frequency of observed outcomes likely to fall within a specified range of their mean value.

The Crater Chebyshev, a lunar feature, recognizes Tchebyshev's many scientific contributions.

WILLIAMS, JOHN BURR (1900–1989)

Author, economist, and investment manager, John Burr Williams was a man of many talents and scholarly accomplishments. Between 1923 and 1940 he earned four degrees at Harvard, including a bachelor's in chemistry, graduate degrees in business and economics, and a doctorate in economics.

In 1938 Williams wrote the *The Theory of Investment Value,* a groundbreaking work on the use of dividend valuation models for common stocks.[3] That was followed in 1954 by "International Trade Under Flexible Exchange Rates," which examined import-export trade and forecast the end of fixed exchange rates.[4]

Williams died just shy of his 89th birthday after more than 60 years as a manager of private investment portfolios. To the end he was active in the stock market and continued his research into the determinants of interest rates and the effect of the money supply on inflation.

Rebalancing the Total Return Portfolio

T HE TOTAL RETURN PORTFOLIO (Chapter 5) requires annual "rebalancing" to ensure that assets remain exposed to those companies with the strongest dividend records and are equally distributed among them.[1] Annual rebalancing instructions for the Total Return Portfolio, along with other important investor services, will be available at our Web site: www.topthedow.com/.

In our earlier discussion we presented the strategy's performance record through 1997, the last year for which return data were available at the time of our analysis. Now that 1998 is history, we can illustrate the step-by-step procedures necessary to update the portfolio.

First, though, let's take a moment to review 1998 performance. Remember, at the start of the year, the Total Return Portfolio was comprised of the 15 DJIA stocks (in equal dollar amounts) with the best 10-year dividend records as of December 31, 1997.[2] As shown in Table E-1, calendar-year returns proved satisfactory, with the Total Return Portfolio posting a 20.31 percent return (excluding brokerage commissions and taxes on dividend income) versus 18.01 percent total return for the Dow Jones Industrial Average.

YEAR-END ADJUSTMENTS
Step 1: Calculate the 10-Year Dividend per Share Increase.
The Total Return Portfolio strategy exploits the linkage between corporate dividend policy and share price. Measuring the strength of a company's dividend policy is a function of (1) the magnitude and (2) the consistency of dividend increases relative to competing investment choices.

183

TABLE E-1
The 1998 Total Return Portfolio

Ticker	Name	Closing Quotations 12/31/97	12/31/98	Appreciation	Dividend Return (%)	Total Return
CAT	Caterpillar	48.50	46.00	-5.2%	2.27%	-2.88%
CHV	Chevron	77.00	82.94	7.7%	3.17%	10.88%
KO	Coca-Cola	66.69	67.00	0.5%	0.90%	1.36%
DIS	Disney	33.00	30.00	-9.1%	0.59%	-8.50%
DD	DuPont	60.06	53.06	-11.7%	2.27%	-9.39%
GE	General Electric	73.38	102.00	39.0%	1.70%	40.70%
HWP	Hewlett-Packard	62.38	68.50	9.8%	0.96%	10.77%
JNJ	Johnson & Johnson	65.88	83.88	27.3%	1.47%	28.78%
MCD	McDonald's	47.75	76.82	60.9%	0.74%	61.62%
MRK	Merck	106.00	147.50	39.2%	1.87%	41.02%
MMM	Minn Mining & Mfg	82.06	71.13	-13.3%	2.68%	-10.65%
JPM	JP Morgan	112.88	105.06	-6.9%	3.40%	-3.53%
MO	Philip Morris	45.25	53.50	18.2%	3.71%	21.94%
PG	Procter & Gamble	79.81	91.31	14.4%	1.27%	15.68%
WMT	WalMart	39.44	81.44	106.5%	0.29%	106.78%
	1998 Total Return Portfolio:			18.49%	1.82%	20.31%
	Dow Jones Industrial Average:	7908.25	9181.43	16.10%	1.91%	18.01%

Rebalancing the portfolio is straightforward and requires knowledge of each company's 10-year dividend record. Once these data are in hand, the process starts by calculating the 10-year percentage increase in each company's dividend per share. For example, despite a deteriorated credit risk exposure in Asia, Russia, and Latin America, J. P. Morgan paid out $3.84 in dividends during 1998 versus $3.59 in the prior year. Compared with its 1988 dividend payout ($1.54), that's a 149.4 percent increase.

Step 2: Handicap the Dividend Records.

As we discussed more fully in Chapter 5, the strategy calls for handicapping the dividend records of the various companies. Companies that have "spotty" records shouldn't receive equal billing with those that raise their payouts by the same gross percentage but do so every year without fail. Consistency bespeaks corporate policy—a policy that serves investors during times of adversity. Notice that our illustrative company, J. P. Morgan, boosted its dividend despite a deteriorated credit environment. As a result, J. P. Morgan maintained its enviable record.

Handicapping company dividend records is accomplished using a "dividend factor" based on the number of years in 10 that dividends increased. While this factor is born of a formula, for convenience we've listed the factor weights in Table E-2.

TABLE E-2
Dividend Factor Weights

Number Years Dividend Increased	Dividend Factor*
10	1.00
9	0.90
8	0.75
7	0.60
6	0.45
5	0.25
4	0.10
3	0.02
2	0.00
1	0.00

* Figures are rounded.

Once determined, each company's factor is multiplied by its 10-year dividend increase (Step 1) to yield the handicapped dividend record. As we can see from Table E-2, businesses that hike their dividend payout every year, like J. P. Morgan, earn full credit (factor weight = 1.0).[3] But companies that miss a year or more are *seriously* penalized even though they may have the same 10-year percentage increase.

Step 3: Rank the Dividend Records.
Once all the handicapped dividend records have been calculated, they must be rank-ordered so as to identify the top 15 companies. Stocks already held in the portfolio are retained while those that fail to "make the cut" are replaced. Rankings for the 1999 Total Return Portfolio appear in Table E-3.

Step 4: Rebalance Company Portfolio Weights.
As a final matter, it's important to adjust the portfolio so that all the stock positions are more or less equally weighted in the portfolio. After adjustments for round-lot considerations, a $150,000 portfolio would have approximately $10,000 invested in each of the 15 stocks. Maintaining equal dollar investments spreads the portfolio risk uniformly across the spectrum of equity positions.

TABLE E-3
Handicapped Dividend Rankings
(10-Year Period Ended December 31, 1998*

	10-year Dividend Increase (%)	Number of Years Dividend Increased	Dividend Factor	Handicapped Dividend Increase	Dividend Rank
Hewlett Packard	757.1%	10	1.00	757.1%	1
Disney	726.1%	10	1.00	726.1%	2
WalMart	675.0%	10	1.00	675.0%	3
Philip Morris	398.5%	10	1.00	398.5%	4
Merck	330.4%	10	1.00	330.4%	5
Johnson & Johnson	304.2%	10	1.00	304.2%	6
Coca-Cola	300.0%	10	1.00	300.0%	7
General Electric	242.5%	10	1.00	242.5%	8
Caterpillar	485.1%	6	0.43	207.1%	9
Procter & Gamble	197.1%	10	1.00	197.1%	10
JP Morgan	149.4%	10	1.00	149.4%	11
McDonald's	147.9%	10	1.00	147.9%	12
DuPont	121.2%	10	1.00	121.2%	13
Minnesota Mining & Mfg	107.5%	10	1.00	107.5%	14
Chevron	91.4%	10	1.00	91.4%	15
United Technologies	79.4%	8	0.76	60.0%	16
Exxon	52.6%	10	1.00	52.6%	17
Alcoa	130.8%	5	0.25	32.7%	18
Goodyear	41.2%	8	0.76	31.2%	19
Boeing	62.8%	5	0.25	15.7%	20
Allied Signal	33.3%	6	0.43	14.2%	21
International Paper	56.7%	4	0.10	5.7%	22
AT&T	10.0%	1	0.00	0.0%	23
Eastman Kodak	-7.4%	2	0.00	0.0%	24
Union Carbide	-21.7%	2	0.00	0.0%	25
General Motors	-20.0%	4	0.10	-2.0%	26
American Express	-30.4%	5	0.25	-7.6%	27
IBM	-60.9%	5	0.25	-15.2%	28
Sears	-54.0%	0	0.00	0.0%	29

*Citigroup (Unranked - historical data unavailable because of 1998 merger)

APPENDIX F

Glossary

Absolute Risk The chance of losing money over the course of a specified investment horizon.

Active Management Investment management strategies that seek excess returns over an appropriate benchmark by favoring certain securities at the exclusion of others. Security positions held in actively managed portfolios tend to be traded more frequently than those held in passively managed strategies.

Annualized Return The smooth, constant annual return required to generate the same overall result as the actual varied annual returns produced (see also Mean, Geometric).

Appreciation Positive change in the value of a security or asset. A measure of the increase in value of an asset excluding income distributions (e.g., dividends).

Arbitrage A zero-risk strategy that allows profits earned from price differentials available in the same security in different markets.

Basis Point The popular measure of interest rate movements. One basis point equals 0.01 percent. Hence 1 percentage point equals 100 basis points. If Treasury yields increase from 5 to 5.5 percent, they move up by 50 basis points.

Bear Market A protracted period of declining prices in a single security, in groups of stocks representing a single industry, or in the general market. Investors are described as *bearish* when they are pessimistic.

Benchmark A point of reference from which comparative measurements can be made. An index against which portfolio performance is evaluated. For example, the performance of a professionally managed large capitalization stock portfolio might be appropriately compared with that of the S&P 500 stock index.

Bottom-up Investing   Portfolio selection strategies that rely on detailed, company-specific information while attaching less importance to industry or general economic conditions.

Bull Market   A protracted period of rising prices in a single security, in groups of stocks representing a single industry, or in the general market. Investors are described as *bullish* when they are optimistic.

Capital Gain   A positive difference between a security's purchase price and current market value. Capital gains are realized when the security is sold; otherwise they are termed "unrealized capital gains."

Cash Equivalents   Short-term money market instruments that enjoy a unique property: freedom from principal risk. Treasury bills are an example.

Common Stock   A class of securities representing a corporate ownership share. Shareholders have voting rights in the corporation and, when issued dividends, receive the distributions on a pro rata basis.

Company-Specific Risk   A circumstance or series of events related to a single company, and not present with similar types of companies, that threatens the value of its securities. A potential stock price decline or inferior performance emanating from events uniquely experienced by a specific company. For example, a management decision to add productive capacity results in bankruptcy.

Consumer Price Index   A measure of the price level of a basket of goods as reported by a monthly survey conducted by the U.S. Bureau of Labor Statistics (see also Inflation).

Corporate Bond   A debt instrument issued by a corporation with various maturities. Interest income is fully taxable.

Correction   A sharp, often short-lived, downturn in the price of a stock or the general stock market.

Correlation Coefficient   A statistical measurement of the degree to which two competing assets move in tandem (i.e., directional movements). Correlation coefficient values can range from +1 (for assets that always move in lockstep) to −1 (for those that always move in opposite directions).

Dow Jones Industrial Average   The oldest and most popular gauge of the U.S. stock market. (See Appendix A.)

Dow Jones Diamonds (Ticker Symbol DIA)   A unit of beneficial interest in a trust that holds the 30 component stocks in the Dow Jones Industrial Average. Diamonds trade like shares of common stocks on the American Stock Exchange and are designed to track the DJIA performance.

Diversification   An investment management strategy that spreads investment risk across a spectrum of competing assets and securities within a portfolio.

Dividend   A pro rata distribution to shareholders. Cash dividends are pro rata distributions of cash from the earnings of a corporation. Stock dividends are pro rata distributions of additional shares of stock.

Dividend Yield   The annual dividend paid on preferred or common stock expressed as a percentage of the share price.

Equities   Ownership interest in a corporate entity (see also Common Stock).

Expected Return   The probability-weighted anticipated outcome.

Fiscal Policy   Legislated policy initiatives involving tax-and-spending programs aimed at managing the nation's economy. Fiscal policy changes are of critical importance to financial market prices.

Frequency Distribution   A graphic depiction indicating the fraction of a population or sample profiling certain characteristics.

Front Running   An illegal practice in the securities industry whereby a registered representative or trader executes a securities transaction for a personal account knowing that a sizable pending order will influence the security's price.

Front-End Load   The sales charge applied to mutual fund sales at the time of purchase.

Fundamental Research   Analysis of company financial statements, products, markets, and management capabilities to assess the company's investment prospects.

Futures Contract   An agreement between two parties to make or accept delivery of a standardized quantity and quality of a commodity or asset at a predetermined price on a specified date. Contract prices are determined through open bidding on a central exchange. Foodstuffs, metals, currencies, and financial instruments are among the commodities traded through futures contracts.

Hedging   Investment strategies aimed at mollifying the risks associated with owning an asset or a portfolio.

Gross Domestic Product   The dollar value of all goods and services produced within the nation's boundaries.

Growth Stocks   Shares of companies that exhibit above-average profit growth, pay little or no dividend, and appreciate relative to stagnant or slower-growing companies.

Index Fund   A mutual fund that seeks to capture a given securities index return (e.g., the S&P 500 stock index) by replicating the positions that comprise the index (see also Passive Management).

Inflation   An observed change in the price of goods and services (see also Consumer Price Index) resulting in a lost purchasing power per currency unit.

Initial Public Offering (IPO)   A stock offering to public investors of a formerly privately held corporation.

Interest   The price of credit. The cost of borrowing money.

Liquidity   The ability to convert investment positions to cash equivalents.

Market Capitalization   The total value of a corporation's stock derived by multiplying the total number of shares outstanding by it share price.

Market Timing   Active investment strategies that seek excess returns over an appropriate benchmark by anticipating turning points in the financial markets. The buying and selling of stocks on the basis of short-term factors rather than long-term assessments.

Mean, Arithmetic   The simple average of a data series determined by dividing the sum of data by the number of values in the series. For example:

Arithmetic Mean = $(1 + 2 + 3 + 4 + 5) \div 5 = 3.0$

Mean, Geometric   Used for calculating compounded rates of return, the geometric mean of a series of n positive values is found by multiplying the values and raising the resulting product to the power of $1/n$ (see also, Annualized Return). For example:

Geometric Mean = $(1 \cdot 2 \cdot 3 \cdot 4 \cdot 5)^{1/4} = 2.61$

Median   The middle value of a data series such that half the observed values are equal to or greater than the median value and half are equal to or less than this central point. When there are an even number of values, the median is the midpoint between the two central values. For example:

Median = $(1, 2, 3, 4, 5) = 3$

Median = $(1, 2, 3, 4) = 2.5$

Mode   The most frequently encountered value in a data series. For example:

Mode = $(1, 2, 3, 2, 4, 2) = 2$

Monetary Policy   Policy initiatives of the Federal Reserve Board aimed at managing the nation's economy through interest rates and the money supply. Monetary policy changes are of critical importance to financial market prices.

Municipal Bonds   Debt obligations of various maturities issued by state and local governments. Interest income is exempt from federal income tax and (usually) state and local taxes if the bond was issued in the taxpayer's state of residence.

Nominal Interest Rate   The gross rate of interest observed in the marketplace.

Passive Management   Investment management strategies that seek to capture a securities index return by replicating the index positions. Security positions held in passively managed portfolios tend to be traded less frequently than those held in actively managed strategies. Passive management is rooted in the belief that efforts to earn an excess return over the general market will prove futile over the course of a market cycle.

Preferred Stock   A class of stock that pays dividends at a specified rate and that enjoys preference over common stock in the payment of dividends. In the event a company's assets are liquidated, preferred stockholders have a prior claim over common stockholders but not over creditors and bondholders. Preferred shares typically do not carry voting rights.

Price/Earnings (P/E) Ratio   The share price of a common stock divided by its earnings per share. When viewed in historical context, it provides a measure of a stock's intrinsic value.

Price/Economy (P/Ec) Ratio   The market capitalization of the stock market divided by Gross Domestic Product. It is a measure of the overall stock market's intrinsic value.

Principal Risk   The chance of losing a portion of an original capital investment.

Real Interest Rate   The nominal interest rate (usually measured by 1-year Treasury bill yields) after taking account of inflation. The rate of interest in excess of inflation (usually measured by the Consumer Price Index).

Relative Risk   The chance of underperforming an appropriate benchmark.

Risk-Adjusted Return   Investment return in excess of that earned on so-called riskless assets (usually Treasury bills).

Stagnation   An economic condition characterized by anemic Gross Domestic Product growth and above-average inflation.

Standard Deviation   A statistical measure of the variability (i.e., Volatility) of investment returns about their arithmetic mean value.

Standard & Poor's Composite   A market capitalization weighted gauge of the U.S. stock market comprised of 500 publicly traded issues, most of which are traded on the New York Stock Exchange. (See Appendix A.)

Standard & Poor's Depository Receipt (Ticker Symbol SPY)   A unit of beneficial interest in a trust that controls a portfolio of common stocks that closely tracks the total return of the S&P 500 stock index. SPDRs (pronounced "Spiders") trade like shares of common stocks on the American Stock Exchange.

Strategic Asset Allocation   A diversification strategy that affixes the portfolio mix of competing assets (e.g., between stocks, bonds, and cash equivalents) over the course of a specified investment horizon. (See Chapter 7.)

Statistical Inference   Formulating generalizations from sample data. Expected Return is an example.

The Street or Wall Street   A colloquial term denoting New York's financial district where the New York and American Stock Exchanges and many of the nation's largest investment bankers are headquartered. The NYSE is actually located on Manhattan's Wall Street (at the corner of Broad Street). Often used as an easy reference to the general stock market.

Systematic Risk   The risk factor associated with the overall stock market.

Tactical Asset Allocation   Short-term diversification strategies that seek to protect or enhance portfolio returns by opportunistically targeting a particular asset, investment style, or security at different stages of an investment cycle. (See Chapter 8.)

Technical Analysis   Research into a security's investment prospects on the basis of trading volume and price movements. Analytical tools include charts and computer programs designed to reveal price trends and turning points.

Ticker Symbol   Identifying letters under which stock are listed or traded. For example, International Business Machines trades under the ticker symbol IBM.

Top-down Investing   Portfolio selection strategies that start by examining prevailing general economic factors and industry conditions in order to identify the companies likely to prosper in the projected business environment.

Total Return   A measure of financial return that takes account of appreciation and income distributions. (See Chapter 5.)

Treasuries   Debt obligations of various maturities issued by the U.S. government. Interest income paid on Treasuries is exempt from state and local taxes.

- Treasury bills are short-term securities with maturities of 1 year or less; the smallest denomination issued is $10,000.
- Treasury notes are intermediate-term securities with maturities ranging from 1 to 10 years; the smallest denomination issued is $1,000.
- Treasury bonds are long-term securities with maturities over 10 years; the smallest denomination issued is $1,000.

Yield Curve   A line chart depicting the relations of yields on fixed income securities with varied maturity dates measured at a specific point in time.

Yield Spread   The yield differential between various securities measured at a specific point in time.

Volatility   Sudden, often violent, price fluctuations. Volatile securities are often preferred by "traders," who buy and sell on short-term price movements.

Notes

PREFACE

1. Benjamin Graham and David L. Dodd, *Security Analysis,* McGraw-Hill Book Company (1951), p. 3. Reprinted with permission of The McGraw-Hill Companies.
2. As John Burr Williams observed in his 1938 doctoral thesis: "A stock derives its value from its dividends, not its earnings." See John Burr Williams, *The Theory of Investment Value,* Fraser Publishing Company (1997), p. 57. Reprinted from the Harvard University Press 1938 edition.
3. Laurence H. Sloan, *Everyman and His Common Stocks—A Study of Long Term Investment Policy,* Whittlesley House, McGraw-Hill Book Company (1931), p. 12. See Appendix D of *Secrets* for a biographical sketch.

CHAPTER 1

1. Benjamin Graham and David L. Dodd, *Security Analysis,* McGraw-Hill Book Company (1934), p. 12. Reprinted with permission of The McGraw-Hill Companies.
2. In his December 5, 1996, address to the American Enterprise Institute (Washington, DC), Greenspan asked "How do we know when irrational exuberance has unduly inflated asset values, which then become subject to unexpected and prolonged contractions as they have in Japan over the past decade?" While any number of observers scoffed, Greenspan's admonition had a strong basis in history. As Graham and Dodd chronicled in 1934, "One of the striking features of the past five years has been the domination of the financial scene by purely psychological elements. In previous bull markets the rise in stock prices remained in fairly close relationship with the improvement in business during the greater part of the cycle; it was only in its invariably short-lived culminating phase that quotations were forced to disproportionate heights by the unbridled optimism of the speculative contingent." Benjamin Graham and David L. Dodd, *Security Analysis,* McGraw-Hill Book Company (1934), p. 11. Reprinted with permission of The McGraw-Hill Companies.
3. Abraham Maslow, *Motivation and Personality,* Harper & Row (1965).

 4. Edgar Lawrence Smith, *Common Stocks As Long Term Investments,* The MacMillan Company (1926), p. 13.
 5. Laurence H. Sloan, *Everyman and His Common Stocks—A Study of Long Term Investment Policy,* Whittlesey House, McGraw-Hill Book Company (1931), p. 35.
 6. Roger W. Babson, *Business Barometers and Investment,* Harper & Brothers Publishers (1951), p. 197.
 7. "How to foretell changes in opinion is the heart of the problem of speculation, just as how to foretell changes in dividends is the heart of the problem of investment." John Burr Williams, *The Theory of Investment Value,* Fraser Publishing Company (1997), p. 34. Reprinted from the Harvard University Press 1938 edition.
 8. Ibid., p. 33.
 9. Laurence H. Sloan, *Everyman and His Common Stocks—A Study of Long Term Investment Policy,* Whittlesley House, McGraw-Hill Book Company (1931), p. 8.
10. Benjamin Graham and David L. Dodd, *Security Analysis,* McGraw-Hill Book Company (1934), p. 3. Reprinted with permission of The McGraw-Hill Companies.
11. The successful investor "must be able to dig for facts, to evaluate them critically, and apply his conclusions with good judgment and a fair amount of imagination. He must be able to resist human nature itself sufficiently to mistrust his own feelings when they are part of mass psychology. He must have courage commensurate with his competence." Benjamin Graham and David L. Dodd, *Security Analysis,* McGraw-Hill Book Company (1951), p. 1. Reprinted with permission of The McGraw-Hill Companies.

CHAPTER 2

 1. Benjamin Graham and David L. Dodd, *Security Analysis,* McGraw-Hill Book Company (1951), p. 8. Reprinted with permission of The McGraw-Hill Companies.
 2. Gross Domestic Product and the National Income and Product Accounts (NIPA) are maintained by the U.S. Department of Commerce, Bureau of Economic Analysis (http://www.bea.doc.gov). Historical data are available since 1928.
 3. This finding is a product of multiple regression analysis, the specification of which is beyond the scope of our discussion.
 4. Adam Smith, *An Inquiry into the Nature and Causes of the Wealth of Nations* (1776), Book IV, Chapter II, Modern Library, Random House (1937).
 5. Irving Fisher, *The Rate of Interest,* The MacMillan Company (1907), p. 336.
 6. Any number of studies report that negative real interest rates do occur, as evidenced during the 1970s. Fisher's observation that interest rates are forward-looking suggests a flaw. The methodology typically employed adjusts the

1-year Treasury bill rate for changes in the Consumer Price Index or other popular inflation measure to produce a negative finding. But inflation indexes reflect historical price movements; in effect, they subtract the past from the future. At best, such studies are a measure of the "ex post" real rate and reveal, albeit with hindsight, the presence of "winners" and "losers." On an ex ante basis, rational lenders would likely eschew the credit market if they *expected* to lose purchasing power.

7. Consider 1980. The yield on 3-month Treasury bills ranged from a low of 6.18 percent (June 13, 1980 close) to a high of 17.14 percent (December 11, 1980 close).

8. Yield differentials between fully tax-exempt municipal bonds, Treasury obligations, and fully taxable corporate bonds also attest to the importance of taxes in determining nominal interest rates, although risk factors associated with different credit instruments account for some of the difference.

9. Paul A. Samuelson, *Economics,* McGraw-Hill Book Company (1948), p. 337. Reprinted with permission of The McGraw-Hill Companies.

10. The Federal Reserve Board controls the discount rate (the interest rate charged to member banks for borrowing from Reserve Banks) and the federal funds rate (the rate of interest charged to banks for borrowing excess reserves from other banks).

11. This finding is a product of multiple regression analysis, the specification of which is beyond the scope of our discussion.

12. See Chapter 10 for a detailed description of the methodology.

13. Laurence H. Sloan, *Everyman and His Common Stocks—A Study of Long Term Investment Policy,* Whittlesey House, McGraw-Hill Book Company (1931), pp. 100–101.

CHAPTER 3

1. Derived from Roman law, the term "fiduciary" refers to "a person holding the character of a trustee, or a character analogous to that of a trustee, in respect to the trust and confidence involved in it and the scrupulous good faith and candor which it requires. A person or institution who manages money or property for another [and] who must exercise a standard of care in such management activity imposed by law or contract." *Black's Law Dictionary,* Henry Campbell Black, M.A., West Publishing Company (1979).

2. *Reports of Cases Argued and Determined in the Supreme Judicial Court of Massachusetts,* Little, Brown and Company (1864), p. 454.

3. Ibid., p. 473.

4. Brokerage schedules often assess a minimum amount per trade (usually $50 to $75) irrespective of the per share commission rate. Imagine a 5 cent per share commission schedule with a $75 minimum ticket charge. Security transactions involving fewer than 500 shares would be subject to the minimum fee. As an example, a buy order for 100 shares of XYZ @ $25 = $2,500 plus the

$75 minimum ticket charge. The commission would equal 2 percent of the principal amount.

5. Every equity position involves a "buy" and a "sell" ticket, hence a "round trip," with both trades subject to a commission charge.

6. Laurence H. Sloan, *Everyman and His Common Stocks—A Study of Long Term Investment Policy,* Whittlesey House, McGraw-Hill Book Company (1931), p. 34.

7. See *"Junk bonds* ride the wave of popularity." Malcolm Foster, Bloomberg News as published in the *Raleigh News and Observer,* July 15, 1997.

8. Roger W. Babson, *Business Barometers and Investment,* Harper & Brothers Publishers (1951), p. xi.

9. Roger W. Babson, *Business Barometers and Investment,* Harper & Brothers (1951), p. 252.

10. Cumulative total returns: DJIA, 120 percent; Lehman Aggregate Bond Index, 36 percent; and Treasury bills, 17 percent.

11. See Chapter 10 for a description of the market and how to derive the implicit interest rate forecast.

12. A $1 dividend compounded at 10 percent per annum for 25 years would grow to $10.83, bringing the "yield on cost" to 10.83 percent.

13. Given a 200 percent turnover, we've assumed that the gains were of the short-term variety and taxed accordingly.

14. James P. Garland, *The Attraction of Tax-Managed Index Funds, Journal of Investing,* Spring 1997, p. 13.

15. Roger W. Babson, *Business Barometers and Investment,* Harper & Brothers Publishers (1951), p. 208.

16. Charles D. Ellis, CFA, "Conceptualizing Portfolio Management," in *Managing Investment Portfolios—A Dynamic Process,* Institute of Chartered Financial Analysts, Warren, Gorham & Lamont (1983), p. 11.

CHAPTER 4

1. Laurence H. Sloan, *Everyman and His Common Stocks—A Study of Long Term Investment Policy,* Whittlesey House, McGraw-Hill Book Company (1931), p. 14.

2. Discussions involving statistical measurements invariably touch on the problem of sample size and whether the number of observations is sufficient to support an inference. In this book, we've elected to illustrate basic concepts by applying them to an abbreviated data set.

3. Laurence H. Sloan, *Everyman and His Common Stocks—A Study of Long Term Investment Policy,* Whittlesey House, McGraw-Hill Book Company (1931), p. 19.

4. The geometric mean of a series of calendar-year returns is found by expressing each year's percentage change as a positive number (e.g., 10% is transformed to 1.10 and −10% to 0.90) and then multiplying the resulting values

rather than adding them. The product of the multiplication is then raised to a power per the formula $(X_1 \cdot X_2 \cdot X_3 \ldots X_n)^{1/n}$, where x is the observed calendar-year return and n is the number of years in the series.

5. Annualized return calculations using monthly or quarterly data require an extension of the formula.

6. Development of the standard deviation and its practical application is attributed to the French mathematician Abraham DeMoivre (1667–1754). See Appendix D for a biographical profile.

7. Given the small sample size involved with our illustration (5), an adjustment is required to the variance. So technically, the standard deviation in this case is not exactly the square root of the variance as shown in Table 4-4, but it's close. With large samples, this distinction is nebulous.

8. A more rigorous measurement of this statistic was advanced by William F. Sharpe (Stanford University Graduate School of Business). Known as the "Sharpe Ratio," the procedure divides the risk-adjusted return (i.e., the excess return over the Treasury bill yield) by the standard deviation. In brief: (Return − Risk-Free Return) ÷ Standard Deviation.

9. "*Sur les Valeurs Limites des Integrales,*" *Journal de Mathématiques* (1874), Ser. No. 2, 19, pp. 157–160. See Appendix D for a biographical profile.

10. Here's how we figured it out. The k in the formula is the interval on either side of the mean return measured in terms of the standard deviation, in this instance, 2. Hence the formula would be:

$$1 - (1 \div (2)^2) = 1 - (1 \div 4) = 1 - 0.25 = 75\%$$

11. The calculation is: $2.5 \div 1.58 = 1.58$ standard deviations.

12. The actual formula is $1 - (1 \div (1.58)^2) = 59.9\%$. That is, at least 59.9 percent of the outcomes should be contained by an interval defined as the mean (10%) $\pm$ 1.58 standard deviations or between 7.5 and 12.5 percent. The remaining outcomes (40.1%) would be expected to fall outside this range.

13. A discussion of "normal distribution" is presented in Chapter 6. See Appendix D for a biographical profile of DeMoivre.

14. The symbol $\pm$ denotes the terminology "plus and minus."

15. The calculation is $1.08 \div 1.075 = 1.005$.

16. The calculation is $(1.023 - 1.0) \div 0.015 = 1.53$.

17. For a detailed description of AIMR's Performance Presentation Standards, visit its Web site at www.aimr.org.

18. For an excellent review of the problem of performance measurement, see James A. White, "Getting Started: When Figuring the Rate of Return Don't Be Confused by the Sales Hype," *Wall Street Journal,* March 30, 1990, p. C1.

19. Irving Fisher, *The Rate of Interest,* The MacMillan Company (1907), p. viii.

20. Benjamin Graham and David L. Dodd, *Security Analysis,* McGraw-Hill Book Company (1934), p. 14. Reprinted with permission of The McGraw-Hill Companies.

CHAPTER 5

1. John Burr Williams, *The Theory of Investment Value,* Fraser Publishing (1997), p. 57. Reprinted from the Harvard University 1938 edition.
2. As Graham and Dodd put it nearly a half-century ago, "The considered and continuous verdict of the stock market is overwhelmingly in favor of liberal dividends as against niggardly ones. The common-stock investor and securities analyst must take this judgment into account in the selection of stocks for purchase." Benjamin Graham and David L. Dodd, *Security Analysis,* McGraw-Hill (1951), p. 432. Reprinted by permission of The McGraw-Hill Companies.
3. Edgar Lawrence Smith, *Common Stocks As Long Term Investments,* The MacMillan Company (1926), p. 80.
4. See Appendix B for historical price and dividend data.
5. Table 5-1 presents an abbreviated version of the spreadsheet. See Appendix E for a complete illustration of the analytical process.
6. The factor formula is given as Dividend Increase · ((Years Increased/Total Years) · (Total Years/Years Increased)).
7. Laurence H. Sloan, *Everyman and His Common Stocks—A Study of Long Term Investment Policy,* Whittesley House, McGraw-Hill Book Company (1931), p. 170.
8. Unfortunately, Travelers Group, which was the top-ranked dividend payer in the Dow at the end of 1997, suffers from a lack of historical data owing to a series of acquisitions. Hence, for the purpose of this exercise, TRV was eliminated from consideration, leaving 29 stocks to select from.
9. Ibid.
10. Benjamin Graham and David L. Dodd, *Security Analysis,* McGraw-Hill Book Company (1934), p. 327. Reprinted with permission of The McGraw-Hill Companies.
11. See Appendix E.
12. Cumulative returns shown for the DJIA assume a 36 percent tax liability on dividends. However, no allowance for capital gains taxes are reflected in the DJIA data.
13. Edgar Lawrence Smith, *Common Stocks As Long Term Investments,* The MacMillan Company (1926), p. 10.
14. Laurence H. Sloan, *Everyman and His Common Stocks—A Study of Long Term Investment Policy,* Whittlesey House, McGraw-Hill Book Company (1931), p. 48.
15. Roger W. Babson, *Business Barometers and Investment,* Harper & Brothers (1951), p. 254.

CHAPTER 6

1. Benjamin Graham and David L. Dodd, *Security Analysis,* McGraw-Hill Book Company (1951), p. 3. Reprinted with permission of The McGraw-Hill Companies.

2. Reliance on observed data to derive probability estimates for the purpose of hypothesis testing is termed "statistical inference."

3. Statistical analysis of historical DJIA monthly returns (1962–1997) reveals the following measurements: mean = 1.19%; median = 1.68%; standard deviation = 4.37%. See Appendix F for definitions and discussion of practical significance.

4. Ibid.

5. The calculation is (1.19% − 7.5%) ÷ 4.37% = 1.4 standard deviations.

6. Numbers may not compute because of rounding.

7. More precisely, the correlation coefficient is 0.88. For a discussion of the correlation statistic, see Chapter 7 at "Correlation Coefficients: The Diversification Search Engine."

8. In practice, equal dollar investments may not be feasible given the need to adjust share quantities to the nearest "round lot" (100 shares).

CHAPTER 7

1. Harry Markowitz, "Portfolio Selection," *Journal of Finance,* Vol. 7, March 1952, p. 77.

2. Known in the medical field as bovine spongiform encephalopathy (BSE), Mad Cow disease is a lethal, progressive ailment that affects the central nervous system of cattle. In March 1996, the British government announced that 10 people in the United Kingdom may have become infected with BSE through exposure to beef. It is believed that the disease spread when the bodies of infected cows and sheep contaminated with a similar illness (scrapie) were rendered and used in cattle feeds. No cases of BSE have ever been found in U.S. herds, according to the U.S. Food and Drug Administration.

3. The risk associated with nondiversified portfolios is also discussed in Chapter 9. Here we focus on avoidance of a self-inflicted problem, whereas the later chapter deals with rectifying a preexisting condition.

4. Harry Markowitz, "Portfolio Selection," *Journal of Finance* Vol. 7, March 1952, p. 89.

5. Roger W. Babson, *Business Barometers and Investment,* Harper & Brothers Publishers (1951), p. x.

6. A beneficial interest in the 30 Dow Jones Industrial stocks is available via a "Diamond"—a listed American Stock Exchange security that trades under the ticker symbol DIA. See Appendix A for a detailed description.

7. That is, their returns either don't fluctuate in the same direction simultaneously or move in opposite directions. Correlation is integral to strategic asset allocation and is discussed more fully in the pages that follow.

8. The standard deviation of the diversified portfolio's quarterly returns was 5.12% vs. 7.84% for McDonald's.

9. McDonald's annualized return was 17.7%.

10. In Wall Street parlance, "stock-specific" or "nonsystematic risk."

11. "Market" or "systematic risk."

12. As we mentioned earlier, discussions involving statistical measurements invariably touch on the problem of sample size and whether the number of observations is sufficient to support conclusions. For the sake of illustration, we've elected to demonstrate basic concepts by applying them to an abbreviated data set.

13. Treasury bills are obligations of the U.S. government that carry a "maturity" of a year or less. Since T-bill investors assume no principal risk (at least as a practical matter), these instruments are deemed to be "riskless" investments.

14. Assuming the DJIA is the equity market benchmark, it would be impossible for the Dow to underperform itself.

15. The probability of rolling a 6 on two successive attempts is less than 3%, while the chance of doing it three times in a row is only 0.4%.

16. Estimation interval: 1962–1997. Multiple-year periods are overlapping.

17. The discussion is intended to demonstrate a methodology for assessing diversification options. The benefit of hindsight is acknowledged.

18. "We should invest across industries because firms in different industries, especially industries with different economic characteristics, have lower covariances than firms within an industry." Harry Markowitz, "Portfolio Selection," *Journal of Finance* Vol. 7, March 1952 (1952), p. 89.

19. McDonald's constitutes roughly 6% of the Total Return Portfolio on an equal dollar weighted basis.

20. Edgar Lawrence Smith, *Common Stocks As Long Term Investments,* The MacMillan Company (1926), p. vi.

21. As proxied by the Russell 2000 index.

22. "The portfolio with maximum expected return is not necessarily the one with minimum variance. There is a rate at which the investor can gain expected return by taking on variance, or reduce variance by giving up expected return." Harry Markowitz, "Portfolio Selection," *Journal of Finance* Vol. 7, March 1952, p. 79.

23. Ralph E. Badger, Harold W. Torgerson, and Harry G. Guthmann, *Investment Principles and Practices,* Prentice Hall (1961), p. 170.

CHAPTER 8

1. Edgar Lawrence Smith, *Common Stocks As Long Term Investments,* The MacMillan Company (1926), p. 116.

2. Benjamin Graham and David L. Dodd, *Security Analysis,* McGraw Hill Book Company (1934), p. 18. Reprinted with permission of The McGraw-Hill Companies.

3. Benjamin Graham and David L. Dodd, *Security Analysis: The Valuation of Common Stocks,* McGraw-Hill Book Company (1951), p. 519. Reprinted with permission of The McGraw-Hill Companies.

4. The market capitalization of the New York Stock Exchange may be found at

its Web site: www.nyse.com. GDP data are available from the Bureau of Economic Analysis at http://www.bea.doc.gov/.

5. Interest rate data are available from the Federal Reserve Board at its Web site: www.bog.frb.us/releases/.

6. The Treasury yield curve appears in the credit market section of the daily financial press.

7. With Treasury securities, maturities of 1 year or less are called "bills." Maturity dates between 1 and 10 years are known as "notes," and instruments with more than 10 years to maturity are termed "bonds."

8. Data are available via the Internet. See footnote 4 for the Web sites.

9. The New York Stock Exchange, of course, is not the entire "stock market." Still, since the market capitalization data are readily available, it is convenient to use these data in the P/Ec ratio formula.

CHAPTER 9

1. Benjamin Graham and David L. Dodd, *Securities Analysis,* McGraw-Hill Book Company (1934), p. 320. Reprinted with permission of The McGraw-Hill Companies.

2. A variety of other factors can spawn concentrated equity positions, including low tax basis considerations and regulatory prohibitions specified under securities law.

3. "The future cannot be analyzed; we can seek only to anticipate it intelligently and prepare for it prudently." Benjamin Graham and David L. Dodd, *Securities Analysis,* McGraw-Hill Book Company (1951), p. 3. Reprinted with permission of The McGraw-Hill Companies.

4. The Empirical Rule is traceable to the Russian mathematician P. L. Tchebyshev's theorem that at least $1-1/k^2$ of a distribution's measurements will lie within k standard deviations of its mean. See "Sur les Valeurs Limites des Intégrales," *Journal de Mathématiques* (1874), Ser. 2, 19, pp. 157–160.

5. Reliance on observed data to derive probability estimates for the purpose of hypothesis testing is termed "statistical inference."

6. The discussion that follows describes a generic approach to diversifying concentrated equity positions. Importantly, most of the rules may be tailored individual investor tolerances.

7. The exception being any transactions dictated by the time default discussed under Rule 4 to follow.

8. Remember, when Microsoft's performance equals that of the Dow, the relative performance factor is 1.

9. The "diversification amounts" found in Table 9-3 are derived from a straightforward formula:

$$\text{ndv}_{3\sigma} \div \text{ndv}_{z\sigma}$$

where ndv = probability that the observed return > Z_σ
Z = observed change measured in standard deviation terms

10. See the "diversification amount" indicated for a 0.1 standard deviation event in Table 9-3.
11. With dividends taken into account, Chevron's calendar-year average return was 20.4 percent versus 19.2 percent for the DJIA.
12. At the time of this writing, December 1992 was the last inception date for which an ensuing 5-year investment period could be measured.
13. Diamonds are units in an investment trust that holds shares of the 30 issues comprising the Dow Jones Industrial Average. They trade like common stocks under the ticker symbol DIA. See Appendix A for a description.
14. Laurence H. Sloan, *Everyman and His Common Stocks—A Study of Long Term Investment Policy,* Whittesley House, McGraw-Hill Book Company (1931), p. 289.

CHAPTER 10

1. Benjamin Graham and David L. Dodd, *Securities Analysis,* McGraw-Hill Book Company (1934), p. 610. Reprinted with permission of The McGraw-Hill Companies.
2. See Chapter 2, especially at footnote 5.
3. As measured by year-over-year changes in calendar-year average 91-day Treasury bill yields.
4. Contracts are traded for March, June, September, and December delivery dates with quotations published in the daily financial press.
5. The calendar-year average T-bill yield is the typical packaging for short-term interest rate forecasts as well as an important official U.S. budget assumption.
6. See the discussion of the standard deviation in Chapter 4.
7. See Appendix B for historical data.
8. Benjamin Graham and David L. Dodd, *Security Analysis,* McGraw-Hill Book Company (1934), p. 18. Reprinted with permission of The McGraw-Hill Companies.
9. This discussion focuses on Individual Retirement Accounts but is applicable to other tax-advantaged accounts such as IRA Rollovers and Simplified Employee Pension Plans (SEPP). The points raised do not apply uniformly to the recently invented Roth IRAs, which are available to qualifying taxpayers and exempt from federal income and capital gains taxes. Readers should consult their tax professional for specific advice.
10. See Appendix B for historical price data.
11. Laurence H. Sloan, *Everyman and His Common Stocks—A Study of Long Term Investment Policy,* Whittlesey House, McGraw-Hill Book Company (1931), p. 28.

APPENDIX A

1. Dow Jones & Company Web site: http://www.dowjones.com.
2. Ibid.

3. For a complete description, visit the American Stock Exchange Web site: http://www.amex.com.
4. SPDRs (referred to as "Spiders") are similar to Diamonds but designed to track the Standard & Poor's 500 stock index. Introduced in 1993, they trade under the ticker symbol SPY. A million units (shares) of Spiders changed hands on the first day of trading.

APPENDIX D

1. *"Security Analysis"* (1934 edition) was reprinted in 1997 by McGraw-Hill (New York).
2. *Economics* (1948 edition) was reprinted in 1997 by McGraw-Hill (New York).
3. *The Theory of Investment Value* was reprinted in 1997 by Fraser Publishing Company (Burlington, VT).
4. John Burr Williams, *International Trade Under Flexible Exchange Rates,* North-Holland Publishing Co. (Amsterdam), 1954.

APPENDIX E

1. Our universe for possible selection was restricted to the constituent stocks in the Dow Jones Industrial Average (as it existed on December 31, 1997) with the exception of Travelers Group, which suffered from a lack of historical data owing to a series of acquisitions. During 1998, Travelers merged with Citicorp to form a financial services giant known as Citigroup (Ticker symbol C).
2. See Chapter 5, Figure 5-8, for rankings.
3. By raising its dividend each and every year during the previous decade, J. P. Morgan would earn a factor of 1.00. So its handicapped 10-year dividend increase would remain at 149.4 percent (149.4% gross increase multiplied by 1.0 equals 149.4% handicapped increase).

Index

About the Authors

CHARLES E. BABIN

Charles E. Babin's *curriculum vitae* traces associations with a number of prominent financial institutions including Natwest Investment Management and State Street Global Advisors. He launched his professional career in 1969 when he joined H. C. Wainwright & Co., an internationally respected investment banking firm, and was admitted to partnership in 1974. In 1978 he cofounded H. C. Wainwright & Co. Economics, a highly regarded economic forecasting and consulting firm that received national attention for its work in modeling the U.S. economy and financial market behavior using objective credit market prices as explanatory variables.

In 1988 he became managing director and principal stockholder of BRS Capital Management, a registered investment adviser formed for the purpose of commercializing the investment disciplines pioneered at Wainwright Economics. These strategies, which continue in operation, successfully averted the effects of the 1987 "crash" and 1990 Gulf War "correction."

A former naval officer and Vietnam veteran, Charles Babin earned his BS and MBA degrees at Boston College. His published work has appeared regularly in the national and local press. In 1978 his analysis of capital spending trends in America—a featured article in the *Journal of Financial Analysts*—was honored with the Financial Analysts Federation's Graham and Dodd Award. He has been a contributing columnist at *Forbes* since 1985.

WILLIAM J. DONOVAN

William J. Donovan is a business writer for the *Providence Journal,* a Pulitzer prize winning newspaper in Rhode Island. During the course of a 14-year career at the *Journal,* he has written extensively about the economy, the government, and personal finance, including such topics as tax reform, personal debt, and mutual funds.

He has taught business journalism at two nationally recognized journalism schools: Boston University and Northeastern University in Boston. In addition, he has lectured at Harvard University on labor economics, focusing on such areas as downsizing, job quality, and how the media portray changes in the labor force. The thrust of his teachings is to help young writers understand the value of business news—including personal finance—to the average reader and develop the skills needed to present such information in a clear and engaging style.

He holds a master's degree in journalism and public affairs from American University in Washington, D.C., and earned bachelor degrees in history and communications at Boston College. He has received journalism awards from the Massachusetts Press Association and the New England Newspaper Association.

Photo by Shelly Babin.